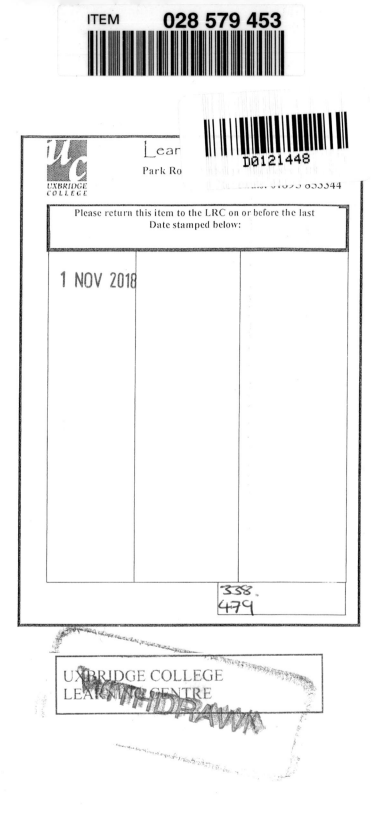

TOURISM AND HOSPITALITY MANAGEMENT

ADVANCES IN CULTURE, TOURISM AND HOSPITALITY RESEARCH

Series Editor: Arch G. Woodside

ADVANCES IN CULTURE, TOURISM AND HOSPITALITY
RESEARCH   VOLUME 12

TOURISM AND HOSPITALITY MANAGEMENT

EDITED BY

METIN KOZAK

Dokuz Eylul University, Foca-Izmir, Turkey

NAZMI KOZAK

Dokuz Eylul University, Eskisehir, Turkey

United Kingdom − North America − Japan
India − Malaysia − China

Emerald Group Publishing Limited
Howard House, Wagon Lane, Bingley BD16 1WA, UK

First edition 2016

British Library Cataloguing in Publication Data
A catalogue record for this book is available from the British Library

ISBN: 978-1-78635-714-4
ISSN: 1871-3173 (Series)

Printed and bound by CPI Group (UK) Ltd, Croydon, CR0 4YY

ISOQAR certified
Management System,
awarded to Emerald
for adherence to
Environmental
standard
ISO 14001:2004.

Certificate Number 1985
ISO 14001

INVESTOR IN PEOPLE

CONTENTS

LIST OF CONTRIBUTORS

Ángela Aguiló Lemoine	University of the Balearic Islands, Spain
Margarita Alemany Hormaeche	University of the Balearic Islands, Spain
Ahmad Azmi M. Ariffin	Universiti Kebangsaan, Malaysia
Ali Bavik	Macau University of Science and Technology, Macau, SAR China
Marlena A. Bednarska	Poznan University of Economics, Poland
Ian Boxill	The University of the West Indies, Jamaica
Teresa Catramby	Federal Rural University of Rio de Janeiro, Brasil
Funda Cengiz	Adnan Menderes University, Turkey
Grace Chan	The Hong Kong Polytechnic University, Hong Kong, SAR China
Athena Lele Chen	The Hong Kong Polytechnic University, Hong Kong, SAR China
Elaine Y.T. Chew	Monash University, Malaysia
Kaye Chon	The Hong Kong Polytechnic University, Hong Kong, SAR China
Antónia Correia	University of Algarve, Portugal
João Duque	University of Lisbon, Portugal
Priscilla Dutra	Federal Rural University of Rio de Janeiro, Brasil
Hilal Erkuş-Öztürk	Akdeniz University, Turkey

Jerónimo Esteve-Pérez	Technical University of Cartagena, Spain
Antonio García-Sánchez	Technical University of Cartagena, Spain
Maria Antonia García Sastre	University of the Balearic Islands, Spain
Basak Denizci Guillet	The Hong Kong Polytechnic University, Hong Kong, SAR China
Cathy H. C. Hsu	The Hong Kong Polytechnic University, Hong Kong, SAR China
Blerton Hyseni	University of Sunderland, UK
Magdalena Kubal	Jagiellonian University in Kraków, Poland
Bob McKercher	Hong Kong Polytechnic University, Hong Kong, SAR China
Michelle T. McLeod	The University of the West Indies, Jamaica
Maurice McNaughton	The University of the West Indies, Jamaica
Ekaterina Miettinen	Karelia University of Applied Sciences, Finland
Priscilla Chau Min Poon	Hong Kong Polytechnic University, Hong Kong, SAR China
Dirisa Mulindwa	University of Sunderland, UK
Vipin Nadda	University of Sunderland, UK
Marcin Olszewski	Poznan University of Economics, Poland
Noor Balkhis Omar	Universiti Kebangsaan, Malaysia
Stephanie Onggo	Monash University, Malaysia
Robert Pawlusiński	Jagiellonian University in Kraków, Poland
Pedro Pimpão	University of Lisbon, Portugal
Roya Rahimi	University of Wolverhampton, UK
H. Kader Şanlıöz-Özgen	Özyeğin University, Turkey

Julia C. Wells	Rhodes University, South Africa
Alan Wong	The Hong Kong Polytechnic University, Hong Kong, SAR China
Carlos Zorrinho	University of Évora, Portugal

ABOUT THE EDITORS

Metin Kozak is Professor of Tourism in the School of Tourism and Hospitality Management, Dokuz Eylul University, Turkey. He holds both Master's and Ph.D. degrees in tourism management. His research focuses on consumer behaviour, benchmarking, destination management and marketing, and sustainability. He acts as the co-editor of *Anatolia: An International Journal of Tourism and Hospitality Research* and has been to various universities in the United States, Europe and Asia as a visiting scholar.

Nazmi Kozak is Professor of Tourism in the School of Tourism and Hospitality Management, Anadolu University, Turkey. He gained both his Master's and Ph.D. degrees in tourism management. His research activities focus on tourism marketing, history of tourism, and bibliometrics. He is the Editor of *Anatolia: Turizm Araştırmaları Dergisi* and the co-editor of *Anatolia: An International Journal of Tourism and Hospitality Research* and has been to several universities in the United States as a visiting scholar.

INTRODUCTION

Over the last few decades, as an inter-disciplinary, multi-disciplinary and trans-disciplinary field (e.g. Jafari, 2003; Tribe & Xiao, 2011; Xiao & Smith, 2006), tourism has become a fashionable topic across a wide range of academic fields. Due to its unique characteristics, tourism is perhaps the only field of academic study that imports more knowledge than it exports to other fields (e.g. Crouch & Perdue, 2015; Joppe, 2012; Wardle & Buckley, 2014). While the field of tourism studies was first developed in the 1940s by scholars with a background in economics, such as Hunziker, Krapf, and Kaspar, since the 1980s it has evolved to become more management-oriented (e.g. Xiao & Smith, 2006). This has opened new avenues, with more professional focus on tourism education at the institutional level, and the development of many training programs at the business or organisational level.

The reason for this is quite simple. Following WWII, tourism was considered the primary and most convenient solution to support the development of nations in economic terms, as more visitors became involved in tourism activities and more destinations were introduced to meet the increase in demand. As a result, it became clear that the lack of managerial skills was an issue that needed to be dealt with firmly and professionally. The emergence of schools at the university level (e.g. the school of tourism and hospitality management, or Master's degrees in tourism or hospitality management) are also clear evidence indicating the perceived strong relationship between tourism and management and between tourism and education/training.

The last decade of the 20th century saw developments not only in tourism education but also in the tourism industry itself. New destinations were established (e.g. Mediterranean, South-east Asian and Asia—Pacific countries) and some others made further progress (e.g. the United States, France, the United Kingdom, Germany, among others). The number of tourist arrivals boomed, and the capacity of destinations increased (Kozak, 2003; Kozak & Baloglu, 2010). However, some additional problems also emerged, such as the shortage of a qualified labour force at all levels, and the lack of knowledge of publicity (Baum, 2015). In response to these problems and their consequences, much attention has been paid to the development of tourism education and the advancement of tourism research in both developed and developing countries. Beginning in the early 1990s, the number of tourism departments and tourism began to rise, reaching its peak in the early 2000s. In addition to a large number of tourism and hospitality businesses, there are now also many worldwide centres with a specific focus on research, consultancy, and education and training.

Like other fields, tourism has two sides, the academic and the practical, and these require further elaboration if they are to become fully complementary (Ayikoru, Tribe, & Airey, 2009; Cooper & Shepherd, 1997). In both academic and practical terms, tourism is a very broad subject. In practical terms, tourism covers a broad range of topics from transport to accommodation, and from food services to hospitality services. In academic terms, the field of empirical investigation covers a long list of research topics. There is also an emerging debate concerning the structural differences between tourism and hospitality studies in contextual settings, with only a limited focus on finding solutions. Regarding the comparison across industries, due to low entry and high exit barriers and easy access to an unskilled labour force, the tourism and hospitality industries are somewhat dissimilar to some other industries (Singal, 2015). However, in terms of an internal industry comparison, while tourism clearly involves hospitality, some scholars studying hospitality suggest that it should be distinguished as an independent field of research (e.g. Pizam, 2009; Pizam & Shani, 2009) with further hospitality-specific journals and books.

The present book aims to address these topics, taking 'tourism' to be a broader field than 'hospitality'. The term 'hospitality' refers to all operations or services encompassing accommodation and food/beverage facilities at the micro level, whereas 'tourism' stands for the other elements at the macro level, including business, destination, and transportation operations. Moving from the generic to the specific, this book is divided into three main parts. Part I starts from a more generic perspective, and is entitled 'Tourism Management'. It comprises seven chapters by 13 scholars. Part II has a more moderate focus, and is entitled 'Hospitality Management'. It includes seven chapters contributed by 15 scholars from across the world. Part III is entitled 'Tourism Education & Training', and covers a range of topics from both tourism and hospitality. This last part consists of six chapters contributed by 13 scholars from four continents.

PART I – TOURISM MANAGEMENT

The dominant chapters of this part are quite diverse, and enriched by the provision of some useful cases across three continents – Europe, Asia and Africa. The coverage of the chapters is also diverse, but each chapter is related to a specific aspect of tourism management, such as quality management, service collaboration, transit tourism, network relationship, social media, cruise traffic or revenue management. Chapter 1, by H. Kader Şanlıöz Özgen, looks at the proportion of the tourism industry among the winning organisations of the European Quality Award. Surprisingly, the proportion remains very low despite the significance of quality standards in tourism operations. Chapter 2, by E. Y. T. Chew and Stephanie Onggo, examines the nature of the service collaboration between healthcare businesses and tourism agencies operating in Malaysia, using the co-evolutionary theory; the study findings confirm a weak collaboration. Chapter 3, by Priscilla Chau Min Poon and Bob McKercher, aims to outline the profile of transit tourists in Hong Kong, primarily dominated by passengers from the United States, Germany, Australia, and New Zealand. Chapter 4, by Maurice McNaughton, Michelle T. Mcleod and Ian Boxill, suggests implementing a tourism open data policy that would allow the practice of data exchange. Chapter 5, by Ekaterina Miettinen, examines the availability of tourism businesses using social media channels in Russia, and shows how social media could help in the development of digital strategies dealing with Russian tourism demand. Chapter 6, by Jerónimo Esteve-Pérez and Antonio García-Sánchez, emphasises the lack of research on the cruise industry, and provides three key stakeholders involved in developing a cruise itinerary. Chapter 7, by Grace Chan and Basak Denizci Guillet, discusses a list of strategies that travel agencies operating in Hong Kong could implement to maximise their profits.

PART II – HOSPITALITY MANAGEMENT

As a sub-division of the tourism industry and as a business operation, hospitality has become more significant over the last three or four decades. In fact, the significance of hospitality dates back many centuries, and the host-guest relationship has long been significant in cultural terms. However, the study of hospitality has in recent years become more business-dominant, due to the transformation of traditional hospitality into modern hospitality management.

The content of Part II is more specific, and addresses several different aspects of modern hospitality management. The topic coverage is quite diverse, ranging from loyalty programs to customer delight, the Asian style of hospitality and its historical development, diversification, and branded contents. Chapter 8, by Pedro Pimpão, Antónia Correia, João Duque and Carlos Zorrinho, monitors the speed of diffusion patterns in loyalty programs launched by hotel chains among adopters and potential adopters. Chapter 9, by Ahmad Azmi M. Ariffin and Noor Balkhis Omar, confirms the strong and positive relationship between surprise and customer delight moderated by the hospitality service. Chapter 10, by Athena Lele Chen and Kaye Chon, assesses the potential transferability of the Asian paradigm in hospitality management concepts to non-Asian countries, by providing a case study of an international hotel chain based in Hong Kong. Chapter 11, contributed by Robert Pawlusiński and Magdalena Kubal, is more historically oriented, and looks at how the hospitality industry in Krakow, Poland, has evolved since the mid-19th century.

Chapter 12, by Hilal Erkuş-Öztürk, determines the factors that influence product and service diversification in the hotel businesses in Antalya, Turkey, and suggests that company type, size, sector-specific knowledge and collaboration with other businesses are worthy of note in this respect. Chapter 13, by Ángela Aguiló Lemoine, Maria Antonia García Sastre and Margarita Alemany Hormaeche, notes the importance of branded contents in increasing the brand visibility of hotel businesses, with specific reference to Ibiza, Spain. Chapter 14, by Ali Bavik, provides an overview of gaps in the existing literature on organisational culture and considers the results of a new scale developed for the purpose of understanding organisational culture in the hospitality industry.

PART III – TOURISM EDUCATION AND TRAINING

On one hand, the tourism industry has gained an international reputation, and many more countries' authorities have tended towards enlarging their existing potential sources. Many people have now experienced tourism services, and the capacity of tourism businesses and destinations has boomed over the past few decades. On the other hand, shortages in the labour force have appeared, and more schools and training programs have been established in order to fill this gap. Such concerns point towards the significance of better educated or trained employees in every single area of the tourism industry. Therefore, Part III is dedicated to underlining the significance of education and training in the tourism and hospitality industry, with specific emphasis on a selected list of case studies conducted in a range of countries.

In terms of context, the chapters in Part III are quite diverse. The discussion includes two mainstream topics. The first is the development of training programs, mostly from an industry perspective. The second is the consideration of students enroled on tourism and hospitality programs at the university level. Chapter 15, written by Funda Cengiz, emphasises the value of developing training programs for disabled tourists at both the business and destination levels, due to the present lack of understanding concerning the needs of such people, both as residents and visitors. Chapter 16, co-authored by Roya Rahimi, Vipin Nadda, Blerton Hyseni and Dirisa Mulindwa, tries to determine the main motivations of South Asian students for studying tourism and hospitality in British universities. Chapter 17, co-authored by Marlena A. Bednarska and Marcin Olszewski, investigates the possible effects of work experience on students' perceptions the attractiveness of a career in hospitality. Chapter 18, by Julia C. Wells, determines the role of education-based tourism in bridging radical divides in South Africa. Chapter 19, by Teresa Catramby and Priscilla Dutra, has a broader focus on tourism education in the Brazilian education system. In Chapter 20, in light of today's multi-cultural working and learning environment, Alan Wong and Cathy H. C. Hsu focus on the role of schools and educators in developing intercultural awareness and skills for hospitality students in China. With contributions from countries ranging from Turkey to China and the United Kingdom, the contents of Part III are also well-established from a geographical perspective.

To sum up, this volume includes chapters dealing with a wide range of topics related to tourism and hospitality management, including education and training. The methodologies of the contributing authors include both qualitative and quantitative methods, and range from survey methods to case studies.

As part of a broad collaborative effort, a number of different perspectives on a wide diversity of topics on tourism and hospitality management and education are presented by researchers from 25 different institutions and 11 countries. As such, the richness of the volume derives not only from the cultural diversity of its contributor, but also to the contents of the chapters (see Chapters 10, 15, 16), which explore the significance of understanding the multi-cultural characteristics of tourism and hospitality industry. In terms of Hofstede's cultural dimensions (Hofstede, 2001; Hofstede,

Hofstede, & Minkov, 2010), there remains much to think about with regard to possible management, marketing and education methods that would develop better communication between service providers and visitors, among service providers, and among visitors, where each of these represents a piece of today's multi-cultural tourism and hospitality world.

The idea of putting together the present volume originated during discussions prior to two conference series held in Istanbul, Turkey, on 4—9 June 2014, namely the Interdisciplinary Tourism Research Conference and the World Conference for Graduate Research in Tourism, Hospitality and Leisure. This series attracted the participation of over 260 scholars from across the world. Selecting some of the papers presented at these conferences has become a traditional way of contributing to the existing body of tourism knowledge, and this volume includes 20 studies by 41 invited contributors. The cluster of chapters included in the book address tourism management, hospitality management, and tourism education and training.

As a result, the audience for this book may include students of tourism and hospitality programs at both undergraduate and postgraduate levels, faculty members with teaching and research commitments, libraries in schools that run tourism and hospitality programs, and practitioners (e.g. destination managers, ministry of tourism staff and individual tourism establishments). This book would serve as an excellent supplement to existing textbooks that examine various aspects of tourism management, particularly in the context of worldwide case studies on tourism, hospitality management, and education. The contributions accommodated in this volume will be a helpful reference resource, full of rich materials that refer to the applications of tourism and hospitality management practices via worldwide case studies.

We acknowledge and thank all the authors for their remarkable contributions and for showing the commitment and continuous cooperation that has been of such help in bringing this proposal to fruition. We would also like to thank Arch G. Woodside for his generous support and Emerald for giving us a unique opportunity to publish this volume in such a smooth and professional manner. Without your endless support, positivity and understanding, we would never have been able to make this happen.

Metin Kozak
Nazmi Kozak
Editors

REFERENCES

Ayikoru, M., Tribe, J., & Airey, D. (2009). Reading tourism education: Neoliberalism unveiled. *Annals of Tourism Research, 36*(2), 191−221.

Baum, T. (2015). Human resources in tourism: Still waiting for change? − A 2015 reprise. *Tourism Management, 50,* 204−221.

Cooper, C., & Shepherd, R. (1997). The relationship between tourism education and the tourism industry: Implications for tourism education. *Tourism Recreation Research, 22*(1), 34−47.

Crouch, G. I., & Perdue, R. R. (2015). The disciplinary foundations of tourism research: 1980−2010. *Journal of Travel Research, 54*(September), 1−15.

Hofstede, G. (2001). *Culture's consequences: Comparing values, behaviors, institutions and organizations across nations* (2nd ed.). London: Sage.

Hofstede, G., Hofstede, G. J., & Minkov, M. (2010). *Cultures and organizations: Software of the mind* (3rd ed.). New York, NY: McGraw-Hill.

Jafari, J. (Ed.). (2003). *Encyclopaedia of tourism.* New York, NY: Routledge.

Joppe, M. (2012). Conference note − Second interdisciplinary tourism research conference. *Anatolia: An International Journal of Tourism and Hospitality Research, 23*(3), 442−443.

Kozak, M. (2003). *Destination benchmarking: Concepts, practices and operations.* Oxon: CABI.

Kozak, M., & Baloglu, S. (2010). *Managing and marketing tourist destinations: Strategies to gain a competitive edge.* London: Routledge.

Pizam, A. (2009). What is the hospitality industry and how does it differ from the tourism and travel industries? *International Journal of Hospitality Management, 28*(2), 183−184.

Pizam, A., & Shani, A. (2009). The nature of the hospitality industry: Present and future managers' perspectives. *Anatolia: An International Journal of Tourism and Hospitality Research, 20*(1), 134−150.

Singal, M. (2015). How is the hospitality and tourism industry different? An empirical test of some structural characteristics. *International Journal of Hospitality Management, 34,* 116−119.

Tribe, J., & Xiao, H. (2011). Development in tourism social science. *Annals of Tourism Research, 38*(1), 7−26.

Wardle, C., & Buckley, R. (2014). Tourism citations in other disciplines. *Annals of Tourism Research, 46,* 163−184.

Xiao, H., & Smith, S. L. J. (2006). The making of tourism research: Insights from a social science. *Annals of Tourism Research, 33*(2), 490−507.

PART I
TOURISM MANAGEMENT

CHAPTER 1

EUROPEAN QUALITY AWARD WINNING COMPANIES: A SITUATIONAL ANALYSIS

H. Kader Şanlıöz-Özgen

ABSTRACT

The European Quality Award came into being in 1992. Since then, 42 organizations from various sectors have attained this internationally recognized award. Although the model of the award is considered as a single-generic framework for organizations of all sectors, the question about the situation of the tourism industry arises since this model is not frequent in tourism establishments. With the aim of revealing the situation of tourism industry, this chapter utilized the list of the award winning organizations and identified their economic sectors with reference to The Statistical Classification of Economic Activities in the European Union (NACE). As a consequence, the study revealed the weak participation of the tourism industry, represented by only two hotels and a conference center.

Keywords: European Quality Award; EFQM Excellence Model; business excellence; service excellence

Tourism and Hospitality Management
Advances in Culture, Tourism and Hospitality Research, Volume 12, 3–17
Copyright © 2016 by Emerald Group Publishing Limited
All rights of reproduction in any form reserved
ISSN: 1871-3173/doi:10.1108/S1871-317320160000012002

INTRODUCTION

The categorization of economic sectors dates back more than 80 years. Since then, researchers have developed several models with adaptations to economic developments. Meanwhile the development of the service sector (SS), together with technological advances has necessitated the diversification of these categories and the establishment of international standards for economic and political issues.

As for quality awards their initiation dates back to the 1950s in the Far East to improve productivity in the manufacturing companies. In the following decades, quality awards and models have advanced in other parts of the world with various sets of criteria or concepts (i.e., value for the customer, leadership, people, creativity and innovation) in addition to productivity. That is, the focus has moved on to processes and results. The European Quality Award (EQA) introduces one of these comprehensive models covering an organization with all stakeholders.

In this context, this study aims to address the situation of the tourism industry as a part of SS among EQA winners. Firstly, the paper summarizes the history of economic sector categorizations in order to determine a framework for an appropriate classification of the winners. The study utilized NACE as the reference set to classify the economic sectors of winning organizations. Upon a data collection process on the award history web page, database and documents, a list and details of award winning companies were obtained. After determining the activities of SS in the NACE codes, the ones related to tourism activities were selected with reference to UNWTO classification of tourism activities. The analysis of the economic sectors of award winning companies revealed the share of SS as slightly higher than other sectors. However, the share of the tourism industry is relatively small, with only two hotels and a conference center.

THEORETICAL CONSIDERATIONS

The very first categorizations of economic sectors include three basic groups, defined in various terms (Katouzian, 1970; Singelmann, 1978): primary, secondary and tertiary (unproductive activities other than primary and secondary ones); agricultural, manufacturing and service; and extractive, transformative and services. These classifications indicate an evolution in production with milestones in economic history (Pine & Gilmore, 1999); an economy based on agriculture until the start of manufacturing in

England in the 18th century and its development in the United States in the 19th century, followed by the increase in service activities in the 1950s.

Due to the development of services, technological advances, and innovations, the distinction between the different sectors becomes ambiguous according to principal or subordinate productions; therefore, three-factor models become inadequate to classify economic sectors (Singelmann, 1978). Consequently, the need for new classification sets with more items arises in order to cover all types of productions or organizations (Castaldi, 2009; Castellacci, 2008; Miozzo & Soete, 2001; Pavitt, 1984). In this context, Pavitt (1984) suggests classifying sectors as supplier dominated (i.e., agriculture), scale intensive (i.e., bulk materials such as gas, durable goods), specialized suppliers (i.e., machinery) and science based (i.e., electronics).

As for the categorization of SS activities, Fisher (1933) identifies them as "facilities for travel, amusements of various kinds, governmental and other personal and intangible services, flowers, music, art, literature, education, science, philosophy and the like". In the following decades, the development in technology, innovation, and services creates the need to classify SS in sub-categories for more purposeful definitions. To this extent, Katouzian (1970) suggests classifying SS activities in relation to other economic sectors as the new services (based on a rise in income and time; i.e., education, entertainment, hotels, restaurants), complementary services (related to manufacturing production; i.e., banking, transportation) and the old services (pre-industrial period; i.e., domestic service). From a different perspective, Singelmann (1978) groups services as distributive (i.e., transportation, communication, and the retail trade), producer (i.e., banking, legal, and real estate), social (i.e., medical, education, and government), and personal (i.e., hotels, eating and drinking places, repair, and entertainment) activities.

More recently, Miozzo and Soete (2001) has extended Pavitt's model to classify services with two slight changes; distinguishing physical and information infrastructure in the scale intensive services and combining science based and specialized supplier services. Castellacci (2008) has added new dimensions to previous models and groups manufacturing and SS in four main sets with subsets for each: (1) advance knowledge providers (intensive business services such as software, engineering and specialized suppliers such as machinery), (2) mass production goods (science based manufacturing such as electronics and scale intensive manufacturing such as motor vehicles), (3) supporting infrastructure services (network services such as telecommunications and physical services such as transport), and (4) personal goods and services (supplier dominated goods such as textiles and supplier dominated services such as hotels and restaurants).

The concern inherent in comparing economic data at an international level leads to the production of an international reference as a standardized tool of statistics. In order to construct a set of activities to be utilized while collecting and reporting economic data, the United Nations (UN) launched the very first classification set on the international standardization of industry activities in 1948 (UN Statistics Division, 1990). Since then, the UN has revised this reference set four times up until to the fourth version in 2008. The UN calls this document the *International Standard Industrial Classification of All Economic Activities (ISIC)*, which the majority of countries in the world utilize.

Currently the ISIC serves as the classification reference for international reports and statistics (Mannetje & Kromhout, 2003). Some countries develop their national classifications (i.e., NACE) derived from the ISIC. NACE includes some identical to ISIC items, and adds some sub-items to the ISIC categories (UN Statistics Division, 2008). The majority of European countries adopt NACE for the publication of statistics (Mannetje & Kromhout, 2003). Concerning the codes related to SS, Veil (1990) identifies the central and broadest classifications including the ones between G and Q with reference to ISIC Rev.3; that is, the codes coming after F represent SS activities (Table 2 indicates the codes with their respective content). Since then, due to the updates of ISIC and NACE depending on the variety of economic activities, particularly in the SS, the list of codes has been extended to the letter U.

Finally, in accordance with Miozzo and Soete's (2001) model and ISIC Rev.3, Castaldi (2009) suggests a more recent model of SS classifications including supplier dominated (direct services to consumers, i.e., hotels, restaurants, rental), scale intensive (i.e., transport, communication, real estate), science based and specialized suppliers (knowledge intensive services, i.e., consultancy, computer related activities). Table 1 presents a summary of the evolution of economic sectors and services classifications.

Being involved in the SS, which in particular dominates the economies of industrialized countries (Ghobadian, Speller, & Jones, 1994; Pine & Gilmore, 1999), the tourism industry is among the world's largest and fastest growing economic activities (Nicolau & Sellers, 2010). In spite of the fact that tourism establishments (airlines, hotels, restaurants) deliver tangible goods (seats, beds, food), economists identify this industry as a part of SS since the offerings are not standardized or inventoried, and delivery occurs on demand as a response to an individual order (Pine & Gilmore, 1999). As seen in the previously mentioned categories, the tourism industry has taken part with its various sectors in the classifications from the early

Table 1.   The Evolution of Economic Sectors and Service Classifications.

Grouping Type	Author(s)	Classification
Three-factor model	Clark (1940), Fisher (1933)	Primary
		Secondary
		Tertiary
	Kuznets (1949)	Agricultural
		Manufacturing
		Service
	Singelmann (1978)	Extractive
		Transformative
		Service
Four-factor model	Pavitt (1984)	Supplier dominated
		Scale intensive
		Specialized suppliers
		Science based
Service sector	Katouzian (1970)	The new services
		Complementary services
		The old services
	Singelmann (1978)	Distributive
		Producer
		Social
		Personal
	Miozzo and Soete (2001)	Scale intensive (physical and information infrastructure)
		Science based
		Specialized supplier services
	Castaldi (2009)	Supplier dominated
		Scale intensive
		Science based and specialized suppliers
Integration of the service sector with other economic activities	Castellacci (2008)	Advance knowledge providers (intensive business services and specialized suppliers)
		Mass production goods (science based manufacturing and scale manufacturing)
		Supporting infrastructure services (network services and physical services)
		Personal goods and services (supplier dominated goods and supplier dominated services)

Source: Produced by the author.

definition of SS to the recent sets. Alongside the crystallization of SS activities within years, the tourism industry's principal activities become part of various classes: transport as distributive or physical supporting infrastructure services, or hotels and restaurants as supplier dominated personal services.

Among the 14 founder companies of the European Foundation for Quality Management (EFQM) from various European establishments at the model development stage, only two run businesses in the SS (one in information technology and one in the airline sector) while the others are manufacturing, medicine, or engineering companies (Conti, 2007). Founded with the participation of 67 European countries in 1989, EFQM established an excellence model (EFQM EM) as a framework for the EQA in 1991 (EFQM, 2014a).

In respect of this model, in October every year since 1992, the EFQM announces the award, the prize winners and finalists. Every year the organizations with over 600 points among the finalists are recognized as prize winners. The organizations with the highest points win the EQA for the subject year, and obtain the award on their highest graded fundamental concept of the model (face-to-face interview with EFQM representative of Turkish Society for Quality − KalDer on 30.01.2014).

Both EFQM and EFQM EM are dynamic entities with regular revisions in their systems for an excellent and sustainable performance. EFQM, as an organization, has started its journey toward excellence by fulfilling the necessities of the model framework (EFQM, 2014b). As for EFQM EM, used by over 30,000 organizations in Europe (EFQM, 2014b), the model has been revised five times (EFQM, 2012) to adapt to global changes in the world. Fundamental concepts have been utilized as components of the evaluation set since 1999. The model has served as a single, generic model for all sectors with a change in the criteria weights (all with 10% of weight except for customer and key results with 15%) since 2010. Today the final version of the model is action-oriented and concentrates on sustainability, the fulfillment of all stakeholders' expectations, and innovation and most of the national quality awards in Europe are based solely or with some modifications on EFQM EM (Mavroidis, Toliopouluo, & Agoritsas, 2007).

The three-year period is a key term for EFQM in order to review their strategies with mission, vision and values (EFQM, 2014a), to adapt the framework to changes if needed (EFQM, 2012) and to determine the validity of EQA (E-mail correspondence with EFQM Center on 16.09.2014). On the other hand, one critical aim of EFQM is to share successful implementations within a network in order to deliver excellence throughout the world. In addition to recognition books and other publications, the foundation has established on its official website a recognition online database where information about applying organizations to EFQM EM takes place. Launched in 2009, this database pertains to organizations back to that year, and is currently at the stage of update and refinement (E-mail correspondences with the EFQM Center on 29.01.2014 and 16.09.2014).

The academic literature on quality management discusses EFQM EM and EQA from various perspectives. A number of conceptual studies (Conti, 2007; Martin-Castilla & Rodriguez-Ruiz, 2008; Ruiz-Carrillo & Fernandez-Ortiz, 2005) aim to explain the basic principles, structures, processes and benefits of the EFQM EM while some other papers (Ghobadian & Woo, 1996; Mavroidis et al., 2007; McDonald, Zairi, & Idris, 2002) compare EQA with other major quality awards indicating its strengths and weaknesses. Martin-Castilla and Rodriguez-Ruiz (2008) provide some further details concerning the model for a clear understanding of its benefits. Their explanatory study presents an analysis of the model criteria with the perspective of intellectual capital and emphasizes its adaptability to strategic management thanks to its dynamic features and comprehensive structure supporting organizational learning regarding stakeholders. Ruiz-Carrillo and Fernandez-Ortiz (2005) prove that EFQM EM has an implicit theoretical basis of a resource-based framework.

The comparable studies (Ghobadian & Woo, 1996; Mavroidis et al., 2007; McDonald et al., 2002) attempt to identify the similarities and differences between EFQM EM and other quality award models, particularly the Malcolm Baldrige award. These findings reveal the distinctive features of this approach such as higher direct weight of customer satisfaction and balance of business results with other criteria, and adaptability of the subcriteria to the specific requirements of companies or countries. Ghobadian and Woo (1996) suggest organizations of all sectors can utilize EFQM EM as a comprehensive tool for total quality management and self-assessment method by making use of the information and experience shared on various media.

A body of empirical research (Bou-Llusar, Escrig-Tena, Roca-Puig, & Beltran-Martin, 2005; Bou-Llusar, Escrig-Tena, Roca-Puig, & Beltran-Martin, 2009; Ehrlich, 2006; Tutuncu & Kucukusta, 2010) supports the findings that EFQM EM is an appropriate framework for total quality management in organizations, since the model includes interrelated elements which have a positive impact on organizational results.

Some meta-analysis studies (Doeleman, ten Have, & Ahaus, 2014; Kim, Kumar, & Murphy, 2010), test EFQM EM in various areas such as education, medicine, non-profit organizations, and manufacturing companies, and put forward the model as an effective management approach. Moreover, researchers prefer utilizing quantitative methods with large-scale data in order to generalize the effectiveness of the model especially in terms of performance measurement. In addition to available findings in the literature, there is a need for future studies in terms of emphasizing the model's comprehensive implementation, together with policy, leadership, and strategy subjects, focusing on longitudinal effects of the EFQM EM process, using analytical, simulation techniques and control groups.

Critical studies (Ghobadian & Woo, 1996; Gomez Gomez, Martinez Costa, & Martinez Lorente, 2011) focus on EFQM EM and EQA winning organizations in terms of the features of the model, size, type, understanding, and performance of the organizations. Ghobadian and Woo (1996) criticize the model as having static criteria and being a process-oriented approach rather than a results-oriented one. However, the model is a clear tool which can also be applicable to small businesses, and aims to construct an organizational structure and process for a sustainable continuation despite external pressures. Gomez Gomez et al. (2011) raise the question about the relationships between the criteria of the EFQM EM as they may not be as valid as proposed. They suggest this fact may occur due to the model itself, or the evaluators' interpretations.

As for the share of the tourism industry in the EFQM-related studies (excluding the ones with a focus on national quality awards using the EFQM EM framework, which were not researched during this study), a literature search reveals only one study (Camison, 1996) with a direct focus on tourism. This empirical research suggests EFQM EM as an effective self-assessment instrument for hotels to improve service quality. Several studies (Doeleman et al., 2014; Gomez Gomez et al., 2011; Tutuncu & Kucukusta, 2008) deal with SS organizations, particularly in the education and health fields, but the tourism industry and its sectors are not represented in the EFQM EM-related academic literature.

METHOD

This study aims to address the situation of the tourism industry among EQA winners as a part of SS. In order to achieve this aim, there is a need for a classification instrument to distinguish the sectors of EQA winners. For this purpose, NACE was chosen as the appropriate classification set since both NACE and EQA concern European countries. After précising the classification instrument, the second step was to determine the relevant codes of NACE including SS and tourism industry activities. Since Veil (1990) suggests codes after F in ISIC are related to SS, this definition was utilized for an appropriate classification of tourism-related activities. ISIC and NACE are similar sets; therefore, the definition of Veil can be used to determine tourism-related activities. Among the codes between G and U, the ones indicating the tourism activities were selected by using the UNWTO terms (UNWTO, 2007). Table 2 shows the tourism-related NACE codes.

After the determination of the relevant NACE codes to SS and the tourism industry, a search was conducted on the EFQM official website which displays EFQM EM implementing organizations on two different pages: Recognition database and award history records. The EFQM database was launched in 2009 and contains detailed information on the organizations from then onwards (E-mail correspondence with EFQM Center 29.01.2014). The page regarding award history provides some information about the award and prize winners together with the finalists from the very first award in 1992. Since the database is subject to revision according to the changes in the model, and contains only the recent applications, history records were taken into consideration upon the advice of EFQM (E-mail correspondence on 29.01.2014).

The EFQM Center notified the author regarding the sectoral classification of the organizations on the recognition database (E-mail correspondence on 16.09.2014) by noting that organizations were responsible for declaring their economic activity with the respective documentation. These records are not reliable in determining the sectoral classification; for instance, the sector of the 2013 award winning hotel is recorded as administration of economic activities whereas the economic sector of a tour operator in Turkey is indicated as a hotel establishment. Therefore, the list of award winning organizations between 1992 and 2013 was taken as reference from the award history page of EFQM official website (EFQM, 2014a).

Once the list of award winning companies was available, the main economic activity of each organization was researched by using the internet. The EFQM has published a recognition book since 2001. The findings from the internet were compared to the sectoral information indicated in these books. Depending on this information, the sectoral division of each organization was identified by using the classification of Veil (1990).

Table 2. Tourism Products and Services in NACE Codes.

Code Letter	Sectors	Tourism Products and Services as Defined by UNWTO
A	Agriculture, forestry and fishing	–
B	Mining and quarrying	–
C	Manufacturing	–
D	Electricity, gas, steam and air conditioning supply	–
E	Water supply: sewerage, waste management and remediation activities	–
F	Construction	–
G	Wholesale and retail trade; repair of motor vehicles and motorcycles	Retail trade of country-specific tourism characteristic goods
H	Transportation and storage	Railway, road, water and air transport services
I	Accommodation and food service activities	Accommodation, food and beverage services for visitors
J	Information and communication	–
K	Financial and insurance activities	–
L	Real estate activities	–
M	Professional, scientific and technical activities	–
N	Administrative and support service activities	Transport equipment rental services; travel agencies and other reservation services activities
O	Public administration and defense; compulsory social security	–
P	Education	–
Q	Human health and social work activities	–
R	Arts, entertainment and recreation	Cultural, sports and recreational activities; other country-specific tourism characteristic goods
S	Other service activities	–
T	Activities of households as employers; undifferentiated goods- and services-producing activities of households for own use	–
U	Activities of extraterritorial organizations and bodies	–

Source: European Commission Competition (2010), UNWTO (2007).

FINDINGS

In spite of the fact that a recognition database presents erroneous data about EFQM applications (EFQM, 2014a), a study was conducted on this database by counting and noting each entry in order to reveal the share of SS. Among 2,684 applications for EQA, SS was represented by the following services and shares: 32% education, 10% health, 10% social, 9% miscellaneous, and 5% the administration of economic programs. Concerning the hotels; there were 36 applications at various stages of the model (16 for recognition of excellence and 20 for commitment to excellence). The applications at the recognition stage came from Germany (5), Ireland (4), Turkey (2) and Austria (2), whereas, 16 commitment applications were from the United Kingdom. As for the tourism industry, 223 applications were ascertained on the database, but this number was ambiguous since transportation was not separated into passenger and materials.

Table 3.   Sectors of EQA Winning Organizations.

Country	Number of EQA Winners	Sector with NACE Codes and Number of Organizations for each Sector
The United Kingdom	16	C:3, H:2, J:3, K:1, M:1, N:1, P:4, Q:1
Turkey[a]	8	C:5, D:1, G:1, S:1
Germany	4	C:2, H:1, I:1
Belgium	2	C:2
Denmark	2	C:1, P:1
France	2	C:1, J:1
Italy	2	C:2
Austria	1	I
Finland	1	C
Greece	1	C
Hungary	1	C
Spain	1	J
Switzerland	1	Q
TOTAL	42	C: 19, D:1, G:1, H:3, I:2, J: 5, K:1, M:1, N:1, P:5, Q:2, S:1

Source: EFQM (2014a, 2014b).
[a]One manufacturing company won EQA twice.

Being a more reliable data source, the EFQM award history page (EFQM, 2014a) stated that 42 organizations won the EQA between the years 1992–2013. Table 3 shows the number and sector of the EQA winners according to the countries and NACE codes.

As seen in Table 3, SS was represented by 22 organizations (52.4%) whereas 19 organizations operated in manufacturing (45.2%) and one organization was active in the D-coded economic sector (delivery of gas). Once the concepts of the awards were investigated, the records indicated that eight organizations won the EQA for leadership-related concepts, while five organizations won for customers and another five organizations for people-related concepts. The tourism industry was represented by two hotels in Germany and Austria and by a conference center in the United Kingdom; thus, only three tourism organizations took part among the 42 award winning ones. No other tourism organization has won the EQA so far.

The award history records also include data regarding the EQA prize winners and finalists. Table 4 shows the situation of the tourism industry organizations in these records. Once these data were analyzed, another hotel establishment was ascertained as a prize winner in 2003 and 2004 (Table 4). No other tourism organization was found in these records.

Table 4. Tourism Industry Organizations in EQA.

Year	Organization Name, Country	EQA Details
2013	Alpenresort Schwarz, Austria	Award and prize winner in adding value for customers and succeeding through the talent of people
2010	Alpenresort Schwarz, Austria	Finalist
2004	Schindlerhof Klaus Kobjoll GmbH, Germany	Prize winner in people development and involvement under the category of independent small and medium enterprises
2003	Schindlerhof Klaus Kobjoll GmbH, Germany	Prize winner in customer focus under the category of independent small and medium enterprises
		(First hotel in Germany to obtain the ISO9001)
2003	Edinburgh International Conference Center Limited	Award and prize winner in people development and involvement under the category of subsidiary small and medium enterprises
1998	Landhotel Schindlerhof	Award winner

Source: EFQM (2014a, 2003, 2004, 2010).

CONCLUSION AND IMPLICATIONS

Aiming to reveal the situation of the tourism industry among EQA winning organizations, this study has made a significant contribution to the literature by ascertaining the share of SS and the tourism industry. Consequently, the study identifies the share of SS organizations as being slightly higher than those in other sectors. On the other hand, tourism industry, compared to its pace of development, owns very little representation within the award winning organizations with only two hotels and a conference center. Despite the fact that one of the founder organizations was an airline company, this sector of the industry does not exist in the award listing. Although there are a number of applications involved in the recognition database, the share of the tourism industry is relatively small (8%) compared to the dominance of SS with various economic activities. The reasons why the tourism industry organizations do not implement EFQM EM are worth studying in order to confirm if the model is an appropriate instrument for all sectors or indeed to adapt it if updates are required.

The academic literature on EFQM EM shows another aspect of this infrequency in the tourism industry by the number of studies carried out on this issue. More academic research, with a focus on implementation of EFQM EM, should also be conducted to disseminate the information about the probable benefits of the model, so the tourism industry will be open and willing to make use of a comprehensive total quality management tool.

As for the limitations of the study, the most critical one was that the data collection process was carried out only on the database of the EFQM Center, and published on either the recognition database or the award history records. Being a framework which has inspired many national quality awards in Europe, EFQM EM is current in many organizations in various economic activities, including the tourism industry. Therefore, more comprehensive research, with a focus on national quality awards would generate more concrete results in terms of the tourism industry's position and the reasons for the infrequency if the share of tourism is still relatively low.

ACKNOWLEDGEMENTS

The author thanks the reviewers and participants of the 7th World Conference for Graduate Research in Tourism, Hospitality, and Leisure,

I. Aguirre and V. Beauduin from EFQM Center in Belgium and O. Argon from KalDer in Turkey for their remarks and significant contribution to the study.

REFERENCES

Bou-Llusar, J. C., Escrig-Tena, A. B., Roca-Puig, V., & Beltran-Martin, I. (2005). To what extent do enablers explain results in the EFQM excellence model? *International Journal of Quality and Reliability Management, 22*(4), 337–353.

Bou-Llusar, J. C., Escrig-Tena, A. B., Roca-Puig, V., & Beltran-Martin, I. (2009). An empirical assessment of the EFQM excellence model: Evaluation as a TQM framework relative to the MBNQA model. *Journal of Operations Management, 27*, 1–22.

Camison, C. (1996). Total quality management in hospitality: An application of the EFQM model. *Tourism Management, 17*(3), 191–201.

Castaldi, C. (2009). The relative rate of manufacturing and services in Europe: An innovation perspective. *Technological Forecasting and Social Change, 76*, 709–722.

Castellacci, F. (2008). Technological paradigms, regimes and trajectories: Manufacturing and service industries in a new taxonomy of sectoral patterns of innovation. *Research Policy, 37*, 978–994.

Clark, C. (1940). *The conditions of economic progress.* London: MacMillan.

Conti, T. A. (2007). A history and review of the European quality award model. *The TQM Magazine, 19*(2), 112–128.

Doeleman, H. J., ten Have, S., & Ahaus, C. T. B. (2014). Empirical evidence on applying the European foundation for quality management excellence model: A literature review. *Total Quality Management & Business Excellence, 25*(5–6), 439–460.

EFQM. (2003). *EFQM recognition book.* Brussels: EFQM.

EFQM. (2004). *EFQM recognition book.* Brussels: EFQM.

EFQM. (2010). *EFQM recognition book.* Brussels: EFQM.

EFQM. (2012). *Excellence in action November 2012.* Brussels: EFQM.

EFQM. (2014a). *European foundation of quality management official website.* Retrieved from www.efqm.org. Accessed on January 17, 2014.

EFQM. (2014b). *EFQM annual report 2013.* Brussels: EFQM.

Ehrlich, C. (2006). The EFQM-model and work motivation. *Total Quality Management & Business Excellence, 17*(2), 131–140.

European Commission Competition. (2010). *List of NACE codes.* Retrieved from http://ec.europa.eu/%20competition/mergers/cases/index/nace_all.html. Accessed on January 24, 2014.

Fisher, A. G. B. (1933). Capital and the growth of knowledge. *The Economic Journal, 43*(171), 379–389.

Ghobadian, A., Speller, S., & Jones, M. (1994). Service quality: Concepts and models. *International Journal of Quality & Reliability Management, 11*(9), 43–66.

Ghobadian, A., & Woo, H. S. (1996). Characteristics, benefits and shortcomings of four major quality awards. *International Journal of Quality and Reliability, 13*(2), 10–44.

Gomez Gomez, J., Martinez Costa, M., & Martinez Lorente, A. R. (2011). A critical evaluation of the EFQM model. *International Journal of Quality & Reliability Management*, *28*(5), 484–502.

Katouzian, M. A. (1970). The development of the service sector: A new approach. *Oxford Economic Papers New Series*, *22*(3), 362–382.

Kim, D. Y., Kumar, V., & Murphy, S. A. (2010). European foundation for quality management business excellence model: An integrative review and research agenda. *International Journal of Quality & Reliability Management*, *27*(6), 684–701.

Kuznets, S. (1949). National income and industrial structure. *Econometrica: Journal of Econometric Society*, *17*, 204–241.

Mannetje, A., & Kromhout, H. (2003). The use of occupation and industry classifications in general population studies. *International Journal of Epidemiology*, *32*, 419–428.

Martin-Castilla, J. I., & Rodriguez-Ruiz, O. (2008). EFQM model: Knowledge governance and competitive advantage. *Journal of Intellectual Capital*, *9*(1), 133–156.

Mavroidis, V., Toliopouluo, S., & Agoritsas, C. (2007). A comparative analysis and review of national quality awards in. *Europe. The TQM Magazine*, *19*(5), 454–467.

McDonald, I., Zairi, M., & Idris, M. A. (2002). Sustaining and transferring excellence: A framework of best practice of TQM transformation based on winners of Baldrige and European quality awards. *Measuring Business Excellence*, *6*(3), 20–30.

Miozzo, M., & Soete, L. (2001). Internationalization of services: A technological perspective. *Technological Forecasting and Social Change*, *67*, 159–185.

Nicolau, J. L., & Sellers, R. (2010). The quality of quality awards: Diminishing information asymmetries in a hotel chain. *Journal of Business Research*, *63*, 832–839.

Pavitt, K. (1984). Sectoral patterns of technical change: Towards a taxonomy and a theory. *Research Policy*, *13*, 343–373.

Pine, P. J., & Gilmore, H. H. (1999). *Experience economy*. Boston: Harvard Business Review Press.

Ruiz-Carrillo, J. I. C., & Fernandez-Ortiz, R. (2005). Theoretical foundation of the EFQM model: The resource-based view. *Total Quality Management*, *16*(1), 31–55.

Singelmann, J. (1978). The sectoral transformation of the labor force in seven industrialized countries, 1920–1970. *American Journal of Sociology*, *83*(3), 1224–1234.

Tutuncu, O., & Kucukusta, D. (2008). The role of supply chain management integration in quality management system for hospitals. *International Journal of Management Perspectives*, *1*(1), 31–39.

Tutuncu, O., & Kucukusta, D. (2010). Canonical correlation between job satisfaction and EFQM business excellence model. *Quality & Quantity*, *44*, 1227–1238.

UN Statistics Division. (1990). *ISIC revision 3*. Retrieved from http://unstats.un.org/unsd/cr/%20registry/regcst.asp?Cl=2. Accessed on January 23, 2014.

UN Statistics Division. (2008). *ISIC revision 4*. New York, NY: United Nations.

United Nations World Tourism Organisation. (2007). *Understanding tourism: Basic glossary*. Retrieved from http://media.unwto.%20org/%20content/understanding-tourism-basic-glossary. Accessed on February 03, 2014.

Veil, E. (1990). *Defining services: An enumerative approach*. Paris: OECD, Department of Economics and Statistics.

CHAPTER 2

SERVICE COLLABORATION BETWEEN HEALTHCARE SERVICE PROVIDERS AND TOURISM AGENCIES

Elaine Y.T. Chew and Stephanie Onggo

ABSTRACT

The aim of this chapter is to understand the nature of business collaboration between healthcare service providers and tourism agencies in Malaysia. Interviews with 17 healthcare service providers in Malaysia reveal that most of the collaboration between healthcare service providers and tourism agencies in Malaysia is informal or loose, despite their intention to leverage on medical tourism for business expansion. Close and tight collaborations are rare. The findings point towards the main reasons behind the rare collaboration which are the high customer orientation of healthcare service providers, the strategic move of business and support for government agenda.

Keywords: Medical tourism; business collaboration; co-evolutionary theory; stakeholder relationships

Tourism and Hospitality Management
Advances in Culture, Tourism and Hospitality Research, Volume 12, 19–30
ISSN: 1871-3173/doi:10.1108/S1871-317320160000012003

INTRODUCTION

Medical tourism is conceptualised as a phenomenon where people travel beyond their own territory to obtain medical, dental and surgical care while simultaneously being holidaymakers (Connell, 2006). Medical tourism is also associated with the health and wellness being of individuals. The medical tourism industry has grown to be one of the fastest-growing parts of tourism internationally (Heung, Kucukusta, & Song, 2010). For some countries, investment in the medical tourism industry may serve as a means to increase GDP, improve services, generate foreign exchange and boost tourism (Ramirez de Arellano, 2007). Countries such as Jordan, Argentina, India, Thailand, Singapore and Malaysia are among the countries that have started developing and promoting their own medical tourism industry (Connell, 2006).

As the term itself suggests, medical tourism comprises of both medical and tourism services, where the combination of medical/health treatment and tourism attractions is considered to be its fundamental pillars (Connell, 2006; Horowitz, Rosensweig, & Jones, 2007; Hume & Demicco, 2007; Loubeau, 2009; Singh, 2008). Thus, despite the core product being medical treatment, attractive hospitality and travel options are also perceived to be crucial elements of medical tourism (Heung et al., 2010). Health and tourism are regarded as interacting with each other to form an integral part influencing service experience and overall satisfaction of medical tourists (Lawton & Page, 1997).

Wang (2012) emphasised that the perceived value of medical tourism is significantly influenced by three critical components − perceived medical quality, perceived service quality and perceived enjoyment. To enhance medical tourism experiences apart from the quality of medical facilities and service delivery, tie-ins with tourism services are offered (Bookman & Bookman, 2007). The whole infrastructure of the tourist industry (i.e. tourism agencies, airlines, hotels, restaurants and transport services) benefits considerably from the new niche (Connell, 2013), and in turn, contributes positively to the country's economy.

To ensure the sustainable performance of medical tourism, the creation and design of medical service packages should be coordinated in tandem with vacation plan to ensure positive experience for medical tourists. There is a need for integration of medical and tourism services as well as the coordination between these industries if the combination of value creations is to be enhanced for medical tourists (Wang, 2012). Therefore, past scholars often emphasise the importance of good coordination between these two distinct industries for the development of the medical tourism industry (Heung et al., 2010).

Yet, past research often offers lop-sided attention to medical services to understand medical tourism. Little is known about the role of the tourism industry. Despite the collaborative platform developed by various governments for enhancing the medical tourism industry, no studies have examined the nature of collaboration between healthcare service providers and tourism agencies to provide wholesome service offerings to international medical tourists. There is also a dire need to understand the motivations driving the nature of collaboration. The absence of such knowledge that is strategically important for maintaining the boom of the medical tourism industry necessitates a study. Thus, it is important to understand how collaborative works between healthcare service providers and tourism agencies have taken place in the development of the medical tourism industry.

THEORETICAL CONSIDERATIONS

Asia, in particular, India, Thailand, Singapore and Malaysia (Hall, 2013), holds the reputation as the key region for medical tourism (Connell, 2006; Hall, 2013). In creating competitive advantage, governments in a few Asian countries (e.g. Thailand, Singapore and Taiwan) have started to play a role in strengthening their own medical tourism industry. Initial government efforts include leading road shows for both industries and providing guidance in the integration of these two distinct industries. Connell (2013) noted that some healthcare service providers and its chains in Thailand have developed functional departments to cater both medical and tourism services. Large-scale healthcare service providers in Singapore provide airport transfers, booking of accommodation and arrangement for local tours.

The key healthcare service providers in these two countries do not own any type of business in the travel industry. They closely integrate their service offerings with different players in the travel industry (i.e. hotels, airlines, tourism agencies) so as to provide superior, integrated service experiences to international medical tourists. In Taiwan, the government has been very proactive in creating a platform for healthcare service providers and tourism agencies to explore the creation of an integrated service. As many as 20 healthcare service providers work together with hotels, airlines and tourism agencies to attract medical tourists (Wang, 2012). From various sources (Connell, 2013; Heung et al., 2010; Ormond, 2011;

Wong & Musa, 2012), it is understood that some Asian countries have been proactively developing this industry to position their country as the ultimate medical tourism destination.

Malaysia shares a similar aspiration to position itself as a medical tourism hub in Asia. In Malaysia, the medical tourism industry is regarded by its government as an important economic area for the country (Hall, 2013) with 671,000 medical tourists in 2012 (Leong, 2013; MHTC, 2013). The Ministry of Health in Malaysia has set up a special government agency to manage medical tourism so as to develop sustainable competitive advantage amidst stiff competition from neighbouring countries like Thailand and Singapore. From an initial small unit to promote medical tourism (MHTC, 2013), the Malaysia Healthcare Tourism Council (MHTC) was established with the objectives of promoting the country's medical tourism as well as supporting industry players (MHTC, 2013).

Despite government and commercial investments to seize lucrative and growing opportunities in the medical tourism industry, not much research attention has been given to understanding the industry (Henderson, 2003; Heung et al., 2010). Past research tends to be conceptual (Runnels & Carrera, 2012; Smith & Forgione, 2007), non-empirical and descriptive in nature (e.g. Carrera & Bridges, 2006; Connell, 2006, 2013; Enderwick & Nagar, 2011; Henderson, 2003; Horowitz et al., 2007; Lee, 2007; Lunt & Carrera, 2010; Tseng, 2013; Whittaker, 2008). The majority focuses on the demand side of medical tourism. This narrow focus is particularly observable in studies that describe the motivations behind the phenomenon of people travelling abroad for medical care (Altin, Singal, & Kara, 2011; Connell, 2006; Henderson, 2003; Horowitz et al., 2007; Reddy, York, & Brannon, 2010).

As such, this study attempts to provide an insight of the current strategic business practices in Malaysia's medical tourism industry. In particular, this study looks into the collaboration between healthcare service providers and tourism agencies by understanding the motivations that drive the strategic collaboration between healthcare service providers and tourism agencies.

METHOD

A qualitative research method was employed in this study as it aims to explore a new area of research. Semi-structured interviews are adopted as interviews provide a better opportunity for respondents to express their experiences in person (Harrell & Bradley, 2009). The probing of respondents in qualitative research, in fact, allows the researcher to develop a higher level of meaning about the motivations for collaboration between healthcare service providers and tourism agencies in delivering wholesome one-stop service offerings to international healthcare tourists. The probing also enables better understanding of how collaborative works between healthcare service providers and tourism agencies have taken place.

Semi-structured interviews are employed to acquire information from marketing managers of 17 healthcare service providers in Malaysia. The selection of medical centres and managers was based on two criteria: (1) the healthcare service providers in Malaysia must be targeting healthcare tourists from abroad; and (2) the representative personnel from the healthcare service providers in Malaysia must have an understanding of the collaboration between healthcare service providers and tourism agencies. Table 1 shows the geographical details of the seventeen participants that are also heavily populated by healthcare service providers.

FINDINGS

This section discusses the findings on the nature of collaboration between healthcare service providers and tourism agencies, and the motivating forces that push for strategic collaboration. Firstly, the findings on the nature of collaboration will be discussed to illustrate how collaboration has taken place in the medical tourism industry, followed by a discussion uncovering the motivations for such collaborations.

Table 1. The Geographical Details of Participants in Malaysia.

No.	Respondent	Geographical Location	No.	Respondent	Geographical Location
1	Respondent 1	Petaling Jaya	10	Respondent 10	Penang Island
2	Respondent 2	Kuala Lumpur	11	Respondent 11	Penang Island
3	Respondent 3	Kuala Lumpur	12	Respondent 12	Penang Island
4	Respondent 4	Kuala Lumpur	13	Respondent 13	Kuala Lumpur
5	Respondent 5	Penang Island	14	Respondent 14	Johor Bahru
6	Respondent 6	Shah Alam	15	Respondent 15	Petaling Jaya
7	Respondent 7	Penang Island	16	Respondent 16	Petaling Jaya
8	Respondent 8	Malacca	17	Respondent 17	Kuala Lumpur
9	Respondent 9	Seremban			

The findings reveal that the nature of collaboration between healthcare service providers and tourism agencies falls into three types or levels — loose, close and tight collaborations. According to the Oxford Dictionary, loose is defined as 'not close, compact or solid in structure or formation' and 'not rigidly organised'. The word 'loose' can be used to describe one of the three types of collaboration between healthcare service providers and tourism agencies. In this study, loose collaboration depicts the lowest or minimal level of collaboration. This study found that some collaboration between healthcare service providers and tourism agencies is rather fragmented and informal.

This type of collaboration is basically characterised by (1) the absence of a contractual agreement with tourism agencies; (2) the absence of a commission fee between the two parties; (3) the mutual support via business recommendation; and (4) the high degree of trust by healthcare service providers towards the service quality of tourism agencies. The absence of a contractual agreement to structure and administrate the strategic collaboration signifies the adoption of a simple business collaboration. It also shows that the business relationship between healthcare service providers and tourism agencies is rather an extension of the current informal relationship that exists prior to the respective parties' corporate decision to expand sales or business into the medical tourism industry.

While being termed as having loose collaboration, this type of collaboration does not necessarily imply that value-added complementary services to international medical tourists are ignored by healthcare service providers. Interestingly, loose collaboration can be a result of a high degree of customer orientation by the healthcare providers. In other words, the proactiveness of healthcare service providers in customer service has led them to learn, absorb and perform complementary services (i.e. booking of accommodation, booking of flight tickets or confirmation of flight tickets) that are traditionally part of tourism agencies' core service offerings. This learning effort also implies that healthcare service providers tend to rely on trusted tourism agencies to provide high quality sight-seeing experience to their customers. In doing so, healthcare service providers are inclined to only seek collaboration with trusted tourism agencies to provide leisure travel so as to complete the integrated medical tourism service.

The second nature of collaboration is coined as close collaboration in this study. In the Oxford Dictionary, 'close' is defined as 'to grapple, engage in close encounter' or 'strong'. Another source describes close as 'to come together' or 'unite' (Dictionary.com). These definitions appear to be relevant in describing the close collaboration observed in this study. These definitions are reflective of our findings for close collaboration.

The findings have shown that there are four characteristics that are typical of the close collaboration between healthcare service providers and tourism agencies. They are: (1) the creation of product bundling; (2) the existence of a contractual agreement with tourism agencies; (3) the commitment for certain activities; (4) the existence of a commission fee. The evidence shows that in a close collaboration, healthcare service providers tend to continue their focus on the core business and make changes to provide extra attention and service to better meet the needs of international medical tourists. With core business in mind, healthcare service providers or tourism agencies tend to create a medical tourism package that combines a health-screening programme with a holiday tour.

The healthcare service providers delegate the delivery/provision of tourism services to tourism agencies. The holiday itinerary depends on the creativity of tourism agencies to attractively feature the integrated packages. In such instances, it is typical to have a contractual obligation to clearly specify both parties' commitment in ensuring the success of the medical tourism package as well as the sharing of business outcomes in the form of a commission fee.

The last type of collaboration is termed as tight collaboration in this study. The term 'tight' is defined as 'concise, condensed or well-structured', 'disciplined or well-coordinated' and 'having close relations or tight-knit' (Oxford Dictionary). Evidence from the interview findings is reflective of the definition of the word 'tight'. The nature of collaboration between healthcare service providers and tourism agencies tends to be more structured through the use of a contractual agreement. Another characteristic underpinning tight collaboration between healthcare service providers and tourism agencies is the allocation of a permanent office or travel service counter for the tourism agent at the premises of the healthcare service providers. In other words, the tourism agent has a permanent presence in the vicinity of the healthcare service provider.

The tight collaboration binds the tourism agent to provide immediate travel advice, convenience and travel services to enquiring patients or customers. In this type of collaboration, healthcare service providers rely on tourism agents for their expertise to deliver the complementary services to international medical tourists. Business focus for both parties is similar to that of close collaboration, in that each party remains focused on the core business and tour-related services. The healthcare service providers still outsource the holiday travel to tourism agents. The tight nature of collaboration between healthcare service providers and tourism agencies is a rare practice. While keen on securing more business by expanding to the medical tourism industry, most healthcare service providers are yet to be willing to commit to such tight collaboration due to certain institutional constraints.

THE MOTIVATION FOR STRATEGIC COLLABORATION

Institutional factors underpinning closer strategic collaboration between healthcare service providers and tourism agencies are identified in Table 2. Healthcare service providers, whose priority is customer satisfaction, believe that there is a need to offer a comprehensive or integrated medical tourism service that is satisfying for medical tourists. One of the most efficient means of doing so is to engage tourism agents to deliver the leisure aspect of the service. Some healthcare service providers also find it more efficient and effective to collaborate with tourism agencies rather than creating their own tourism department which is not their core expertise. Additionally, the collaboration is undertaken as an attempt to contribute to the national agenda, either to the industry itself or to the government.

Table 2. The Motivations for Closer Collaboration with Tourism Agencies.

No.	Themes	Sub-Categories
1	Customer-oriented	(a) Attempt to provide solutions to patients' and companions' requests
		(b) The provision of more convenience to customers
2	Strategic move	(a) Efficiency seeking
		(b) Resource seeking
		(c) Network seeking
		(d) Market seeking
		(e) Risk management
		(f) Product promotion effectiveness
		(g) Cost efficiency seeking
3	Contributory effort to national agenda	(a) To the industry
		(b) To the government

High Customer Orientation

The healthcare service providers who engaged in close(r) collaboration with tourism agents tend to place a high priority on patients' needs and consideration beyond medical service. They tend to see the benefit of having a single point of contact to cater to medical and travel needs of patients. Evidence from interviews shows that healthcare service providers that are customer-oriented are more inclined to provide complementary services to medical tourists and have closer collaboration with tourism agencies. Therefore, these healthcare service providers attempted to offer services beyond the core business. A large number of healthcare service providers that are customer-oriented are proactive in assisting customers to solve any matters in relation to logistics and travel (e.g. accommodation, air travel, visa extension and leisure).

A popular means is to offer a medical tourism package that combines healthcare and travel services. In the perception of medical tourists, the healthcare provider provides an integrated service while in terms of operation, the leisure service is outsourced to tourism agents. A less adopted way is to seek long-term commitment of tourism agents to offer services at the premises of the medical centre. By allocating a physical service office or counter for tourism agents in the vicinity of the medical centre, medical tourists can obtain advice and travel services in a short time without the need to travel out of the medical centre. Medical tourists could directly enquire about tour-related services from tourism agents.

Strategic Move

Many healthcare service providers interviewed in this study have tried to penetrate into the Indonesian markets. Some attempted to develop new markets in tier two cities in Indonesia while others tried to expand market share in tier one cities. Considering that aggressive market entry via foreign direct investment is a huge investment exercise that requires substantial corporate resources, relying on local/Indonesian tourism agents was seen as a better move to achieve market-seeking and efficient-seeking business objectives. Healthcare service providers can leverage on the resources of local/Indonesian tourism agents. Tourism agents possess strengths and are endowed with various resources such as travel expertise, wide distribution channels, wide networks and understanding of local markets.

Collaboration with tourism agents as a means to achieve market expansion and market penetration represents a less risky corporate strategy in an efficient way. Moreover, the political environment in Indonesia is often crowded with various issues that are concerns for foreign direct investment. Therefore, besides engaging tourism agents to better serve medical tourists in tour-related services, healthcare service providers also see the strategic role of tourism agencies in supporting the implementation of corporate strategies and attainment of business objectives. The various strategic benefits motivate a large number of healthcare service providers to closely collaborate with tourism agencies in Malaysia and Indonesia.

Contributory Effort to National Agenda

The evidence also points towards contributory efforts in support of the national agenda in making Malaysia a medical tourism hub. Healthcare service providers, especially the wholly owned entities, can afford to run business as usual without catering to the different needs of international medical tourists. However, healthcare service providers also see their role as supporting the government's national goal. Therefore, they perceive that to better cater to the needs and requests of international medical patients, there is a necessity to engage with tourism agencies to provide a wholesome medical tourism experience to international medical patients. Furthermore, healthcare service providers as national entities of the country feel the responsibility to contribute to the country's economy by integrating tourism services into core services — medical services.

CONCLUSION AND IMPLICATIONS

To recapitulate, the scope of this study is to understand the nature of collaboration between healthcare service providers and tourism agencies in Malaysia to provide one-stop service offerings to medical tourists. The scope also covers the motivating forces for the two parties' collaboration. The findings contribute to the tourism literature and business literature.

From the 17 interviews, the collaboration between healthcare service providers and tourism agencies in Malaysia appears to be considerably loose, where in most cases, no formal agreement = prevails between them. The primary motivations for closer collaboration are a high degree of customer orientation, strategic move and response to national agenda.

The study has practical implications. The fragmented service offerings for medical tourism should be integrated further to better serve medical patients. Healthcare service providers and tourism agencies, as the main key players of the medical tourism industry, should undertake such initiatives more seriously. Considering the strategic intent of many healthcare service providers in this study to secure a share of the Indonesian market, the government agency should create a new platform for strategic alliances to occur among key players in the medical tourism industry.

REFERENCES

Altin, M., Singal, M., & Kara, D. (2011). *Consumer decision components for medical tourism: A stakeholder approach (Graduate Student Research in Hospitality and Tourism)*. Retrieved from Scholar Works website http://scholarworks.umass.edu/cgi/viewcontent.cgi?article = 1286&context = gradconf_hospitality

Bookman, M. Z., & Bookman, K. R. (2007). *Medical tourism in developing countries*. New York, NY: Palgrave Macmillan.

Carrera, P. M., & Bridges, J. F. (2006). Globalization and healthcare: Understanding health and medical tourism. *Expert Review of Pharmacoeconomics & Outcomes Research, 6*(4), 447–454.

Connell, J. (2006). Medical tourism: Sea, sun, sand and ... surgery. *Tourism Management, 27*, 1093–1100.

Connell, J. (2013). Contemporary medical tourism: Conceptualisation, culture and commodification. *Tourism Management, 34*, 1–13.

Enderwick, P., & Nagar, S. (2011). The competitive challenge of emerging markets: The case of medical tourism. *International Journal of Emerging Markets, 6*(4), 329–350.

Hall, C. M. (2013). *Medical tourism: The ethics, regulation, and marketing of health mobility*. London: Routledge.

Harrell, M. C., & Bradley, M. A. (2009). *Data collection methods − Semi-structured interviews and focus groups*. Retrieved from National Defense Research Instituted (RAND) website http://www.rand.org/content/dam/rand/pubs/technical_reports/2009/RAND_TR718.pdf

Henderson, J. C. (2003). Healthcare tourism in Southeast Asia. *Tourism Review International, 7*(3–4), 3–4.

Heung, V. C., Kucukusta, D., & Song, H. (2010). A conceptual model of medical tourism: Implications for future research. *Journal of Travel and Tourism Marketing, 27*(3), 236–251.

Horowitz, M. D., Rosensweig, J. A., & Jones, C. A. (2007). Medical tourism: Globalization of the healthcare marketplace. *Medscape General Medicine, 9*(4), 33.

Hume, L. F., & Demicco, F. J. (2007). Bringing hotels to healthcare: A RX for success. *Journal of Quality Assurance in Hospitality & Tourism, 8*(1), 75–84.

Lawton, G., & Page, S. (1997). Evaluating travel agents' provision of health advice to travellers. *Tourism Management, 18*(2), 89–104.

Lee, C. (2007). Medical tourism, an innovative opportunity for entrepreneurs. *Journal of Asia Entrepreneurship and Sustainability*, *3*(1), 110–123.

Leong, T. (2013, September 12). Malaysia looks to make RM630 million from lucrative medical tourism market. *The Malaysian Insider*. Retrieved from http://www.themalaysianinsider.com/business/article/malaysia-looks-to-make-rm630-million-from-lucrative-medical-tourism-market

Loubeau, P. R. (2009). The globalization of dental care: An opportunity for Croatian tourism. *Turizam: Znanstveno-StručniČasopis*, *57*(2), 193–199.

Lunt, N., & Carrera, P. (2010). Medical tourism: Assessing the evidence on treatment aboard. *Maturitas*, *66*, 27–32.

MHTC. (2013). About us. Medical Healthcare Travel Council. Retrieved from http://www.mhtc.org.my/

Ormond, M. (2011). Medical tourism, medical exile: Responding to the cross-border pursuit of healthcare in Malaysia. In C. Minca & T. Oakes (Eds.), *Real tourism: Practice, care and politics in contemporary travel*. London: Routledge.

Ramirez de Arellano, A. (2007). Patients without borders: The emergence of medical tourism. *International Journal of Health Services*, *37*(1), 193–198.

Reddy, S. G., York, V. K., & Brannon, L. A. (2010). Travel for treatment: Students' perspective on medical tourism. *International Journal of Tourism Research*, *12*(5), 510–522.

Runnels, V., & Carrera, P. (2012). Why do patients engage in medical tourism? *Maturitas*, *73*(4), 300–304.

Singh, P. K. (2008). *Medical tourism: Global outlook and Indian scenario*. New Delhi: Kanishka Publishers.

Smith, P. C., & Forgione, D. A. (2007). Global outsourcing of healthcare: A medical Tourism decision model. *Journal of Information Technology Case & Application Research*, *9*(3), 19–27.

Tseng, H. (2013). Medical health care tourism: Why patients go overseas and nurse practitioners need to know. *International Journal of Healthcare Management*, *6*(2), 132–135.

Wang, H. Y. (2012). Value as a medical tourism driver. *Managing Service Quality*, *22*(5), 465–491.

Whittaker, A. (2008). Pleasure and pain: Medical travel in Asia. *Global Public Health*, *3*, 271–290.

Wong, K. M., & Musa, G. (2012). Medical tourism in Asia: Thailand, Singapore, Malaysia and India. In M. C. Hall (Ed.), *The ethics, regulation, and marketing of health mobility*. London: Routledge.

CHAPTER 3

THE TRANSIT TOURISTS IN HONG KONG

Priscilla Chau Min Poon and Bob McKercher

ABSTRACT

This chapter aims to identify the characteristics of transit tourists in Hong Kong. It shows that the USA, Germany, Australia, New Zealand, and India are the major generating regions of transit tourists. Transit tourists have more than 10 hours of transit-wait at the Hong Kong International Airport before connecting flights to the destination regions. Significant differences exist in travel and trip-breaking patterns among transit tourists from different generating regions. This study not only provides insights on the spatial movement of transit tourists but also serves as a prologue to future discussions on transit tourism, an emerging phenomenon of urban tourism.

Keywords: Transit tourism; transit passengers; airport hub; tourist arrival; urban tourism

Tourism and Hospitality Management
Advances in Culture, Tourism and Hospitality Research, Volume 12, 31–46
Copyright © 2016 by Emerald Group Publishing Limited
All rights of reproduction in any form reserved
ISSN: 1871-3173/doi:10.1108/S1871-317320160000012004

INTRODUCTION

Urban centers are commonly recognized as the origins of outbound tourists and the destinations for inbound tourists, but these centers are often neglected for their importance as transit destinations. Assuming multifunctional roles, urban centers not only play a strategic role in influencing tourist arrival for leisure and business purposes, but also play a significant role in influencing transit visitation. McKercher (2001) argues that numerous destinations serve two purposes: as a main destination for visitors and as a secondary or through destination for people on touring trips or traveling to other countries. He also postulates that through travelers are a significant market, both in terms of total tourist number and total tourist expenditures.

Since deregulation and privatization in the late 1970s, the air transport sector has been evolving rapidly as a result of lesser restrictions on fare controls, more efficient service provision and higher market penetration (Dwyer & Forsyth, 2010; Graham, Papatheodorou, & Forsyth, 2008; Morley, 2003). The consequent impact of this development is improvement of accessibility and connectivity of near or far destinations. The outcome is the development of air transportation hubs, which promote tourism flows and transit routes.

An air transportation hub helps configure new tourism spaces (Redondi, Malighetti, & Paleari, 2012); and generates an emergent market of transfer passengers who make fair contribution to the transit destination, particularly with incremental visitor arrival. The volume of transit traffic has also become an important performance indicator of numerous airlines and hub airports.

In the last two decades, many Asian cities, including Hong Kong, have expanded their airport systems to accommodate the growing demands of travelers and to compete as air transportation hubs (Park, 2003). Opened in 1998, the Hong Kong International Airport has established an efficient hub airport in the Asia Pacific region (Hong Kong Airport Authority, 2011). In June 2006, Cathay Pacific Airlines, Hong Kong's home carrier, took over the entire ownership of Dragon Air, which enabled the former to connect to its international network with the short-haul services of the latter to Mainland China and secondary regional destinations (Cathay Pacific Press Release, 2006). This move not only expanded the hub-and-spoke network of Cathay Pacific but also strengthened the hub position of the Hong Kong International Airport.

Hub positioning is especially relevant for tourism development because it attracts origin-and-destination passengers, as well as transit-and-transfer passengers. In 2011–2012, there was a record of 54.9 million airline passengers arriving at and departing from the Hong Kong International Airport (Hong Kong Airport Authority, 2011), of which one-third or 18 million were transit-and-transfer passengers.

With reference to Hong Kong Tourism Board Statistical Review reports, the number of visitors to Hong Kong has been growing year on year. The number of tourist arrival in 2012 was 48.61 million (Hong Kong Tourism Board, 2011). While the reports contain bulks of tourism data on incoming visitors, they do not, however, contain detailed statistics of transit visitors. Hence, there is no way of tracing the market size of the transit passenger segment or knowing its rate of development in an upward or downward development.

In the academic arena, the existing academic literature is focused on origin-and-destination passengers who comprise the majority of users of the airport and consumers of tourism attractions. The literature on transit tourism is limited and only a few studies on transit passengers have been conducted. The present study investigates the characteristics of a group of transit tourists at the Hong Kong International Airport; and it aims to acquire some insights of the transit passenger segment.

THEORETICAL CONSIDERATIONS

Leiper (1979) conceives the basic model of the geographical elements of tourism (Fig. 1). This model indicates that transit routes are vital elements in the tourism system. Transit routes link the paths of traveler-generating regions with tourist destination regions, along with the tourist travel. These routes include stopover points, which may be used for convenience or because of the existence of attractions. Traveler-generating regions are permanent residential bases of tourists, the locations of the basic tourist markets, or the sources of potential tourism demand. Tourist destination regions are defined as locations that attract tourists to stay temporarily. The efficiency and characteristics of transit routes influence the quality of access to particular destinations and the size and direction of tourist flow.

Tourism involves the movement of people through time and space either between their homes and destinations or within destination areas

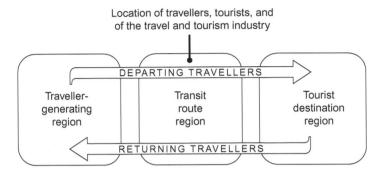

Location of travellers, tourists, and
of the travel and tourism industry

DEPARTING TRAVELLERS

Traveller-
generating
region

Transit
route
region

Tourist
destination
region

RETURNING TRAVELLERS

ENVIRONMENTS: Human, sociocultural, economical, technological,
physical, political, legal etc.

Fig. 1. Geographical Elements of Tourism.

(McKercher & Lew, 2008). McKercher and Lew study the movement of people using different itineraries and conclude that these itineraries have four types of commonalities and features. The first type involves a single destination. The second type involves a transit leg area, followed by a circle tour within the destination, and stopping overnight at different places. The third type involves a circle tour with or without multiple access and egress points. The last type is hub-and-spoke itineraries. The focus of this study is the second type of itinerary that includes a transit stop and a circular tour.

Liasidou (2013) claims that recent developments in the airline industry have given rise to new types of tourists who differ in terms of the ways they devise their own travel itineraries. According to his study, tourists as consumers are familiar with current advancements in the airline and tourism industries and have the power to determine their holiday itineraries. Hence, the power of travelers in breaking trips for visiting the transit regions becomes an optimistic sign for developing transit tourism.

However, transit passengers receive scant attention not only among academic researchers but also among destination marketers. Limited literature exists on transit passengers while most of existing literature is focused on origin-and-destination passengers, which comprise the majority users of the airport. Tang (2003) studies the barriers for visiting a transit region by interviewing the transit passengers who originated from Taiwan and waited at the Hong Kong International Airport for connecting flights to China. Correia, Wirasinghe, and De Barros (2008) highlight the relative importance of individual terminal facilities for transit-and-transfer passengers who arrive and depart through different terminal buildings. Other related studies investigate the level of service of airports for transfer passengers (De Barros, Somasundaraswaran & Wirasinghe, 2007; Park & Se-Yeon, 2011). To date, little is known of the transit passenger segment in terms of their profile and the characteristics of their travel.

AIR TRANSPORT AND TOURISM

Air transportation deregulation and privatization during the past three decades have led to increasingly globalized hub-and-spoke networks of airports (De Barros et al., 2007). It has also brought about an increasing number of code-sharing flights through joint operating agreements, which can instantly expand the network of an airline and, thus, bring benefits to passenger flows (Duval, 2013). A study also shows that passengers are generally better off when airlines are allowed to form alliances because it increases network effects, densities on different links, and joint pricing of complementary links (Pels, 2001).

Redondi et al. (2012) define a hub airport as an airport where traffic is concentrated to foster connections, typically to intercontinental long-haul destinations. The presence of origin-and-destination passengers and transit-and-transfer passengers provides a hub airline with sufficient traffic volume to offer more routes and frequencies to long-haul destinations compared with the volume that would have been provided based on origin traffic alone. They conclude that the concentration of transiting traffic represents a tourist market to be tapped.

It is necessary to highlight that a hub airport is associated with an integrated interchange point. In addition to origin-and-destination passengers, it generates a high proportion of transit-and-transfer passengers. Moreover, the volume of transit-and-transfer passengers becomes the indicator of hub activity. However, the volume of transfer passenger is rarely publicly announced and made available for conducting studies.

TRANSIT TOURISM AS AN URBAN TOURISM PHENOMENON

Urban centers are commonly recognized as the origins of outbound tourists and the destinations for inbound tourists (Page & Hall, 2003). However, an oversight is often made on these centers as transit destinations. According to Law (2002), urban centers that are gateway cities will generally become the focal points of tourist-transport interchanges and termini for layover or transit. Hence, they are often the first and last legs of a journey or an en route stop on a long journey. Thus, urban centers not only play an important role in driving tourist arrival, but also in influencing transit stop. However, the extent to which these centers can establish themselves as something more than a hub or a gateway (i.e., destinations in their own right) depends on their ability to provide facilities and attractions that appeal to the connecting traffic (Lohmann, Albers, Koch, & Pavlovich, 2009).

McKercher (2001) argue that many destinations serve two purposes: one as a main destination for visitors and the other as a secondary or through destination for people on touring trips or traveling to other. In his study of main-destination visitors and through travelers to a regional Australian centre, he reveals that the latter is a significant market, both in terms of total tourist number and total tourist expenditures. It is of no doubt that urban centers, assuming the hub and gateway functions, are especially relevant for tourism development. However, the emerging phenomenon of transit tourism is neglected.

DEFINITION OF TRANSIT PASSENGERS

Beaver (2005) defines a transit passenger as a passenger who has disembarked from a mode of transport at an intermediate point, but who will be continuing his journey through a connecting flight. By referring to the glossary of term normally adopted by the air transport industry, a transit stop is a scheduled en route stopping station on a flight; the transit time is the time an aircraft remains in transit at the station in question; and a connecting carrier is a carrier on which the passengers and their baggage or the cargo are to be transferred for onward connecting transportation (International Air Transport Association, n.d.).

A transit passenger differs from an origin-and-destination passenger, whose journey begins or ends at that place. Transit passengers are confined in the transit lounge and have limited scope of expanding transit-waiting time. Hence, their mobility is constrained while on transit. Subject to visa requirements for entry to a country, transit passengers who choose to leave the transit lounge have to clear immigration and custom formalities at the airport of the transit region before they can enter the city. After visiting the city, they re-enter the airport for connecting flights and continue their onward journey. Transit passengers are subject to an airport tax when they re-enter the airport.

In the context of Hong Kong, nationals of approximately 170 countries and territories may visit Hong Kong visa-free for a period ranging from 7 to 180 days (Hong Kong Immigration Department, n.d.). In accordance to the Air Passenger Departure Tax Ordinance in Chapter 140 of the Hong Kong Law (Hong Kong Department of Justice, n.d.), a tax is imposed on passengers departing by air from Hong Kong and for purposes connected therewith. However, effective 29 September 2003, a tax exemption is granted to passengers who arrive in Hong Kong by aircraft, pass through Hong Kong arrival immigration controls, and depart from Hong Kong by aircraft within the same day. In accordance with the Hong Kong Law, same day refers to the same calendar day (i.e., within Hong Kong time from 00:00 to 23:59).

For the purpose of this study, transit tourists are confined to those who leave the airport transit lounge during transit-wait, pass through Hong Kong immigration controls, and re-enter the airport to catch connecting flights for departure on the same day of arrival (i.e., before 23:59).

METHOD

Using secondary data provided by the sole operator of the Hong Kong Transit Tour, this study investigates the characteristics of transit tourists in Hong Kong. Finn (2000) remarks that secondary data collection should always come before primary data collection because considerable time, effort, and money can be saved.

The Hong Kong Transit Tour was operated exclusively for transit passengers at the Hong Kong International Airport, which enabled them to have a quick tour of the city during transit-wait. The tour was offered at a cost to bona-fide transit passengers, who must have at least 5 hours of transit time. Detailed tour information was posted on websites and at the airport service counter of the Hong Kong Tourism Board, DMO of Hong Kong.

The Hong Kong Transit Tour operator had a service counter at the Hong Kong International Airport arrival hall, where transit passengers could make walk-in bookings upon arrival. Prior to putting the transit passengers on the tour, the tour operator would collect details of their flight schedules and transit hours to ensure that they had sufficient time to complete the tour and return to the airport timely for connecting flights. A survey in the form of a structured questionnaire was used in the data collection, and it was conducted face-to-face by the service counter staff member to every transit passenger who paid to join the Hong Kong Transit Tour. Questions in the survey included the date of participation, nationality and country of residence of passenger, information on the port of origin and port of destination, flight numbers of arrival and connecting flights, and transit duration by hours.

With the data in the questionnaires, the tour operator would compile the monthly transit tourist records. This study adopts the transit tourist records from April 2011 to March 2012, a full fiscal year in Hong Kong. The large dataset of 3,704 counts were analyzed on aggregated and disaggregated levels. Firstly, the traveler-generating regions and source markets were analyzed on an aggregate level. The sample was then divided into market specifics, namely, International and Asian market specifics. At this disaggregate level; it was further differentiated into two groups to analyze passenger characteristics, namely, travel party, transit hours, trip-breaking pattern and transit routes.

All quantitative data were coded and analyzed using Statistical Package for Social Science (SPSS) software. The use of SPSS enables the researcher "… to score and analyze quantitative data very quickly and in many different ways" (Bryman & Cramer, 2001) through descriptive statistics. The advantage of descriptive statistics is its ability to reduce a large set of data into results that can be clearly and concisely presented (Argyrous, 2011).

For ease of reporting, the transit passenger-generating countries in Asia are termed "Asian market," whereas those from Europe, North America, and Australasia are termed "International market."

FINDINGS

The 2011−2012 record of 3,704 transit tourists on the Hong Kong Transit Tour was used for analysis. The findings on the characteristics of transit tourists, including tourist profile, transit pattern, duration of transit-wait time and transit route, are presented in the following section.

1. *Generating regions of transit tourists.* Out of a total of 3,704 transit tourists who participated in the tour during transit-wait, 80% originates from North America, Europe, and Australasia, whereas 13% from Asia.
2. *Country of residence of transit tourists.* Travelers from the USA (32%), Germany (13.6%), and Australia (12.8%) are the most common, followed by New Zealand (4.7%), Canada (4.5%), the Netherlands (3.7%), and France (3.6%). Overall, the long-haul market comprises

75% of the total number of transit tourists. For the Asian market, India is the largest market on the tour, which comprises 10.8% of the total participation. Only a small percentage of other Asian countries are represented.

3. *Nationality of transit tourists.* The top four nationalities on the Hong Kong Transit Tour are Indians (22%), Americans (21%), Germans (14%), and Canadians (4.3%).

4. *Party size.* The travel party size of all transit tourists ranges from 1 to 24 persons. Single person comprises 40% of the total participants, whereas a travel party of 2 persons represents 38% of the sample. A significant difference is determined in the travel party size between the Asian and International markets. An independent sample t-test shows the result of $t(414.56) = -2.49$, $p < 0.029$. The mean for the Asian market is 1.94 persons or less than 2 persons in the party size, whereas the mean for the International market is 2.23 persons or more than 2 persons.

5. *Duration of transit-wait time.* The transit-wait time of the transit tourists ranges from a minimum of 6 hours to a maximum of 24 hours. The mean is 12 hours. Fig. 2 shows that 80% of transit tourists have more than 10 hours of transit-wait time, which is an extremely long transit time when compared with the norm of three hours in air transport management practice (www.iata.org). Those with 12 hours or more transit time comprise the largest group on the transit tour. The analysis indicates a significant difference between the Asian and International markets in terms of transit hours. An independent sample t-test generates the result of $t(652.1) = -2.69$, $p = <0.000$. The result indicates that Asian market has a shorter transit time (mean of 11 hours and 47 minutes) than International market (mean of 12 hours and 10 minutes).

6. *Pattern of participating in transit tour on outbound and return trips.* The outbound trip (flying out of the place of origin) and return trip (returning to the place of origin) produce tourism inflows into the transit destination. Greater inflow is observed for the outbound trip. This is reflected by the 74.1% of transit tourists who participated in the Hong Kong Transit Tour on the outbound trip, whereas 25.9% did it on the return trip. A chi-squared test proves a significant difference between the Asian and International markets in breaking their long distance trips. A cross tabulation shows 86.7% of International transit tourists took the transit tour on the outbound trip, whereas 13.3% of Asian transit tourists took the tour on the return trip, as presented in Table 1.

7. *Flight pattern of transit tourists.*
   a) *Outbound flights (from the place of origin)*

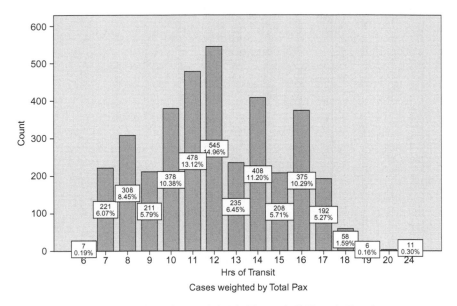

Fig. 2. Duration of Transit-Wait Time of all Transit Tourists.

About 88% of transit tourists departed from the place of origin (arrived at Hong Kong International Airport) by Cathay Pacific (CX) and 11% by non-CX (Dragonair and other airlines) flights.

b) *Connecting flights (at the Hong Kong International Airport)*

The analysis indicates that 53% of transit tourists were connecting with Cathay Pacific flights (online transfers), 10% with Dragonair (inter-line transfer between Cathay and Dragonair), and 24% with other airlines (non-Cathay or Dragonair). Chi-squared analysis reveals a significant difference between the Asian and International markets in making transfer connections. The ratio of the International market taking CX–CX, CX–KA, and CX–Others for flight connection is 6:1:3, whereas a ratio of 5:1:4 for Asian market. A higher percentage of the International market made an online connection, that is CX–CX.

8. *Seasonality.* December is the peak month for the Hong Kong Transit Tour business, with the highest monthly record of 770 persons. The second peak season is June and July, with a total of 777 persons for two months. The number of transit tourists in the two-peak seasons contributes to 47% of the total number of transit tourists on the tour (3,704 passengers) for that year. Further study of the summer peak season in

Table 1. Pattern of Participation in Transit Tour by International Trasnsit Tourists on Outbound Trip and by Asian Transit Tourists on Return Trip.

		Outbound = 0, return = 1		Total
		0	1	
Int.	Count	2614.0	563.0	3177.0
	Expected count	2353.9	823.1	3177.0
	% within Asia non	82.3%	17.7%	100.0%
	% within outbound = 0, return = 1	96.3%	59.3%	86.7%
	% of Total	71.4%	15.4%	86.7%
Asia	Count	100.0	386.0	486.0
	Expected count	360.1	125.9	486.0
	% within Asia non	20.6%	79.4%	100.0%
	% within outbound = 0, return = 1	3.7%	40.7%	13.3%
	% of Total	2.7%	10.5%	13.3%
Total	Count	2714.0	949.0	3663.0
	Expected count	2714.0	949.0	3663.0
	% within Asia non	74.1%	25.9%	100.0%
	% within outbound = 0, return = 1	100.0%	100.0%	100.0%
	% of Total	74.1%	25.9%	100.0%

June and July shows that transit tourists from the USA (44%) and Australasia (21%) comprise over 60% of the two-month total. Asian tourists from India only account for 15%. In the December peak month, Asian tourists from India comprise 55% the monthly total. International tourists from Australasia make up 31% of the total.

9. *Transit route of transit tourists.* The analysis reveals two primary transit routes, namely, the North-South route and the South-North route, as presented in Table 2.

  i. North—South route

    a) Travelers originating from the USA and Canada comprise the largest group on the transit route from North America to India and South Asia, there are 1,333 passengers representing 89% of loading.

    b) Travelers originating from Europe dominate the transit route from Europe to Australasia and the Pacific Islands, there are 924 passengers representing 81% of loading.

Table 2. Transit Routes of All Transit Tourists.

Departing for		Australia, NZ, or Pacific	Europe	India/SA	SEA	US/Can
Originating from	US/Canada	32	0	*1,333*	95	1
	SEA	3	4	4	0	13
	Russia	3	0	0	0	0
	North Asia	0	0	7	0	0
	Nordic	2	0	0	0	0
	Middle E	0	2	0	0	4
	Indo China	0	0	0	0	1
	India/SA	*103*	0	0	0	78
	Europe	*924*	0	9	48	0
	China	0	0	16	0	1
	Australia	11	*151*	134	9	68
	Africa	77	0	0	1	1
Total		1,155	157	1,503	153	167

ii. South-North route
   a) Travelers originating from Australia comprise the largest group on the transit route from Australia and to Europe, there are 151 passengers representing 98% of loading.
   b) Travelers originating from India are the largest Asian group on the route from South Asia and to North America, there are 78 passengers representing 46% of the loading.

DISCUSSION

The tour admits bona fide transit visitors with a minimum of 5 hours of transit, but the analysis indicates that more than 50% of transit tourists on the tour had more than 12 hours of transit-wait at the Hong Kong International Airport. This finding reveals that transit tourists need a significantly larger safety net when a discretionary transit activity intercepts the transit-wait.

After completing the Hong Kong Transit Tour, transit tourists return to the airport on the same day to catch their connecting flight and continue their onward travel. In tourism statistics, they are counted as same-day visitors who have stayed for at least 0.5 day in the city and spent at least HK

$270 per person (tour fee of the Hong Kong Transit Tour) during transit-wait. The transit tourists of Hong Kong Transit Tour for the 12 months of study generated a total of HK$1 million (cost of Transit Tour at HK$270 x 3,704 tour passengers) in term of tourism receipt for Hong Kong. Transit tourists generate incremental arrival and incremental tourism spending, which are key performance indicators of the tourism economy.

The analysis shows the two-peak seasonality for transit tourism, one in the months of June and July and the other in December. The two-peak seasonality reflects the demand in the destination regions. The push factors from the demand side of the generating region are causing the seasonality rather than the pull factors from the supply side of the transit destination. The school holiday season in July for the USA and Germany pushes up transit tourist arrival in the summer months, whereas the school holiday season in Australasia and India boosts transit tourist arrival in the winter months.

The pattern is assumed to be driven by institutional seasonality rather than natural seasonality. Natural seasonality is caused by regular variation in climatic conditions, whereas institutional seasonality is caused by human decisions and calendar (Butler, 1998). However, the dataset for this study is not adequate to reveal if people visiting a destination in different seasons have different preferences (Baum & Lundtorp, 2001) or if different airline ticketing systems have conditioned trip breaking of transit travel.

CX–CX online connection and CX–KA interline connection at the Hong Kong International Airport generated 70% of the total number of transit tourists. CX and KA flights are full-service airlines, which play a pivotal role in developing hub positioning and transit tourism. The study also reveals that low-cost carriers (LCCs) do not have influence in transit tourism.

By analyzing the trip-breaking patterns of transit tourists, the findings indicate that they are numerically and spatially concentrated on two primary transit routes:

1. The north-south-bound route between North America to India and South Asian cities, and
2. The north-south-bound route between Europe and Australasia (known as the Kangaroo route).

On the north-south transit route, the travelers originating from North America arrive at Hong Kong International Airport between 5:30 and 8:00 in the morning, and then connect flights to India between 6:00 and 11:00 in the evening. The travelers originating from Europe arrive between the same times but connect flights to Australia between 9:00 pm to mid night.

On the south-north transit routes, the travelers from Australia also arrive between 5:30 and 8:00 in the morning, and then connect flights to Europe before midnight.

Combining a transit stop with a destination region makes a multi-destination trip. According to Lue, Crompton, and Fesenmaier (1993), multiple-destination trips are the outcome of a choice process in which an individual decides a combination of destinations and the benefits sought, which may be a single benefit in multiple destinations or multiple benefits in multiple destinations.

CONCLUSION AND IMPLICATIONS

Tourist arrival and tourism expenditures are two key performance indicators of tourism economy of urban centers. McKercher (2001) states that transit passengers (through travelers) are contributing significantly to total tourist number and total tourist expenditures. With better understanding of the trip characteristics of transit passenger segment, better demand numbers can be forecasted for generating incremental tourist arrival and tourism receipt of urban centers.

Pearce (1995) stresses the need for better understanding of spatial movement of tourists from the generating region to the destination region, which has been underscored for some time. From this study, the distinctive spatial movement of transit passengers reveals the preference for multi-destination itineraries. It summons marketing organizations of transit regions to develop complementary itineraries with destination regions, which will appeal to transit passengers looking for multiple benefits in multi-destination travel.

This study of transit tourists in Hong Kong provides academics with an interest in the emergent market segment of transit passengers and the potential development of transit tourism. The spatial and temporal movement of transit passengers will shed new light to the current body of knowledge in urban tourism. This study calls for better theoretical and behavioral understanding of transit tourists and more applied contributions in planning and development of transit tourism, a new tourism phenomenon that will extend the current body of knowledge in urban tourism.

ACKNOWLEDGMENTS

The authors thank Vigor Tours of Hong Kong for the dataset of the Hong Kong Transit Tour, without which, this study could not have been conducted.

REFERENCES

Argyrous, G. (2011). *Statistics for research: With a guide to SPSS* (3rd ed.). London: Sage.

Baum, T., & Lundtorp, S. (2001). *Seasonality in tourism*. Oxford: Elsevier.

Beaver, A. (2005). *A dictionary of travel and tourism terminology*. Oxon: CABI.

Bryman, A., & Cramer, D. (2001). *Quantitative data analysis with SPSS release 10 for Windows: A guide for social scientists*. New York, NY: Routledge.

Butler, R. (1998). Seasonality in tourism: Issues and implications. *Tourism Review, 53*(3), 18−24.

Cathay Pacific Press Release. (2006). Hong Kong strengthens its role as the premier Asia-Pacific regional aviation hub under shareholding realignment. Retrieved from http://downloads.cathaypacific.com/cx/press/JointPressRelease_Eng_1.pdf. Accessed on May 12, 2013.

Correia, A. R., Wirasinghe, S. C., & De Barros, A. G. (2008). A global index for level of service evaluation at airport passenger terminals. *Transportation Research Part E: Logistics and Transportation Review, 44*(4), 607−620.

De Barros, A. G., Somasundaraswaran, A. K., & Wirasinghe, S. C. (2007). Evaluation of level of service for transfer passengers at airports. *Journal of Air Transport Management, 13*(5), 293−298.

Duval, D. T. (2013). Critical issues in air transport and tourism. *Tourism Geographies, 15*(3), 494−510.

Dwyer, L., & Forsyth, P. (2010). *Tourism economics and policy* (Vol. 3). Clevedon: Channel View Publications.

Finn, M. (2000). *Tourism and leisure research methods: Data collection, analysis, and interpretation*. Harlow: Pearson Education.

Graham, A., Papatheodorou, A., & Forsyth, P. (Eds.). (2008). *Aviation and tourism: Implications for leisure travel*. Farnham: Ashgate Publishing.

Hong Kong Airport Authority. (2011). E_Annual Report_Full.pdf. (2011/2012). Retrieved from http://www.hongkongairport.com/eng/pdf/media/publication/report/11_12/E_Annual%20Report%20Full.pdf

Hong Kong Department of Justice. (n.d.). Bilingual Laws Information System. Retrieved from http://www.legislation.gov.hk/eng/home.htm?SearchTerm = cap140. Accessed on May 12, 2013.

Hong Kong Immigration Department. (n.d.). General Visa Requirements. Retrieved from http://www.gov.hk/en/nonresidents/visarequire/general/. Accessed on May 17, 2013.

Hong Kong Tourism Board. (2011). *Annual report 20110/2011*. Retrieved from http://www.discoverhongkong.com/au/about-hktb/annual-report/annual-report-20102011.jsp. Accessed on May 11, 2013.

International Air Transport Association. (n.d.). *Passenger-glossary-of-terms*. Retrieved from www.iata.org. Accessed on May 11, 2013.

Law, C. M. (2002). *Urban tourism: The visitor economy and the growth of large cities*. Andover: Cengage Learning EMEA.

Leiper, N. (1979). The framework of tourism: Towards a definition of tourism, tourist, and the tourist industry. *Annals of Tourism Research, 6*(4), 390−407.

Liasidou, S. (2013). Decision-making for tourism destinations: Airline strategy influences. *Tourism Geographies, 15*(3), 511−528.

Lohmann, G., Albers, S., Koch, B., & Pavlovich, K. (2009). From hub to tourist destination − An explorative study of Singapore and Dubai's aviation-based transformation. *Journal of Air Transport Management, 15*(5), 205−211.

Lue, C.-C., Crompton, J. L., & Fesenmaier, D. R. (1993). Conceptualization of multi-destination pleasure trips. *Annals of Tourism Research, 20*(2), 289−301.

McKercher, B. (2001). A Comparison of main-destination visitors and through travelers at a dual-purpose destination. *Journal of Travel Research, 39*(4), 433−441.

McKercher, B., & Lew, A. A. (2008). Tourist flows and the spatial distribution of tourists. In A. A. Lew, C. M. Hall, & A. M. Williams (Eds.), *A companion to tourism* (pp. 36−48). Oxford: Blackwell Publishing.

Morley, C. L. (2003). Impacts of international airline alliances on tourism. *Tourism Economics, 9*(1), 31−51.

Park, J. W., & Se-Yeon, J. (2011). Transfer Passengers' perceptions of airport service quality: A case study of Incheon International Airport. *International Business Research, 4*(3), 75.

Page, S. J., & Hall, C. M. (2003). *Managing urban tourism*. Farnham: Pearson Education.

Park, Y. (2003). An analysis for the competitive strength of Asian major airports. *Journal of Air Transport Management, 9*(6), 353−360.

Pearce, D. G. (1995). Tourism today: A geographical analysis, (Ed. 2), xii + 202 pp.

Pels, E. (2001). A note on airline alliances. *Journal of Air Transport Management, 7*(1), 3−7.

Redondi, R., Malighetti, P., & Paleari, S. (2012). De-hubbing of airports and their recovery patterns. *Journal of Air Transport Management, 18*(1), 1−4.

Tang, E. (2003). *Why transit passengers don't visit Hong Kong?* (2010, June 14). Retrieved from http://theses.lib.polyu.edu.hk/handle/200/3405. Accessed on May 12, 2013.

CHAPTER 4

AN ACTOR NETWORK PERSPECTIVE OF TOURISM OPEN DATA

Maurice McNaughton, Michelle T. McLeod and Ian Boxill

ABSTRACT

This chapter explores the data exchange relationships between stake-holders in a tourism domain as a means of assessing the potential application of open data initiatives. Social network analysis is utilized to analyze network relationships and explain the pattern and consequences of these relationships. Based on centrality and other network attributes, the analysis highlights the key influencers in the tourism data ecosystem examined, and suggests that initial steps towards implementing a tourism open data policy should focus on opening up tourism asset data, and relaxing current restrictive data exchange practices. The agency with responsibility for collecting and disseminating tourism asset data, is well positioned to become the data broker in an emergent tourism open data ecosystem.

Keywords: Open data policy; tourism assets; stakeholders; networks; actor network theory

Tourism and Hospitality Management
Advances in Culture, Tourism and Hospitality Research, Volume 12, 47–60
Copyright © 2016 by Emerald Group Publishing Limited
All rights of reproduction in any form reserved
ISSN: 1871-3173/doi:10.1108/S1871-317320160000012005

INTRODUCTION

Open Government Data, defined as policies and practice where government data is published online in a structured, machine readable format that is available for anyone to access, consume, and reuse, has emerged as a significant global policy and technological trend within the last five years. While its genesis was in the accountability/transparency agenda (see, for instance, US Open Data Directive, 2009), open data is increasingly being seen as a powerful entry point and enabler for Governments and civil society partners to collaborate around the use of ICT to improve public sector efficiency, service delivery and innovation. Several studies (Capgemini Consulting, 2011; Vickery, 2011) underscore the potential for Open Data to create new jobs and generate economic value. The recent McKinsey (McKinsey Global Institute, 2013) study estimates US$3.2 trillion of economic value in the potential use of Open Data in seven "domains": *education, transportation, consumer products, electricity, oil and gas, health care, and consumer finance.* Tourism is not a commonly referenced industry in the emerging Open Data discourse and applications. However, for Jamaica and the Caribbean, tourism is likely to be a much more significant domain of interest for considering value-creating Open Data initiatives, given the importance of the industry to national economies.

The tourism industry in general, and the hospitality industry in particular, functions most effectively with the free flow of information about the tourism product, service providers and consumer experiences. Recent studies in the United Kingdom showed that most search activity conducted online was making travel plans (84%), followed by getting information about local events (77%), looking for news (69%) and finding information about health or medical care (68%) (Buhalis, Jun, & Limited, 2011). Ready access to current information provides the basis for awareness, choice, and improved service delivery between the prospective tourist and operators in the industry, including hotels, attractions and other service providers such as restaurants, transportation, and entertainment operators. Freely accessible information can help businesses in the tourism industry to improve their competitive position (Cooper, 2006; Novelli, Schmitz, & Spencer, 2006).

This study examines the opportunities and potential impact for Open Data policy and initiatives within the tourism industry in Jamaica. Not dissimilar to other tourism jurisdictions, there are relatively well-developed processes and mechanisms for collecting, analyzing, and publishing operational data and statistics within the industry. To explore the nature of data and information sharing within the industry and identify key actor roles, and sources of constraints and inefficiencies that potentially lead to information asymmetry, the lens of actor network theory and social network analysis techniques are applied, similar to McLeod, Vaughan, and Edwards (2010). This allows for the mapping and analysis of the stakeholder relationships in the tourism industry that are involved in providing tourism data for the day-to-day operations, management and development of the industry.

THEORETICAL CONSIDERATIONS

An assessment of the potential economic value of Open Data in any specific industry setting is usually best informed by an assessment of the context and dynamics of the local industry, within which the Open Data initiatives are being considered (Helbig, Cresswell, Burke, & Luna-Reyes, 2012). Helbig et al prescribe "information polity" as a heuristic device which includes an understanding of the actors, their roles and governance relationships, and the current state of data, information and knowledge assets, flows and degrees of asymmetry that exists within the ecosystem.

Actor network theory has been applied to the tourism context to provide fresh theoretical and methodological perspectives regarding tourism activity (McLeod, 2013; Van der Duim, Ren, & Jóhannesson, 2012). This theory explains the agency that both human and non-human elements have and therefore a specific tourism context is "translated" by the enactment and ordering of both agencies to bring about "touristscapes" (Van der Duim, 2007). Ordering is a key concept (Law, 1994) for understanding actor network theory as order is enacted or performed through the relationships between actors. Of particular significance is the notion that actors can be human/non-human and include people, objects, spaces, materials, and technologies that have ontological parity in the actor network. Entities such as institutions, people, data, and technologies can be equally influential in enacting and performing (Ren, Jóhannesson, & van der Duim, 2012) network roles. This theory can therefore be adapted to explain how a data ecosystem is enacted.

The key actors who initiate and/or influence the data & information exchange processes under study can be identified, and data can be represented as an Actor, as well as information flows represented as associations (relationships) between Actors. As an illustration of this approach, Haug (2012) notes the enactment of risk based on the network of actors including people, mountain and the weather at Besseggen, Norway. Within this network both human and non-human actors have the same ontological position in their capability to act. By using this approach, the components of risk can be understood and therefore the eventuality of risk can be mitigated through an increased awareness of the influence of certain actors (Haug, 2012).

METHOD

Jamaica's tourism industry contributes in excess of 20% to the country's GDP and also creates direct and indirect employment opportunities estimated at 23.4% of the country's labor force (World Travel and Tourism Council, 2014). There are three main resort areas: Montego Bay, Negril, and Ocho Rios on the north coast of the island. The capital city of Kingston in the south is a hub of business tourism, while Portland in the eastern part of the island is the home of nature-based tourism activities.

An understanding of the principal organizational stakeholders, their roles and responsibilities in the Governance arrangements of the industry, is an important component of defining the context within which Open Data initiatives will be situated. In particular, the responsibilities of stakeholders in the collection/production, management and dissemination of data in order to serve the needs of the wider industry interests in service delivery and decision-making, is relevant to an Open Data assessment. The following key stakeholders in the Jamaican tourism industry were identified, including Government agencies as well as civil society groups.

Jamaica Tourist Board (JTB): The JTB is responsible for the worldwide tourism marketing and promotion for Jamaica. It is the principal agency for collection and management of tourism related data and collects data and produces statistical summaries of industry performance (i.e., revenues, expenditure, stopover/cruise arrivals, etc.).

Tourism Product Development Company (TPDCO): TPDCo has responsibility for the diversification, development and improvement of the tourism product. They provide support to the accommodation and ancillary industries in the form of advice and training, and supports the development of community-based tourism related projects through its entrepreneurship programs. TPDCo also has a dual role as the effective regulatory body of the industry by virtue of which, it collects and manages information on major tourism assets and products, including all registered hotel properties, attractions, craft markets, as well as registered operators such as transportation providers and artisans;

Tourism Enhancement Fund: Responsible for the allocation of financial resources, collected through a small fee levied on incoming airline and cruise passengers, to support the industry, including development funds, country advertising, and micro-finance for small operators.

Caribbean Tourism Organization: the Caribbean's tourism development agency comprising membership of over 30 countries and territories, that facilitates collaboration in tourism among the member countries and other interests; CTO collates and publishes regional statistics as provided by member countries including: *Tourism Stop Over Arrivals, Tourist Arrivals by Month, Tourist Arrivals by Main Market, Cruise Passenger Arrivals.*

Aside from these principal Government agencies, several industry groups exist that represent the collective interests of various segments within the tourism industry:

Jamaica Hotel and Tourist Association: representative body for hotel owners;

Jamaica Association of Villas and Apartments (JAVA): which acts as a clearing house for the rental of privately owned cottages and apartments (300 members); and

Transportation sub-sector: Jamaica U-Drive Association/Jamaica Rent-A-Car Association and Jamaica Union of Travellers Association (JUTA).

A questionnaire was sent to each of the key agencies/stakeholders to seek to understand the nature of data being collected and managed within the industry, including: *Source & Type of Data; Purpose and Primary Users; Means of dissemination; Any Access Restrictions; Typical Cost and/ or Challenges in collecting the data.* In total seven organizations were contacted, including the three principal government agencies and four representative industry groups. Complete information, suitable for analysis was received from five organizations.

In addition to the surveys, consultative sessions were conducted with representatives of the various organizations, where they were provided with a background regarding Open Data, and briefed on the study and its rationale. This qualitative discourse provided additional insight on some of the data/information constraints within the industry and potential use-cases and outcome/impact opportunities for Open Data. The dialogue also underscored some of the rationale (mostly policy/privacy-related) for restrictions on dissemination of raw data that currently exist. Table 1 summarizes the qualitative insight on some of the key data sources available

Table 1. Key Tourism Datasets and Open Data Considerations.

Dataset	Agency	Feasibility		Potential Benefits and Opportunities
		Policy/practice	Technical	
Tourism industry Stats. Stopover/cruise arrivals data compiled from the register of immigration (i.e., entry points: airport, harbor).	Jamaica Tourist Board	Data aggregated and published as industry performance statistics and reports	Anonymized landing card data is received in raw format and processed/published as statistical reports	+ Availability of this information as raw data can support apps development, and enhance sector reporting, analysis and visualization + Better data for tourist-related businesses to do targeted marketing, plan and price their services − Minimal Risk of competitor analysis since this data is already published in aggregate through the JTB website and regionally through Caribbean Tourism Organization
Tourism Industry Stats: Stopover/cruise arrivals data compiled from member countries of CTO	Caribbean Tourism Organization	Compiled aggregate statistical data from member countries, published on CTO website by country		+ Availability of individual country data can support apps development, and enhance sector reporting, analysis and visualization to provide better data for tourist-related businesses to do targeted marketing, plan and price their services
Licensed/Regulated Tourism Entities: The name, contact information, type of entity, owners, type of activity services offered, location (which includes resort area), mailing	TPDCo	General listings are shared but no specific details of their regulatory status and the outcome of the Product Quality Assessment General listings are shared on request but no specific details of the	Data is collected through several processes including: license application & regulatory oversight process; Information submitted from operators, regulatory agencies and insurance companies	+ Availability of this entity data (properties, attractions), especially with geo-locations information can support a range of apps development opportunities that can provide enhanced product information for prospective and current visitors, as well as improve service delivery

address, Jamaica Tourist Board Licence status		regulatory status on the outcome of the Product Quality Assessment	regarding certificates/permits or licences; Data shared on request in PDF format	+ Provide additional mechanisms for promotion of tourism products/services, especially smaller properties, community-based services and niche offerings + Provide better information services to potential tourists as well as to visitors exploring options, once on-island.
Transport operators: Data on drivers of contract carriages who members of the organization	Jamaica Union of Travelers Association (JUTA) Jam. U-Drive Ass./Jamaica Rent-A-Car Association	Data is collected through registration forms completed by members, and is primarily for Internal use and supporting the licensing process, as well as information queries from GOJ agencies.	+ Availability of this transport operator data can support a range of apps development opportunities that can provide enhanced service availability information for prospective and current visitors, as well as improve service delivery

within the industry, and potential open data opportunities as tabulated from the responses and discussions with various agencies.

To facilitate the use of social network analysis (SNA), the survey respondent data elements were coded as shown in Appendix, to represent the data exchange relationships between the various actors in the tourism data ecosystem. SNA is a theory and method which examines the antecedents and consequences of the relationships between actors (Borgatti & Halgin, 2011). This technique allows a view of a network of relationships but has its limitations in terms of translating the orderings within an actor network. Nonetheless, the prominence of certain items in terms of where these are situated in the network can assist with understanding the actor network. The main advantage of social network analysis in the context of actor networks is that it allows the identification of key actors that can enact certain consequences or role influence within the network. The literature shows that the networking element of actor network theory, social network analysis, can be applied to understand actor networks. Rydin (2012) used SNA to understand planning practice in an actor network. She used the centrality measure of betweenness to identify those actors with central roles in the actor network. Betweenness is used to measure the potential to control network flows (Borgatti, Everett, & Johnson, 2013) whereas there are other centrality measures which can be used to explain an actor's prominence.

Network prominence of an actor is the basis for which SNA was applied to explain the influence of tourism stakeholders and actors on the data ecosystem. In particular, key actors can be identified within a network of actors using social network analysis. These key actors can be potentially important for influencing or controlling the network activities. Centrality determines the prominence of an actor in the network based on that actor's network position (Borgatti et al., 2013). Borgatti et al. (2013) suggest that measures of centrality are calculated with respect to one single relation and therefore centrality relates to the contribution a node makes to network structure. This contribution can be ascribed a value which can explain the potential consequences of the actor network. Centrality measures are examined using UCINET software (Borgatti, Everett, & Freeman, 2002). In UCINET software degree centrality is simply the number of alters connected to an actor. These connections can be directed and within directed networks there are either incoming and/or outgoing links. The degree centrality of a directed network can therefore be divided into an in-degree (incoming links) and an out-degree (outgoing links).

FINDINGS

There are nine (9) centrality structural positions in this actor network (Table 2). Centrality relates to the power an actor has to influence the resources in a network (Borgatti et al., 2002). In this network the key influencers which can control a tourism open data system are dt1 (assets), dd1 (e-mail), dr1 (yes, restrictions) since it was revealed that these actors had the highest in-degree value of 5 (Table 2). The gov1 (TPDCo) and gov2 (JTB) nodes are essential actors for outgoing resources with 14 and 13 out-degree centrality values, respectively. The private sector associations (pri1, pri2 and pri3) are less prominent than the public sector actors in terms of their influence in the tourism data network. The normalized degree centrality values are the degree centrality divided by the highest possible degree centrality score. With a network of 33 actors the highest centrality value is 32 and therefore the normalized out-degree value for actor gov1 is 14/32 times 100 which equals 43.75. This means that gov1 has achieved 43.75% of the possible optimal centralization in the network which represents this actor's level of influence in the tourism open data network.

Influential actors in the network can also be viewed from the in-degree perspective. In Fig. 1 those actors with the highest normalized in-degree values are central to the network and are dr1 (yes, restrictions), dt1 (e-mail) and dd1 (assets). This means that these actors can enact either positively or negatively (as is the case with restrictions) on network outcomes. While these actors exert network influence the level of this influence over all other actors in the network is 15.63%.

Table 2. Tourism Open Data Actor Network (Degree Centrality).

	OutDegree	InDegree	NrmOutDeg	NrmInDeg
gov1	14	0	43.75	0
gov2	13	0	40.63	0
pri1	9	0	28.13	0
pri2	8	0	25.00	0
pri3	9	0	28.13	0
dt2, dt3, ds2, du1, du3, du6, du7, du8, dt7, dd4, dd3, dt8, du4, du12, du13	0	1	0	3.13
du2, ds1, du9, du5, du10, ds3, du11	0	2	0	6.25
dd2, dd5, dr3	0	3	0	9.38
dt1, dd1, dr1	0	5	0	15.63

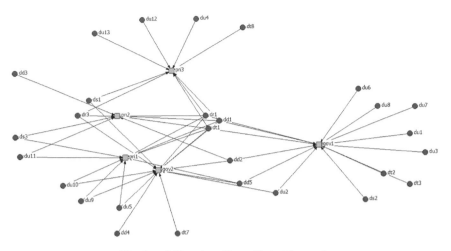

Fig. 1. A Tourism Open Data Network.

CONCLUSION AND IMPLICATIONS

The foregoing analysis illustrates the usefulness of Actor Network Theory in representing an existing data ecosystem and rendering it amenable to well-established social network analytic techniques. The flexibility to equally represent both human and non-human actors and their agency within a specific network context provides a powerful conceptual framework for modeling the tourism domain under study and identifying the factors that could enable or constrain value-adding open data initiatives.

The analysis highlighted a cluster of actors that exhibited relatively high normalized, in-degree attributes, which reflects significant influence on the overall network performance. These actors represent *dt1 (tourism data assets), dd1 (e-mail exchange), dr1 (yes, data restrictions)*. Interpreting these attributes in the real-world tourism industry context: The data on tourism assets (properties, attractions) is a valuable network resource that is currently disseminated and used across the network. Enhanced availability and access to this information through an open data portal, especially with geo-location tags could support a range of innovation opportunities that provide enhanced product information as well as improved service delivery (reservations, transportation) for prospective and current visitors. Other opportunities include additional mechanisms for increased visibility and promotion of tourism products/services, especially smaller properties, community-based services and niche offerings. However, the current restrictive practice of disseminating this information on-demand, via e-mail exchange, in the format of PDF documents, considerably limits its usability and usefulness.

The Government agency TPDCO has emerged as the most influential actor as a source of data (out-degree centrality). As a result of their role as the effective regulatory body of the industry by virtue of their responsibility for the licensing and other oversight processes, TPDCO has become the central repository for much of the data on the Tourism product, including properties, assets and licensed operators. This places them in a unique position to be also the data broker for the industry and to become the focal point for the development of a Tourism Open Data ecosystem. Their designated role for supporting the development of community-based tourism related projects through entrepreneurship programs enhances this positioning as a potentially key open data catalyst. This role is equivalent to the concept of a "keystone species" (Nardi & O'Day, 1999) which are considered critical to the effective functioning and development of ecosystems because their presence performs some vital function. Such enabling actors can "create value" for their ecosystems in a variety of ways, including the creation of platform technologies that offers solutions to others in the ecosystem (see Iansiti & Levien, 2004). The creation of an open data portal could become such an enabling platform in an emergent tourism open data ecosystem.

Open Data is still a relatively new political, social and economic phenomenon. As it evolves from the initial pre-occupation with publishing open government data portals, key stakeholders such as governments, citizens and multilateral agencies, are becoming increasingly interested in more analytic methods for evaluating the value potential and impact of open data initiatives. The purpose of this study was to examine the potential for Open Data within the tourism industry in Jamaica, using Actor Network Theory as the lens and social network analysis as the means by which we examine, represent and interpret this potential.

The analysis illustrates the use of network attributes such as centrality, the existence of brokers to assess the characteristics of an open data ecosystem, identify the influential actors and opportunities for improved network effectiveness. In this particular case, asset data, that is, data on the tourism product including accommodations, attractions and transportation assets are an important information element. The analysis shows that the Government agency, TPDCo, consistent with their role as the effective regulatory body of the industry, is uniquely positioned to be the data broker for the industry and to become the focal point for the development of a Tourism Open Data ecosystem.

A strategic, value-driven approach to open data policy and initiatives within the industry could realize a range of benefits opportunities including: increased visibility and clientele for smaller tourism operators; enhanced tourism product information and diversity of choices for discriminating tourists; and, improved quality of service delivery in support services such as transportation, entertainment and merchandising. All of this should ultimately create a more competitive tourism product in a crowded global market.

A limitation of this study arises due to the application of this analytic technique being driven primarily from a supply-side perspective only, based on some of the key producers of data. In this case, use distribution becomes a proxy for the value of data. An extension of this study to survey data consumers and their perception of the value and opportunities associated with access to data and its use will likely enhance the analysis.

ACKNOWLEDGMENTS

The authors wish to thank the following Organizations for their responsiveness and engagement in supporting the study: Jamaica Tourist Board (JTB); Tourism Product Development Company (TPDCO); Tourism Enhancement Fund; Jamaica Association of Villas and Apartments (JAVA); Jamaica U-Drive Association/Jamaica Rent-A-Car Association; Jamaica Union of Travellers Association (JUTA); and Countrystyle Community Tourism Network (CCTN). This study was undertaken with the kind support and funding from the Economic Commission for Latin America and the Caribbean (ECLAC) and W3C Brazil as part of the Open Data for Development project in Latin America & the Caribbean (OD4D).

REFERENCES

Borgatti, S. P., Everett, M. G., & Freeman, L. C. (2002). *UCINET 6 for Windows: Software for social network analysis*. Harvard: Analytic Technologies.

Borgatti, S. P., & Halgin, D. (2011). On network theory. *Organization Science*, *22*(5), 1168–1181.

Borgatti, S. P., Everett, M. G., & Johnson, J. C. (2013). *Analyzing social networks*. London: Sage.

Buhalis, D., Jun, S. H., & Limited, G. P. (2011). E-tourism. In C. Cooper (Ed.), *Contemporary tourism reviews* (p. 38). Oxford: Goodfellow Publishers.

Capgemini Consulting. (2011). The open data economy unlocking economic value by opening government and public data.

Cooper, C. (2006). Knowledge management and tourism. *Annals of Tourism Research, 33*(1), 47–64.

Haug, B. (2012). Enacting risk at Besseggen. In R. van der Duim, C. Ren & G. T. Jóhannesson (Eds.), *Actor–network theory and tourism: Ordering, materiality and multiplicity* (pp. 80–93). Oxon: Routledge.

Helbig, N., Cresswell, A. M., Burke, G. B., & Luna-Reyes, L. (2012). *The dynamics of opening government data.* Center for Technology in Government, University at Albany, SUNY, New York, NY.

Iansiti, M., & Levien, R. (2004). Strategy as ecology. *Harvard Business Review, 82*(3), 68–81.

Law, J. (1994). *Organising modernity: Social ordering and social theory.* Oxford: Blackwell Publishers.

McKinsey Global Institute. (2013). *Open data: Unlocking innovation and performance with liquid information.* Retrieved from http://www.mckinsey.com/insights/business_technology/open_data_unlocking_innovation_and_performance_with_liquid_information

McLeod, M. T. (2013). A review of "actor-network theory and tourism, ordering, materiality and multiplicity". *Tourism Management, 37*, 48–49.

McLeod, M. T., Vaughan, D., & Edwards, J. (2010). Knowledge networks in the tourism sector of the Bournemouth, Poole, and Christchurch conurbation: Preliminary analysis. *The Service Industries Journal, 30*(10), 1–17.

Nardi, B. A., & O'Day, V. L. (1999). *Information ecologies: Using technology with heart.* Cambridge, MA: MIT Press.

Novelli, M., Schmitz, B., & Spencer, T. (2006). Networks, clusters and innovation in tourism: A UK experience. *Tourism Management, 27*(6), 1141–1152.

Ren, C., Jóhannesson, G. T., & van der Duim, R. (2012). How ANT works. In R. van der Duim, C. Ren, & G. T. Jóhannesson (Eds.), *Actor-network theory and tourism: Ordering, materiality and multiplicity* (pp. 13–25). Oxon: Routledge.

Rydin, Y. (2012). Using actor-network theory to understand planning practice: Exploring relationships between actants in regulating low-carbon commercial development. *Planning Theory, 12*(1), 23–45.

US Government. (2009). *US open government directive.* Retrieved from http://www.whitehouse.gov/omb/assets/memoranda_2010/m10-06.pdf. Accessed on January 11, 2014.

Van der Duim, R. (2007). Tourismscapes an actor-network perspective. *Annals of Tourism Research, 34*(4), 961–976.

Van der Duim, R., Ren, C., & Jóhannesson, G. T. (2012). *Actor-network theory and tourism: Ordering, materiality and multiplicity.* Routledge.

Vickery, G. (2011). *Review of recent studies on PSI re-use and related market developments.* Paris: Information Economics.

World Travel and Tourism Council. (2014). *Travel and tourism economic impact 2014 Jamaica.* World Travel and Tourism Council, UK.

APPENDIX

	dp	dp1	dp2	dp3	dp4	dp5	dp6	dp7	dp8	dp9	dp10	du11	du12	du13
Data provider	dp	Gov. Agency	Operators	Community	Tourist	Media	Regional Agency							
Data type	dt	Assets	Services	Regulatory	Performance	Contact	Experience	Statistics	Taxes					
Data sources	ds	TPDCo	JTB	Operators	Tourists	Immigration	CTO							
Government agency	gov	TPDCo	JTB	Ministry of Tourism	PIOJ	STATIN	Public Health	Immigration	Fire Dept.					
Primary users	du	TPDCo	JTB	Ministry of Tourism	Operators	Tourists	PIOJ	STATIN	Public Health	General Public		Investors	Internal Banks	Ministry of Finance
Dissemination	dd	E-mail	Web	Telephone	Publications	Reports								
Restrictions	dr	Yes	No	Privacy	Competitive	Reports								
Private sector agency	pri	JUTA	JAVA	JUDA										

CHAPTER 5

MARKETING OF TOURISM PRODUCTS THROUGH THE RUSSIAN SOCIAL MEDIA CHANNEL VKONTAKTE

Ekaterina Miettinen

ABSTRACT

Nowadays, social media influences tourists in their decision making process and plays an important role in the digital marketing strategy of tourism service providers. The purpose of this study is to examine the presence of tourism businesses in the most popular social media channel in Russia — VKontakte (VK). The data consist of Finnish and Russian groups devoted to tourism in VK: 10,000 Finnish groups and 5,000 Russian groups were found and the 12 most popular out of each group were chosen for the analysis. The findings show that VK is widely used by Finnish and Russian tourism firms, but there is still potential for more effective implementation of the channel. The group discussions on the most popular topics can provide firms with useful knowledge for planning their digital strategies for the Russian market.

Keywords: Social media; Russian market; social media; Russian tourists

Tourism and Hospitality Management
Advances in Culture, Tourism and Hospitality Research, Volume 12, 61–80
Copyright © 2016 by Emerald Group Publishing Limited
All rights of reproduction in any form reserved
ISSN: 1871-3173/doi:10.1108/S1871-317320160000012006

INTRODUCTION

Today Russia is the most important target market for the Finnish tourism industry. From the practical marketing point of view, the Russian tourism in Finland is a current topic. It is argued that Russians keep the tourism of Finland alive. According to the Border Interview Survey 2012 by Statistics Finland and the Finnish Tourist Board (Statistics Finland, 2013), visitors from Russia are the largest visitor group. The number of visitors from Russia was 3.6 million in the year 2012. Travel from Russia to Finland increased by 10% compared to 2011.

Malankin (2012) studied over 200 works about Russians and offered her view about their travelling habits, consumer behaviour and expectations. She described the Russian tourists as open, curious and spontaneous. The Russians do not really plan their holidays; they look through the information they can find and make their decision right away. Finland is criticized by Russians for a lack of information. During their holidays, The Russians are used to spending money, drinking and eating well. They are surprised by the too peaceful nightlife in Finland and the lack of activities offered to them. As all clients, generally, the Russians also like to be extremely valued; they appreciate it significantly (Malankin, 2012).

Nowadays, Russia is one of the biggest suppliers of tourists to the foreign market (Furmanov, Balaeva, & Predvoditeleva, 2012, pp. 2–3). According to the Federal State Statistics Service of Russia (2013), in the year 2012, the most popular travel destinations for Russians were Finland (+18%), Turkey (−6%) and China. According to the Russia Tourism Strategy to 2020 (2014), Russia was in the top ten list for the leading countries of tourist arrivals and the fifth for the tourists' consuming in 2012. Russia is on its way towards building a unique tourism industry consisting of natural, social, economic, cultural and historical resources. Domestic tourism should be affordable for the Russians. Nowadays, people with an average income often choose an outbound destination for the "quality-price" criterion (Boiko, 2009). In this study, the focus is on tourism in Russia and in Finland through the social media channel VKontakte (hereby abbreviated as VK).

The object of this study is social media groups connected to Finnish and Karelian tourism in the most popular channel VK of Russia. The main research questions are:

- What kinds of groups can be found in VK that are connected to the tourism of Finland and what are the main topics that people discuss?

- What kinds of groups can be found in VK that are connected to the tourism to the Republic of Karelia and what are the main topics people discuss?
- What kind of advice on marketing can be given to: a) the tourism entrepreneurs in Finland and b) the tourism entrepreneurs of the Republic of Karelia, based on knowledge from these groups?

THEORETICAL CONSIDERATIONS

The promotional effectiveness of organisations in social media is quite new. Researchers have just started to examine different social media platforms and their impact on the promotional aims of organisations (Paek, Hove, Jung, & Cole, 2013). Although started as an entertainment tool, social media is widely used for business purposes because of time, audience, relation and costs (Kirtiş & Karahan, 2011).

There is still no definition for social media which would be agreed by all parties (Zhu & Wang, 2013). Safko and Brake (2009, p. 6) define social media as "activities, practices, among communities of people who gather online to share information, knowledge, and opinions using conversational media." Conversational media is a Web-based tool that helps to create and transmit content in the form of words, pictures, video and audio (Safko & Brake, 2009). Kirtiş and Karahan (2011) suggest that in social media, a group of internet-based service users interact with other users online through blogs, by sharing contents and communicate with friends over social networks.

According to Safko and Brake (2009), the most important purpose of social media from the business point of view is to engage the audience. They define four categories of engagement with social media: communication, collaboration (special social media tools for collaboration among work teams, buyers and sellers, companies and customers), education (customer education and employee training) and entertainment (entertainment definitely helps to sell products).

Social Media in Russia

TNS is the leading media and market research company in Russia. It provides monthly internet statistics for the Russian market. In October 2013,

44.2 million people (12 years and older) used the internet at least once a month, and 42.4 million people at least once a week (TNS Russia, 2013).

During the past years, the number of Internet users in Russia increased, up 17% in 2010−2011 and 12% in 2011−2012. Almost all users (94%) have access to the internet at home (Yandex, 2013).

Mail.ru Group is the most popular site in Russia (Table 1). The products of Mail.ru consist of email and portal services, social networks, instant messaging, online games, search and e-commerce and other communication and entertainment platforms (Wikipedia, 2014). Yandex is the largest search engine in Russia and provides internet-based services and products: web

Table 1.   Top 20 sites in Russia. December 2012. (comScore, 2013).

Top 20 Sites in Russia	Total Unique Visitors (000)	% Growth	Avg Minutes per Visitor	Avg Pages per Visitor
Total Internet Audience: Age 15 +	61,345	15	1,565.0	2,938
Mail.ru Group	52,396	17	371.1	733
Yandex Sites	52,124	16	91.6	173
Google Sites	45,838	21	97.9	94
Vk.com	43,959	19	390.7	612
Microsoft Sites	27,370	47	16.9	12
Wikimedia Foundation Sites	25,750	17	14.4	14
Ucoz Web Services	23,900	12	5.7	13
Ros BusinessConsulting	20,073	−2	22.8	32
Rambler Media	18,383	2	23.5	33
Avito.ru	16,402	60	37.2	83
SUP Meida	15,891	9	16.2	20
Facebook.com	14,675	25	29.0	54
Gazprom Media	13,189	5	9.3	12
Technorati Media	13,133	37	2.8	5
Map Makers Sites (Gismeteo)	10,971	81	11.0	18
MIH Limited	10,851	101	13.1	26
Kinopoisk.ru	10,363	40	12.8	19
LiveInternet	9,159	6	7.0	14
VGTRK Sites	8,339	28	12.5	16
Pronto Moscow	8,313	25	9.5	18

search, free mail hosting, mapping service, a transaction service similar to PayPal, and various productivity-enhancing apps (Clay, 2013).

According to the TNS statistics (2013) the market leader of social media is VK, with over 40 million users. VK is a social network that originated in Russia in 2006 and became extremely popular among users from post-Soviet countries. VK is a Russian version of Facebook. In Russia, the global success Facebook has its lowest penetration in Europe at 18.8%, currently ranking behind the leaders VK, Odnoklassniki and Mail.ru (comScore, 2013).

As for the site structure, VK resembles Facebook greatly. Each user has his/her own profile. In addition, one can create a "group profile" and invite fans there. A membership in those groups can be open for everybody or private, meaning that people can only join by invitation.

Odnoklassniki means "schoolmates" and was founded in 2006 as a part of the Mail.ru platform. This channel focuses on sharing photographs and is full of flashing images. Users can rate other people's photos, chat and get information on who has viewed their profile. Facebook became popular when it started to use a Russian interface. The user profile among Russians in Facebook is young people who have friends abroad. Livejournal, owned by SUP Media, differs from the other social media channels with the profile of the online community where users can keep their blogs, diary or journal. Twitter enables users to update profiles and microblog, and to send and read "tweets".

Groups in Social Media

The growth in social media usage has forced businesses to accept it as a communication channel to stay in touch with present and potential clients. Among the different tools used in social media, the most effective one is the creation of a group. The purpose of a group is to gather people with shared interests to discuss issues. The group is used as a platform for communication. It is not quite effective to create a group just around a brand. Users probably would not be interested in Colgate toothpaste, but everybody is interested in how to keep teeth healthy. Therefore, advertising should not be too straightforward. There are different strategies for creating a group: (1) by the company and hosted by the company workers, (2) by the company with hosting outsourced to an agency, (3) unofficially by the company workers, and (4) by active users (Danchenok & Nevostruev, 2011).

FINDINGS

In the beginning of the study, the groups found on VK devoted to tourism in Finland were searched for. About 10,000 were found. The criteria for choosing were based on the name (should have "Finland" in it), content (devoted to those who travel to Finland, not living in the country) and the number of members in the group (only groups with more than 3,000 members got on the list). The first group analysis was done in April 2013 and updated in November 2013.

According to the list presented in Table 2, groups can be divided into four subgroups according to what kind of information is delivered and transmitted in the group discussions:

- Subgroup 1: General information about Finland (Shopping, Sales and Rest in Finland, The land of Finland, Finland, Finland Guide, Stop in Finland).
- Subgroup 2: Information about a certain region in Finland (Finland in VKontakte – visit Mikkeli, Finland/Lappeenranta and Imatra Region/ GoSaimaa, About Helsinki, Finland/Himos).
- Subgroup 3: The group is devoted to shopping and contains plenty of advertisements (Check in Finland – the best holiday in Finland).
- Subgroup 4: The group is devoted to entertainment and is unfocused (To conquer Finland, Fuck yeah Finland).

CHANGES IN THE NUMBER OF MEMBERS

In November 2013, the most popular groups belonged to the subgroups 1 and 2. In the subgroup 1, advertising is presented in articles and blogs rather than in direct advertisements. The content of these groups provides the possibility for many tourism entrepreneurs to offer information about their services: shopping, seasonal touristic activities, cultural attractions, accommodation, competitions, discussions and advertisements.

In several groups the number of users changed dramatically from April to November. The number of users grew in groups such as "Shopping, sales, trips and rest in Finland" (+7,941 users), "Finland/Lappeenranta and Imatra region/GoSaimaa" (+14,829 users), "The land of Finland" (+3,533 users).

For the group, "To conquer Finland", the number of users had decreased (−453) and in December 2013, it did not exist anymore.

Table 2. Groups in VK Connected to Tourism to Finland: vk.ru.

Name of the Group/ VKontakte Name	Description	Number of Members	
		Apr 2013	Nov 2013
Finland in VKontakte, visit Mikkeli / *Финляндия ВКонтакте, Миккели VisitMikkeli.fi*	http://vk.com/visitmikkeli, support for the site: www.visitmikkeli.fi — Popular group for tourists, the most of the new members are from Mikkeli region	14,599	14,281 (−318)
Shopping sales, trips and rest in Finland / *Шоппинг, скидки, поездки и отдых в Финляндии!*	http://vk.com/checkfinland — Group that offers useful information about Finland, what to do, where to go and what to see.	9,027	16,968 (+7,941)
Finland / *Финляндия*	http://vk.com/finland_suomiSupport for the site: www.russian.fi — Finnish news, sales, cultural offers, possibility to ask questions, not well-structured	8,449	8,776 (+327)
To conquer Finland / *Взять Финляндию на абордаж!*	http://vk.com/club22298, support for the site: www.finndeal.ru — Finnish news, advertisements of private people offering services connected to Finland, not focused.	8,067	7,614 (−453)
Finland/Lappeenranta and Imatra Region/GoSaimaa / *Финляндия|Регион Лаппеенранта и Иматра|GoSaimaa*	http://vk.com/gosaimaa, support for the site: www.gosaimaa.com — Information on the activities in South Finland. Works as an online customer service in Russian for those interested in Lappeenranta.	6,873	21,702 (+14,829)
Stop in Finland. Truth about Finland / *Stop in Finland − вся правда о Финляндии!*	http://vk.com/stopinfin, support for the site: www.stopinfin.ru/	6,376	6,113 (−263)
About Helsinki, capital city with style	News about shopping, activities, and culture in Helsinki, well-structured. http://vk.com/prohelsinki, support for the site: www.helsinki.ru	6,297	8,473 (+2,176)

Table 2. (*Continued*)

Groups in VKontakte Related to Tourism in Finland

Name of the Group/ VKontakte Name	Description	Number of Members	
		Apr 2013	Nov 2013
Про Хельсинки! Про Столицу со вкусом™ Helsinki	News about shopping, activities, culture in Helsinki, well-structured.		
The land of Finland	http://vk.com/stranafi, support for the site: www.strana.fi	6,165	9,698 (+3,533)
Suomi maa	Tourism-oriented group, peaceful, well-structured, many pictures of Finnish nature and different places in Finland		
Fuck yeah, Finland!	http://vk.com/suomifyeah	5,947	7,342 (+1,395)
Vittu Joo, Suomi!	The group is full of entertaining stuff: Finnish music, films, design		
Finland/Himos/Downhill Skiing Resort	http://vk.com/himosholiday, support for the site: www.%20Himosholiday%20ru	4,547	4,238 (−309)
Финляндия|Himos|Химос|Горнолыжный курорт	The group about activities in Himos throughout the year.		
Finland guide. I leave for Finland.	http://vk.com/club6361288, support for the site: www.igotofin.ru	4,905	4,951 (+46)
Путеводитель по Финляндии — Я е ду в Финляндию.	The group is closed. I waited for my acceptance to the group to see what the group is about.		
Check in Finland — the best holiday in Finland!	http://vk.com/checkinfinland, support for the site: www.checkinfinland.ru	3,097	3,054 (+407)
Check in Finland — лучший отдых в Финляндии	The group is oriented on shopping in Finland, plenty of advertising, not much tourist information.		

"Finland in VKontakte, visit Mikkeli" (−318 users), "Finland/Himos/ Downhill skiing" (−309 users) are groups that support a special region or resort in Finland. This decrease could be explained by the fact that users were not so well activated by the moderators regarding questions, advice or competitions. It is likely that no advertising budget was used for promoting the group. Naturally, user numbers increase close to the New Year's season and is quite constant during non-touristic seasons.

DISCUSSION TOPICS

The most popular topics were analysed inside the groups connected to tourism in Finland (Table 3). Data were gathered in April-May 2013. Groups from Table 2 were analysed, and the most popular topics were chosen on the basis of the number of comments. Only the topics with over 20 comments were chosen. One topic often consisted of several discussions. All discussions were created by the moderators of the groups. The Russian members of the groups (from Finland or Russia) answered and asked questions and continued discussions.

The topics which gathered more than 20 comments were examined. The discussions concentrated on topics such as health care in Finland, shopping, things that surprised tourists in Finland, questions and answers about Finland, traffic and accommodation.

Shopping: The most popular topic, which gathered 98 comments, was shopping. People gave the addresses of good shops with cheap prices and high-level brands. Out of all the shopping products, the most attention was paid to Swan's down coats, wedding dresses and sports equipment:

> **N.D.:** What are the prices for Finnish swan's down coats???? We are going to travel at the beginning of January ... (http://vk.com/topic-19035_1315875?offset = 20)

> **A.S.:** We are going to travel on the 19th of December. Where can we buy sports clothes in Helsinki? (http://vk.com/topic-19035_1315875?offset = 40)

People also needed more information on the tax free and invoice systems:

> **T.V.:** Regina, I didn't actually understand, what is this VAT refund system? Do they really check everything on the boarder? (http://vk.com/topic-19035_1315875?offset = 80)

Table 3. Discussions in VK about tourism in Finland: vk.ru.

Group Name/Name IN VKontakte	Members Nov 2013	Topic	Comments	Amount of Comments
Finland	8,776	Health care in Finland	Prices for health care, insurance, medicine, surgery, feedback, doctors (their educational level and proficiency)	22
Финляндия		Shopping	Prices, brands, sale, clothes for young persons, wedding dresses, Swan's down coats, loyalty customer cards, shops and shopping centre, low-price shops: where?, sport equipment, delivery of goods, tax free – invoice	98
Check in Finland – the best holiday in Finland!	3,504	What did surprise you in Finland?	Comfortable traffic and clear traffic signs, honesty and friendliness of people, clean and peaceful cities, clear water, beautiful nature, ecology, reindeers	40
Check in Finland – лучший отдых в Финляндии		Questions and answers about Finland	Visas, attractions, spa, parks, holidays with children, accommodation, traffic, sale, opening hours of shops, boat trips from Finland, plane tickets from Finland, parking in Finland, museums	74
Stop in Finland. Truth about Finland	6,113	To Finland by car	Border rules, traffic, motorbikes in Finland, parking, fines	29
Stop in Finland – вся правда о Финляндии!		Public transport in Helsinki	Season tickets, tickets/prices and where to buy, travel cards, timetable, getting to the airport, bus stops	71
Finland in VKontakte, visit Mikkeli Финляндия ВКонтакте, Миккели VisitMikkeli.fi	14,281	Accommodation	What, where; Prices; Where to stay near Mikkeli	25

Health care: Health care in Finland gathered 22 comments; people were interested in prices, the possibilities of giving birth in Finland and surgeries of different kinds:

> **E.O.:** Valentina, hi! I gave birth to my first baby in Finland. Everything was on a high level, the service, the attention from the nurses. With my husband, we got only positive emotions. (http://vk.com/topic-19035_1339228)

The level of proficiency of Finnish doctors did not get much positive attention:

> **J.K.:** Really the level of medicine here is very weak. Children always get Panadol, adults get Panadol as well, if the situation is really serious then they give you antibiotics, but they don't examine you or do any tests. (http://vk.com/topic-19035_1339228)

> **A.O.:** In Finland for any kind of problems you always get Burana or Panadol. (http://vk.com/topic-19035_1339228)

Despite the situation with the Finnish doctors, Russians were satisfied with the level of technical equipment in Finnish hospitals:

> **E.O.:** Svetlana, you've been told right, Finnish hospitals are well-equipped ... (http://vk.com/topic-19035_1339228)

Positive surprises: The things that surprised tourists in Finland were aspects connected to traffic: good roads, drivers obeying the rules and reindeer walking down the streets:

> **T.K.:** When I first came to Finland I was surprised how traffic is organised on the crossroads! I wish we had the same in Saint Petersburg! (http://vk.com/topic-31796237_27334999)

Clean nature, tap water that everyone can drink, peacefulness and the friendliness of people in Finland were also issues discussed under the topic, "What surprised you in Finland?"

> **I.A.:** First of all I was impressed by the ecology of the country, cleanliness, order everywhere. Even the railway station was so clean, I think the cleanest in the whole of Europe. Water is also very clean, you can drink it straight out of the tap. There are very high level products in here that I like. From the first impression people are calm, well-behaved and friendly. (http://vk.com/topic-31796237_27334999)

Questions and answers about Finland: Under the topic, Questions and answers about Finland, there was discussion on such issues as visas, accommodation, traffic, sales, tickets, parking rules, and holiday activities. Group members gave advice to each other and compared how differently things were organized in Finland and Russia:

> **F.R.:** How much time do I need to get a Finnish visa? Thank you.

L.A.: Good afternoon! Is it possible to visit the art gallery Retretti in Punkaharju? The web site doesn't work. Is the gallery open? What are the opening hours?

Other topics connected to transport were: getting to Finland by car and public transport in Helsinki.

GROUPS IN VK CONNECTED TO TOURISM TO THE REPUBLIC OF KARELIA

In April 2013, about 5,000 groups with the word "Karelia" in their title were found in VK. 13 groups were connected to the Republic of Karelia as a tourist destination and had over 3,000 members. These 13 groups were analysed in this study. The first two, "Karelia: Petrozavodsk" and "Karelia-21 century/Petrozavodsk", are built mostly around the happenings in the capital of the Republic of Karelia – Petrozavodsk. Furthermore, the groups which are used as a promotional channel for firms offering cottage rental services are as follows: "Karelia: Rest in the comfortable cottages by the lake", "Cottages, rest, excursions and fishing in Karelia" and "Rest in Karelia: cottages, fishing, hunting".

Tour operators offering package tours and activity services also use VK as a promotional channel in the groups "Active Holiday in Karelia", "Rest in Karelia" and "Travel agency Karelia". Groups for people just interested in Karelia and its nature consist of plenty discussions and some advertising materials. These groups are "Karelia", "Ladoga lake", "Karelia: active holiday in Karelia" and "Karelia! Ladoga lake! Skerries!".

DISCUSSION TOPICS

The most popular topics analysed within the selected groups were connected to tourism to the Republic of Karelia (Table 4). The data were gathered in November 2013. The groups in Table 5 were analysed, and the most popular topics were chosen on the basis of the number of comments. Only topics with at least 40 comments were selected. One topic often consisted of several discussions. The discussion was started by moderators or group members.

Most of the people discussed different places to visit in Karelia: alone, with friends or with the family. They were interested in different kinds of holidays, from cheap to expensive ones, in winter and in summer:

Table 4. Discussion Topics in VK about Tourism to the Republic of Karelia: vk.ru.

Group	Members Nov 2013	Topic	Comments	Nr. Of Comments
Karelia: active holiday in Karelia	4,429	Where to go in Karelia?	How to get to specific destinations by a car and other transportation	127
			The best lake in Karelia	
Карелия!!! Активный отдых и Карелии.			Attractions	
			Prices	
			Accommodation	
			Best fishing, where?	
Karelia! Ladoga lake! Skerries!	3,432	Hotels and other accommodation in Karelia	Best tour operators	88
Карелия!			Best cottages to rent	
Ладожское озеро!Шхеры!			Hostels	
Cottages, rest, excursions and fishing in Karelia	13,530	Water trip in Karelia	Canoe trips	65
Коттеджи, Отдых, экскурсии и Рыбалка и Карелии			Best lakes for canoe trips	
			Water safety issues	
Travel agency "Karelia"	5,323	Where to go in Karelia?	Best peaceful place	63
Туристическая компания Карелия			Fishing permission	
			Good roads	
Ladoga Lake	6,743	Ruskeala	What to see in Ruskeala?	40
Ладожское озеро			What to do in Ruskeala?	
			How to get to Ruskeala?	
			Where to stay?	

Table 4. (*Continued*)

Group	Members Nov 2013	Topic	Comments	Nr. Of Comments
Rest in Karelia Отдых и Карелии	5,554	Rent a cottage without electricity	Unique chance to rent a cottage in a village without electricity and neighbours	40
Rest in Karelia: cottages, fishing, hunting Отдых и ареали: коттеджи, рыбалка, охота	9,025	Where to go in the Republic of Karelia during self-organised trip?	Beautiful place where one can get by him/herself Activities Public transport	33

Table 5. Groups in VK Related to Tourism in the Republic of Karelia.

Name of the Group	Groups in VKontakte Related to Tourism in the Republic of Karelia	
	Description	April 2013 Members
Karelia: Petrozavodsk *Карелия: Петрозаводск*	http://vk.com/petrozavodsk News about Petrozavodsk	40,744
Karelia-21 century/Petrozavodsk *Карелия — 21 Век/Петрозаводск*	http://vk.com/karelia_xxi_vek News about Petrozavodsk, the most beautiful places in the Republic of Karelia.	26,267
Karelia: Rest in the comfortable cottages down the lake *Карелия: Отдых и уютных коттеджах на берегу реки*	http://vk.com/club5431137 The group is created for private company purposes to support cottage renting business, many pictures of the Republic of Karelia	18,102
Cottages, rest, excursions and fishing in Karelia *Коттеджа, Отдых, экскурсии и Рыбалка в Карелии*	http://vk.com/munozero The group is created for private company purposes to support the renting of cottages business in the area of lake Munozero	13,530
Karelia *Карелия*	http://vk.com/karelia_otdih General information about RK, support for the site: www.karjalan.ru	13,138
Rest in Karelia. Tours, Accommodation, Hotels. *Отдых и Карелии. Туры. База отдыха. Гостиницы.*	http://vk.com/all_karelia Official group for the private company, offering cottages and other touristic services, http://baza-karelii.ru/	9,025
Ladoga Lake *Ладожское озеро*	http://vk.com/club19649 Group for people who have fallen in love with Lake Ladoga or are interested in Karelian nature. Plenty of pictures and discussion	6,743

Table 5. *(Continued)*

Name of the Group	Description	April 2013 Members
Active holidays in Karelia	http://vk.com/karelia.activetravel	5,911
Активный отдых и Карелии	Official group for a private company offering activity services for tourists: www. activetravel.ru	
Rest in Karelia	http://vk.com/club2651460	5,554
Отдых и Карелии	Official group for a private company offering activity services for tourists	
Travel agency "Karelia"	http://vk.com/club44077146	5,323
Туристическая компания Карелия	Official group for a tour operator offering package tours, http://www.t-karelia.ru	
Karelia: active holiday in Karelia	http://vk.com/club12281	4,429
Карелия!!! Активный отдых и Карелии.	Group for people who are interested in Karelia and spending a holiday in Karelia. Information about the region.	
Karelia! Ladoga lake! Skerries!	http://vk.com/ladoga812	3,432
Карелия! Ладожское озеро!Шхеры!	Group for people who are interested in the history and geography of Karelia and the skerries in Lake Ladoga	

K.Z.: Sergey, hello! Could you help please, where in Samozero can we visit by car and have rest, and fish? Thanks in advance ... (http://vk.com/topic-12281_10842?offset = 120)

Many tourists wanted to stay in calm places with no neighbours:

M.B.: Albert, we need a beautiful, peaceful place, far from civilization, with winter fishing, skiing etc. Thanks! (http://vk.com/topic-12281_10842?offset = 60)

A.K.: I am searching for a place in Karelia, not more than 600 km from Saint Petersburg with the minimum number of tourists, for staying in a tent. The more difficult to get there the better: that means less tourists. (http://vk.com/topic-12281_21031660)

Many users told about the most beautiful places they had visited in the Republic of Karelia:

N.A.: Interesting places in Karelia situated in Zaonezhye ... (http://vk.com/topic-12281_10842?offset = 60)

Hotels and other accommodation: The group members were asked to write opinions on different accommodation options in Karelia as well as accommodation providers. During this discussion, people wrote their impressions on hotels, hostels and different firms organising accommodation:

A.V.: Yesterday we stayed in the village Matrosi, Prjazinskaja Street 106, Guest House (Skif Tour). We went on a dog safari. It is very comfortable inside; you feel at home. (http://vk.com/topic-12281_1297646)

Trips to Karelia: Different kinds of trips were discussed under the topics, "water trips in Karelia" and "where to go during the self-organised trip in Karelia?". Most of the members asked for advice on a specific destination or a place.

K.A.: Could someone tell is it better to take an instructor with the water tour, or is it better to go by ourselves, even though we don't have any experience? (http://vk.com/topic-12281_1389579)

S.M.: Hello everyone!!! Does anybody know two or three good routes in Karelia for a first time trip for seven to eight days? (http://vk.com/topic-12281_1389579)

O.K.: I would like to have a rest on the shungite lakes, in a tent. Where can I go from Saint Petersburg? (http://vk.com/topic-12281_22349518)

Exotic Karelia: The whole topic and 40 comments were devoted to the special exotic offer for tourists — a unique house in the middle of nowhere, without any electricity and neighbours for 20 kilometres. The price was 2,000 rubles per night for a house. The provider could drive the tourist only to a place 10 km from the house, and afterwards, the tourist should ski or use snowshoes, because no one keeps the roads clear. "For those who really want to feel a real village ...". The reaction of the members was excited and people asked many questions:

> **A.S.**: Hello. I liked the offer very much. How can we get there? I come from Uljanovsk, but at least how can we get there from SPB? What is the weather like there in July-August?

CONCLUSION AND IMPLICATIONS

According to the data analysed in the previous chapter, many companies from Finland and Russia use VK as a marketing tool for promotional and information purposes. Groups in VK that are linked to Finnish tourism are more widely used than groups about the Republic of Karelia. The Finnish groups are mostly used as a promotional tool for the webpage or an online client communication tool.

Here are the tips for entrepreneurs on how to succeed in the most popular social media channel in Russia, VK. Attention is paid especially to those who offer services for tourists:

- The name of the group should include the main idea of the group.
- The group should be moderated and well organised. This means that there should be a moderator who answers the questions, updates the information and deletes inappropriate comments.
- Too much selling took enthusiasm away from the group members; people are more likely to participate in a discussion, not in straight advertising.
- VK is a Russian-speaking channel. There is no reason to create a group in English or other languages. All the groups that were examined in this study use only Russian.

As this study has showed, Russians use groups in VK as a channel for discussion. Discussions can be created by a moderator or a group member. The topics of the discussions about Finland are different from each other. They include comments regarding shopping and the environment in Finland, visa and border procedures, prices and people. The most popular topic is shopping in Finland. People in the groups of the Republic of Karelia are interested in nature tourism, activities near lakes and forest and travelling by their own transport. They are mainly seeking active relaxation. The most popular topics in these groups are recommendations for the best places to visit and where to go. There is a difference in the nature of the groups for Finland and Russia. The members of the groups connected to the Republic of Karelia more actively comment, whereas in the groups related to Finland the members tend to observe more.

Groups in the social media channel VK are used for interacting with potential and real consumers. It is used as an additional tool that supports the webpage of a company or an organisation. When marketing the tourism services for group members their preferences should be taken into account. The moderator of the group can get information on the age and home city of the members. Attention should be focused on the popular discussion topics. According to Gretzel, Fesenmaier, Formica, and O'Leary (2006), the technological marketing tool potential should be used by organisations. Users interact with each other; they create and share content, and the tourism service provider cannot ignore this.

ACKNOWLEDGMENTS

This study was part of the Product development and development of market insight and e-marketing of rural and nature tourism (RUNAT) project managed by the University of Eastern Finland.

REFERENCES

Boiko, A. (2009). *Forming the tourist clusters as an instrument of tourism development in Russia*. Novosibirsk: Siberian Academy of Public Administration.

Clay, D. (2013). *Yandex searches past its language barrier*. Retrieved from http://tech.fortune.cnn.com/2013/11/13/yandex-searches-language-barrier/

comScore. (2013). *Europe digital future in focus*. Retrieved from http://www.comscore.com/Insights/Presentations_and_Whitepapers/2013/2013_Europe_Digital_Future_in_Focus

Danchenok, L. A., & Nevostruev, P. J. (2011). Strategii sozdanija soobcestv v socialnih setjah. *Otkrytoe Obrazovanie, 3*, 52−56.

Federal State Statistic Service. (2013). *Russia in figures*. Retrieved from http://www.gks.ru/bgd/regl/b13_12/IssWWW.exe/stg/d01/5-01.htm

Furmanov, K., Balaeva, O., & Predvoditeleva, M. (2012). Tourism flows from the Russian federation to the European union. *Anatolia: An International Journal of Tourism and Hospitality Research, 23*(1), 1−15.

Gretzel, U., Fesenmaier, D. R., Formica, S., & O'Leary, J. (2006). Searching for the future: Challenges faced by destination marketing organizations. *Journal of Travel Research, 45*(2), 116−126.

Kirtiş, A. K., & Karahan, F. (2011). To be or not to be in social media arena as the most cost-efficient marketing strategy after the global recession. *Procedia — Social and Behavioral Sciences, 24*, 260–268.

Malankin, M. (2012). *Venäläiset matkailun asiakkaina*. Mikkeli: Mikkelin ammattikorkeakoulu tutkimuksia ja raportteja.

Paek, H.-J., Hove, T., Jung, Y., & Cole, R. T. (2013). Engagement across three social media platforms: An exploratory study of a cause-related PR campaign. *Public Relations Review, 39*(5), 526–533.

Russia Tourism Strategy to 2020. (2014). *Strategia razvitia turizma Rossijskoi Federacii na period do 2020 goda*. Retrieved from http://www.russiatourism.ru/data/File/news_file/2014/strategia.pdf?sphrase_id=38705

Safko, L., & Brake, D. K. (2009). *The social media bible*. Hoboken, NJ: John Wiley.

Statistics Finland. (2013). *Border interview survey 2012*. Retrieved from http://tilastokeskus.fi/til/rajat/2012/rajat_2012_2013-05-30_tie_001_en.html

TNS Russia. (2013). *Web index report 10/2013*. Retrieved from Retrieved from http://www.tns-global.ru/services/media/media-audience/internet/information

Wikipedia. (2014). *Mail.ru*. Retrieved from http://en.wikipedia.org/wiki/Mail.Ru

Yandex. (2013). *Development of internet in Russia's regions*. Spring 2013. Retrieved from http://download.yandex.ru/company/ya_russian_regions_report_2013.pdf

Zhu, M., & Wang, Q. (2013). Trends of web 2.0: Get close to social media. 2013 International Conference on Advances in Social Science, Humanities, and Management (ASSHM 2013), 449–445. Atlantis Press: Beijing.

CHAPTER 6

KEY STAKEHOLDERS IN CRUISE TRAFFIC: AN APPLICATION TO SPANISH CRUISE PORTS

Jerónimo Esteve-Pérez and Antonio García-Sánchez

ABSTRACT

The cruise tourism industry has experienced a positive evolution, with an average annual growth rate in the worldwide number of cruise passengers of 7.84% between 1990 and 2013. This chapter presents an empirical analysis particular to Spanish cruise ports and their associated tourist hinterlands. With regard to cruise ports, an evolution analysis and port portfolio analysis technique using the growth-share matrix for the period 2000−2013 is applied in order to identify the competitive positions of a range of 18 ports in the Spanish Mediterranean coast. While for the tourist hinterland of each port is characterized the geographical area encompassed. The results obtained identify the different competitive positions of ports and the different types of hinterlands characterized.

Keywords: Cruise tourism; cruise ports; tourist hinterland; portfolio analysis

Tourism and Hospitality Management
Advances in Culture, Tourism and Hospitality Research, Volume 12, 81−93
Copyright © 2016 by Emerald Group Publishing Limited
ISSN: 1871-3173/doi:10.1108/S1871-317320160000012007

INTRODUCTION

The cruise tourism industry comprises all economic units that provide goods and/or services to cruise passengers. On a cruise, companies successfully combine sets of inland destinations and port cities with various amenities on board the cruise vessel to create the cruise product. Cruises have experienced significant growth during the last two decades. From 1990 to 2013, the number of cruise passengers worldwide has grown at an average annual rate of 7.84%. In the last 20 years, the five-year periods from 1999 through 2003 and from 2004 through 2008 registered the highest growth with an average annual rate of 10.25% and 10.76%, respectively. This positive development has meant that cruise tourism is the fastest growing tourism subsector. Furthermore, forecasts indicate an average annual growth of 2.85% until 2018, a growth that would result in more than 24.15 million cruise passengers worldwide by 2018 (Cruise Market Watch, 2014).

The key elements associated with the cruise product are the vessel and the itinerary that determines the homeport and the ports of call (Wild & Dearing, 2000). The set of port cities and their respective tourist hinterlands delimit the area that cruise passengers can visit. The inland destinations coupled with the services offered on the vessel define the experiences and activities that one can perform on a cruise. Rodrigue and Notteboom (2013) assert, in accordance with the prior sentence, that this industry sells itineraries, not destinations. The three key stakeholders involved in setting up a cruise itinerary are the cruise line, the port and the cruise destination or region visited by cruise passengers in each call (i.e., called tourist hinterland).

The purpose of this chapter is to characterize each of the stakeholders listed above and carry out an empirical analysis applied to the Spanish coast about cruise ports and associated tourist hinterland. This work is aimed at cruise tourism researchers and agents involved in this industry.

THEORETICAL CONSIDERATIONS

The cruise vessel is directly related to the transport component present in the cruise product, along with the tourists' attraction relating to the vessel itself, as it can be considered as a destination in itself, hence the current conception of the marine resort. To benefit from economies of scale, vessels have increased in the size over the past two decades, thereby increasing passenger capacity. Examples of this trend are the *Genesis Project* developed by Royal Caribbean International, which owns the ships Oasis of the Seas and Allure of the Seas, the largest in the world, each of these vessels has a capacity of 5,400 passengers (Royal Caribbean Cruises Limited, 2007), and the Norwegian Epic owned by Norwegian Cruise Line, with a capacity of 4,100 passengers (Norwegian Cruise Line, 2014). This has made the cruise product more accessible to the consumer and no longer reserved as a highly elitist product only for the wealthy and the elderly (Soriani, Bertazzon, Di Cesare, & Rech, 2009).

The cruise lines market is characterized by aggressive acquisitions, mergers, internationalization strategies and corporate concentration (Gui & Russo, 2011). In June 2013, the cruise lines market was divided into three multi-brand groups, known as The Big Three, which comprised 78.26% of total passenger cruise ship capacity, and a fourth group of independent cruise companies with the remaining share of 21.74%.

Carnival Corporation & Plc. is the largest worldwide operator composed of ten cruise lines that report a market share of 48.09%; Royal Caribbean Cruises Limited with five cruise companies and an associated market share of 21.67% is the second largest worldwide operator; and finally, Genting Hong Kong Limited with two brands and a share of 8.49% is the third largest, thus forming The Big Three. MSC Cruises stands out in the group of independent companies due to its fleet size and associated capacity that give it a market share of 6.88%.

Moreover, the concentration is evident not only in the current fleet but also in the order book for new cruise vessels. Cruise lines are in charge of investing in the construction of new ships that are associated with their itineraries. In October 2014, there are 18 cruise ships under construction, 12 of which belong to The Big Three. This concentration means that 84.60% of the new passenger capacity will enter into service from November 2014 to November 2016 (Cruise Market Watch, 2014).

All spatial flows, with the exception of those developed by own means, involve movements between terminals. In the case of passenger transport, more specifically in cruise traffic, the passenger terminal is part of a complex and versatile enclosure: the port. It is often stated that ports exceed the simple function of providing services to ships, passengers and cargoes at the pier. Port functions, services and activities are defined by spatial dimensions, ranging from simple berthing facilities to value-added services (Vaggelas & Pallis, 2010).

The ports play a key role in the maritime transport associated with a cruise itinerary, constituting the link with the tourism component that develops on land. Ports also act as a link between the tourist hinterland and the cruise vessel. Thus, taking as a reference the port definition given by UNCTAD (1991) and particularizing it to a cruise port similarly yields the following:

> A cruise port is the area where the interface between sea and land transport modes is performed, and as such being an intermodal transport node. Passengers are embarked and disembarked from the cruise ship and then forwarded to/from the hinterland with the use of transport modes available between the hinterland and the port.

The definition above applies to the two main types of cruise ports: homeports, from which starts and ends the cruise itinerary, and ports of call, which are intermediate calls in the itinerary. Homeports connect the cruise passenger source markets with the cruise vessel. Ports of call connect the cruise vessel with the tourist hinterland. The global cruise port system is characterized by a high level of concentration and clustering (Rodrigue, Comtois, & Slack, 2013). Furthermore, the number of homeports is much lower than the number of ports of call. The Caribbean Sea is the top cruise destination, with a market share of 34.4%, followed by the Mediterranean, which recorded a market share of 21.7% in 2013 (CLIA, 2014). In 2013, 10 ports on the Mediterranean accounted for 87.67% of the total home in/out passengers compared with the approximately 150 ports able to accommodate cruise ships in this region (MedCruise, 2014).

From a spatial point of view, the evaluation of the attractiveness of a port of call focuses on three geographical areas: the port area, the port city and the area of influence near the port known as the tourist hinterland (Lekakou, Pallis, & Vaggelas, 2009). Generally, it is very difficult to delimit the hinterland of a port; the hinterland varies with respect to commodity, time and transport mode. Moreover, market dynamics can alter the hinterland, so it is not a static and inelastic character concept (OECD, 2009). The tourist hinterland associated with ports of call is defined as the geographic area available to be visited (i.e., via excursions) by cruise passengers during a call in the port (Esteve-Perez & Garcia-Sanchez, 2014). It is possible to distinguish two types of tourist hinterlands associated with one port: primary hinterlands and competitive hinterlands (Rodrigue, Comtois, & Slack, 2013). A primary hinterland is the area that is available to the cruise passengers calling at a specific port, while a competitive hinterland is the area that is available to cruise passengers from more than one port.

The hinterland of a homeport has a dynamic character associated with the creation of new air routes or increased transport modes and infrastructure with respect to the source markets. Furthermore, it can also be extended with the emergence of new source markets. The main constraint associated with delimiting the tourist hinterland of a port of call is the ship's call length. There may be a port with nearby tourist attractions that are not accessible due to a lack of land transport infrastructure that permits visiting them within the time interval that the ship remains in port. It may also happen that a port has important tourist attractions, but at a distance that even with adequate transport infrastructure are impossible to reach during the call. The development of land transport infrastructure can generate an expansion of the tourist hinterland; therefore, attractions that were not possible to visit before could be accessed in a timely manner. Along with this development, the development of new tourist attractions near the port also generates a hinterland's expansion. Furthermore, in the tourist hinterland definition also has a remarkable influence on the ship's operational pattern in port, so that a change in it would bring a change in the size of the tourist hinterland. For example, the vessels of contemporary segment cruise lines remains in port between 8 and 10 hours compared with luxury segment cruise lines that implemented overnight stays in ports of call with the consequent opportunity to expand the tourist hinterland's size.

The integration of the tourist hinterland concept and the role played by the port in the tourist flow to this hinterland is based partly on Baird (1997) and Gui and Russo (2011). Five resulting categories of ports stem from this synergy of concepts, which include the black hole, semi-black hole, balanced, semi-gateway and gateway concepts. In a black hole port, the port city destination is endowed with important tourist attractions, so cruise passengers have no interest to visit attractions located inland. At the other extreme, a gateway port functions as a transport link, which is used to reach the main tourist attractions located outside the port city. A balanced port has an equal share of tourist attractions in the port city and in the surrounding area; consequently, both are similarly rich in terms of tourist attractions. A semi-black hole port offers not only a port city endowed with important tourist attractions that are worth visiting by most cruise passengers but also a hinterland that offers certain attractions that are visited by niche groups of passengers. In contrast, the semi-gateway port is established when core destinations are far from the port; however, the port city itself is also endowed with significant attractions that appear marketable.

METHOD

The empirical analysis focuses on the cruise ports of the Spanish coast and tourist hinterland associated with them. The empirical analysis related to the cruise ports comprises two steps. The number of cruise passengers is the variable used to perform both steps. This variable is selected because it has the highest precision in measuring the cruise traffic registered in each port. The source of information of this variable is the public organization *Puertos del Estado* (2014) from the Public Works Ministry of the Spanish Government. The number of cruise calls and the amount of gross tonnage of calling ships are also variables that could measure cruise traffic, but these two variables show a high degree of uncertainty due to the differences existing in the size of vessels and the occupation rate.

In the first step, an evolution study of this maritime traffic in the Spanish Port System between 2000 and 2013 is conducted. In the second step, a port portfolio analysis is developed to identify the competitive positions of each of the Spanish Mediterranean cruise ports and to determine the concentration of the cruise traffic in this littoral zone. This analysis is based in the growth-share matrix initially introduced by Boston Consulting Group (BCG) in 1968 (Henderson, 1979); in this case, the analysis used the version adapted to the port industry. The matrix represents the average annual growth ratio and the average market share per year vertically and horizontally, respectively, for the period of analysis. Each of the four matrix quadrants corresponds to a competitive position; the four categories are high potential, star performer, mature leader and minor performer (Haezendonck, 2001). The majority of applications of this matrix in the research field of port industry focus on cargo traffic and more particularly containerized cargo. This technique has been applied in the port industry's research works developed, for example, by Winkelmans and Coeck (1993), Park (2006) and Haezendonck, Verbeke, and Coeck (2006). The first application to passenger cruise traffic dates back to 2013 in the work of Bagis and Dooms (2013), which analyzed the competitive position of six cruise ports in the Eastern Mediterranean region.

The empirical analysis related to tourist hinterland also comprises two steps. In the first step, the tourist hinterland of the cruise ports on the Spanish Mediterranean coast is delimited. In addition, the hinterland has been classified as primary, competitive, or both. In the second step, the ports are classified according to their function in the tourist flow following in both specifications the classifications mentioned above.

FINDINGS

The Spanish Port System consists of 46 ports that are managed by 28 port authorities, considering the Landlord Port system present in Spain.

The growth trend of cruise industry has not gone unnoticed in Spain, with 33 ports registering cruise traffic. Between 2000 and 2013, the number of cruise passengers in Spanish ports increased at an average annual rate of 11.59%, much higher than the number of cruise passengers worldwide that has grown during the same period at an average annual rate of 7.84%. In 14 years, the number of cruise passengers arriving to the Spanish ports nearly quadrupled, reaching 7,675,511 in 2013. In addition, the strategic location of Spain, including the Balearic and Canary Islands, allows Spanish cruise ports to have a significant presence in the cruise itineraries that run through Northern Europe and the Mediterranean, and repositioning cruises between America and Europe.

Considering the configuration of the Spanish coast, it is possible to define three groups of ports. One group consists of the 24 Spanish Mediterranean and Andalusian Atlantic ports, another comprises the 11 ports bordering the Cantabrian Sea and the Galician Atlantic coast, and the third group includes the 11 Canary Islands ports. During the period 2000—2013, the Mediterranean coastal ports and the Andalusian Atlantic ports concentrated approximately 75% of the total cruise passengers, followed by the Canary Islands with 20% and the Cantabrian and Galician Atlantic coast ports with just 5%. During this period, 2000—2013, the trend registered in the three littoral areas has been positive, with an average annual growth of over 10%.

The Mediterranean and Andalusian Atlantic coast comprises 18 ports that register cruise traffic. This set of ports is included primarily in Western Mediterranean itineraries. In the Canary Islands, eight of its 11 ports accommodate cruise ships encompassing the seven islands that make up the archipelago. The ports of the Canary Islands play an important role in itineraries that include calls to Morocco and other Atlantic Islands (i.e., Madeira and the Azores) and in repositioning cruises between Europe and America. The Cantabrian Sea and the Galician Atlantic coast comprise 7 of its 11 ports that register cruise traffic. These are included primarily in itineraries that run through Northern Europe and the British Isles.

The significance of cruise traffic in Spanish ports is also evident in homeports. Spain has homeports in its three littoral areas. The number of passengers starting or ending their cruise itinerary on a Spanish port has annually increased, with an average annual growth rate of 13% between 2000 and 2013. In this period, home in/out passengers has represented annually, on average, 32% of total cruise passengers, the Mediterranean coast accounted for the largest amount.

Based on the cruise passenger concentration, 75%, and the high growth registered in the period 2000—2013 with an average annual rate of 11.09% on the Mediterranean and Andalusian Atlantic coast, both the port portfolio analysis and the tourist hinterland analysis are performed focusing on this littoral area, see Fig. 1. In addition, this littoral area has the largest number of cruise ports in the Spanish coast. The analysis compares the average market shares and average growth rates of the ports considered. For this purpose, the average growth rate per year and the average market share in the period 2000—2013 are represented and each matrix quadrant is identified with a competitive position to interpret the performance of the ports that making part of the analysis.

The ports of the Mediterranean and Andalusian Atlantic coast are divided into three competitive positions, see Fig. 2. Four ports are located at the mature leader quadrant; they accounted for a market share of 85.9% in the period 2000—2013. Barcelona and Palma de Mallorca stand out among these with a market share of 43.71% and 27.56%, respectively.

Fig. 1. Map of the Cruise Ports Located in the Spanish Mediterranean and Andalusian Atlantic Coast. *Source*: Author's elaboration adapted from Puertos del Estado (2012).

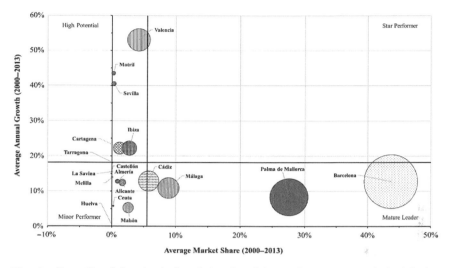

Fig. 2. Port Portfolio Analysis of the Spanish Mediterranean and Andalusian Atlantic Coast Cruise Ports (2000–2013). *Source*: Author's elaboration.

These sets of ports are must-see ports in the Spanish coast of the Western Mediterranean. This role has been maintained between 2000 and 2013 given the balance recorded between growth and market share.

Six ports have a high potential position. The port of Valencia has the largest market share in this quadrant with 4.17% and shows a dynamic behavior with the largest growth during the period 2000–2013. Their trend may consolidate it as a must-see port in the near future. This port is followed by Ibiza (Balearic Islands) and Cartagena. Both ports have similar growth rates of approximately 22.2%. The above three ports account for a market share of 8.07%.

The remaining eight ports are included in the position of minor performer, with an average market share of 5.41% all together. The cruise traffic in some of these ports is not a significant line of business with irregular amounts over the period.

The results obtained show a high concentration of cruise traffic in this littoral area, with 7 of 18 ports accounting for 93.97% of the cruise passengers. Barcelona, Palma de Mallorca, Málaga and Valencia have an established role of homeports. Barcelona, in 2013, was the fourth largest cruise port in the world and the largest in Europe and the Mediterranean Sea (Barcelona Port Authority, 2013), as a result of the higher growth of the cruise traffic in Spain compared to the average worldwide rate. Moreover, Cádiz port plays an important role, due to its geographical position at the gates of the Mediterranean Sea and the Atlantic Ocean, in repositioning cruises between the Mediterranean and the Caribbean or South America and vice versa.

Taking into account the concept of tourist hinterland and the types of ports based on the tourist flow towards the hinterland, both concepts have been applied to the Mediterranean and Andalusian Atlantic cruise ports. Most of the 15 ports analyzed have rich tourist hinterlands encompassing a wide geographical area. Usually, the tourist hinterland comprises several towns in the province where the port is located. However, there are also ports in which the hinterland extends to other provinces; as well as several ports that share the same tourist hinterland or at least a part of it, resulting in primary and competitive hinterlands. Table 1 specifies the hinterlands of each port as primary, competitive, or both.

In addition, this Spanish littoral area has the five categories of ports from the tourist flow point of view towards the hinterland, see Table 1. On the one hand, there are powerful tourist destinations such as Barcelona that focus the most attention of cruise passengers arriving at their ports (black hole ports), as well as nearby ports that act as semi-gateways to these destinations, such as the port of Tarragona with the shore excursion to Barcelona. There are also semi-black hole ports, as the case of Sevilla, in which the port city destination prevails, and niche groups of passengers are attracted to another inland destinations. On the other hand, the port of Motril acts as a gateway to the destination cities located inland and more specifically to the city of Granada. Finally, there are also balanced ports as Cádiz, where shore excursions are equally distributed between the port city and towns of the province in which the port is located.

CONCLUSION AND IMPLICATIONS

The success of a cruise itinerary involves effective interaction between the three main stakeholders responsible of its design. In the cruise lines segment, there is a high level of horizontal concentration, both in the current cruise ship fleet and in the order book of new ship constructions. With respect to cruise ports, there is a high regional concentration, with a market share of the two main worldwide destination regions of 56.1% in 2013. Furthermore, the number of homeports is much lower than ports of call; consequently, homeports have higher decision power in designing

Table 1. Type of Tourist Hinterlands and Type of Ports According to Tourist Flow.

Port	Type of Hinterland (Primary or Competitive)	Type of Port According to Tourist Flow
Alicante	Primary	Balanced
	Competitive	
Almería	Primary	Semi-gateway
	Competitive	
Barcelona	Competitive	Black hole
Cádiz	Primary	Balanced
	Competitive	
Cartagena	Primary	Semi-black hole
	Competitive	
Ceuta	Primary	Black hole
Ibiza	Primary	Black hole
Mahón	Primary	Balanced
Málaga	Primary	Balanced
	Competitive	
Melilla	Primary	Black hole
Motril	Competitive	Gateway
Palma de Mallorca	Primary	Semi-black hole
Sevilla	Competitive	Semi-black hole
	Primary	
Tarragona	Primary	Semi-gateway
	Competitive	
Valencia	Primary	Black hole

Source: Author's elaboration.

itineraries. Tourist hinterlands have a dynamic character primarily associated with the availability of transport infrastructure and tourist attractions. Furthermore, several ports may share the same hinterland or at least a part of it resulting in a competitive hinterland.

The dynamism of the cruise industry has not gone unnoticed in Spain; the number of cruise passengers quadrupled between 2000 and 2013. The three Spanish coastal areas register cruise traffic and have homeports. The positive trend in cruise traffic in Spain also has been evident in the number of home in/out passengers with an average annual growth rate of 13%

between 2000 and 2013. The cruise ports on the Spanish Mediterranean and Andalusian Atlantic Coast and its associated tourist hinterland comprised 75% of cruise passengers in Spanish ports in the period 2000–2013. In addition, they have positive competitive positions, divided primarily into mature leaders and high potential, the ports with these positions accounted for a market share of 94.6%. So, there is a high cruise traffic concentration in this littoral area. Moreover, the ports with the largest shares are associated with the role of must-see ports. They also have a wide hinterland resulting in primary and competitive hinterlands. Additionally, the five categories of ports associated with the role played in the tourist flow to the hinterland are also identified.

REFERENCES

Bagis, O., & Dooms, M. (2013). Turkey's potential on becoming a cruise hub for the East Mediterranean region: The case of Istanbul. Paper presented at International Association of Maritime Economists (IAME) Conference, Marseilles, France, 3–5 July.

Baird, A. (1997). An investigation into the suitability of an enclosed seaport for cruise ships: The case of Leith. *Maritime Policy and Management, 24*(1), 31–43.

Barcelona Port Authority. (2013). *Cruises*. Retrieved from http://www.portdebarcelona.cat/es/web/Port%20del%20Ciudada/cruceros. Accessed on March 20, 2014.

CLIA. (2014). *CLIA 2014 State of the cruise industry report*. Fort Lauderdale: CLIA.

Cruise Market Watch. (2014). *Growth of the Cruise Line Industry*. Retrieved from http://www.cruisemarketwatch.com/growth/. Accessed on October 13, 2014.

Esteve-Perez, J., & Garcia-Sanchez, A. (2014). Cruise market: Stakeholders and the role of ports and tourist hinterlands. *Maritime Economics & Logistics*, Epub ahead of print 21 August, doi:10.1057/mel.2014.21

Gui, L., & Russo, A. P. (2011). Cruise ports: A strategic nexus between regions and global lines – Evidence from the Mediterranean. *Maritime Policy and Management, 38*(2), 129–150.

Haezendonck, E. (2001). *Essays on strategy analysis for seaports*. Louvain: Garant Publishers.

Haezendonck, E., Verbeke, A., & Coeck, C. (2006). Strategic positioning analysis for seaports. *Research in Transportation Economics, 16*, 141–169.

Henderson, B. D. (1979). *Henderson on corporate strategy*. Cambridge: ABT Books.

Lekakou, M. B., Pallis, A. A., & Vaggelas, G. K. (2009). Which homeport in Europe: The cruise industry's selection criteria. *Tourismos: An International Multidisciplinary Journal of Tourism, 4*(4), 215–240.

MedCruise. (2014). *Cruise activities in MedCruise ports: Statistics 2013*. Piraeus: MedCruise.

Norwegian Cruise Line. (2014). *Ships*. Retrieved from http://www.ncl.co.uk/ships/norwegian-epic/. Accessed on October 3, 2014.

OECD. (2009). *Port competition and hinterland connections*. Round Table 143. Paris: OECD.

Park, R. K. (2006). A trend analysis of competitive positioning in Korean seaports by using the BCG matrix with CCR, BCC and scale efficiency scores. *Journal of Korea Trade, 10*(3), 1−19.

Puertos del Estado. (2012). *Los Puertos: Motores del Desarrollo y de la Dinamización Económica.* Madrid: Puertos del Estado.

Puertos del Estado. (2014). *Port traffic statistics − Monthly statistics of cruise passengers.* Retrieved from http://www.puertos.es/estadisticas/estadistica_mensual/index.html. Accessed on February 20, 2014.

Rodrigue, J. P., Comtois, C., & Slack, B. (2013). *The geography of transport systems* (3rd ed.). Abingdon: Routledge.

Rodrigue, J. P., & Notteboom, T. (2013). The geography of cruises: Itineraries, not destinations. *Applied Geography, 38,* 31−42.

Royal Caribbean Cruises Limited. (2007). *Annual report 2007.* Miami: RCCL.

Soriani, S., Bertazzon, S., Di Cesare, F., & Rech, G. (2009). Cruising in the Mediterranean: Structural aspects and evolutionary trends. *Maritime Policy and Management, 37*(3), 235−251.

UNCTAD. (1991). *Handbook on the management and operation of dry ports.* Geneva: UNCTAD.

Vaggelas, G. K., & Pallis, A. A. (2010). Passenger ports: Services provision and their benefits. *Maritime Policy and Management, 37*(1), 73−89.

Wild, P., & Dearing, J. (2000). Development of and prospects for cruising in Europe. *Maritime Policy and Management, 27*(4), 315−333.

Winkelmans, W., & Coeck, C. (1993). Strategic Positioning Analysis as an Evaluation Instrument for Effective Port Policy. *Planologisch Nieuws, 13*(3), 263−270.

CHAPTER 7

REVENUE MANAGEMENT: PROFIT OPTIMISATION FOR HONG KONG TRAVEL AGENCIES

Grace Chan and Basak Denizci Guillet

ABSTRACT

Increasing operational costs and narrowing profit margins are forcing many Hong Kong travel agencies out of business. Studies have demonstrated the strategic importance of revenue management (RM) implementation for travel agencies that wish to remain competitive. Hong Kong travel agencies should learn from these examples and modify their existing practices. As travel agencies have many of the characteristics of traditional and non-traditional RM industries, they should be able to adopt the RM operational strategies that have been successful in other industries. This study's methodology is qualitative; in-depth interviews are conducted with 10 industrial professionals. The results provide valuable insights into RM implementation in Hong Kong travel agencies. The implementation strategies discussed here include the use of perishable inventories, predictable demand, segmentation, reservations made in advance, limited capacity and appropriate cost and pricing structures,

Tourism and Hospitality Management
Advances in Culture, Tourism and Hospitality Research, Volume 12, 95–111
ISSN: 1871-3173/doi:10.1108/S1871-317320160000012008

all of which aid in profit optimisation. The results indicate that RM can improve travel agencies' competitive stance and enhance profit maximisation. RM practitioners need to fully understand the concept and techniques and have the determination to develop and promote the system among personnel at every level of the travel agency.

Keywords: Revenue management; travel agencies; revenue optimisation

INTRODUCTION

Revenue management (RM) has been successfully used by airlines, car rental firms, cruise lines, restaurants and hotels. Its principles can be applied to any service industry characterised by segmented markets, reservations, low marginal costs and fixed capacity, perishable inventories and substantially fluctuating demand. Over the past decade, numerous travel agencies have gone out of business, partly due to their reliance on commissions to cover their fixed and variable costs and their use of price-downward strategies. Are these systems still relevant? How do travel agencies currently earn their livings?

Previous RM studies have focused on the successful application of RM in hospitality businesses (Jancey, Mitchell, & Slamet, 1995; Kimes, 2011). Unlike previous RM studies, this study discusses the application of RM in Hong Kong travel agencies and provides insights for industry practitioners.

Two previous studies conducted in Canada (Anderson & Xie, 2009; Marcus & Anderson, 2008) discussed RM in travel agencies. They focused on North America, and assumed that all travel agencies could make use of the observed strategies (e.g. inventory allocation). Both studies highlighted the use of room-risk agreements to manage packages and resell bundled vacations. Although these discussions of service capacity management and inventory allocation are useful, information on appropriate pricing strategies, predictable demand and market segmentation remains limited. RM is a comprehensive concept, not limited to capacity management, and travel agencies need to understand market segmentation, pricing approaches to designing products, market demand and the strategies that stimulate demand.

SHRINKING MARGINS OF SMALL- AND MEDIUM-SIZED ENTERPRISES

The majority of travel agencies in Hong Kong are small- and medium-sized enterprises (SMEs) run privately or by a family (Information Service Department, HKSAR Government, 2012). The shrinking margins of travel agencies can be attributed to zero commissions from suppliers, low profit margins and downward price trends. Many travel agencies earn up to 10% commission on each sale, but some brochures contain non-commissionable products, such as insurance. In Hong Kong, many travel agencies have moved away from overdependence on airline commissions. Instead, they are concentrating on more lucrative market segments, such as cruises, which offer rebates for 15% commission and vacation packages (Airlines Business, 2000).

Recently, the distribution sector in tourism has grown, giving travel intermediaries the power to influence and direct consumer demand (Sharpley, 2004). Many Hong Kong travel agencies that want to retain their customers and increase customer expenditure are marking up airline tickets by only 5–7% and hotel rooms by 10%. Unlimited discount products and downward price trends are another reason for shrinking margins. The economic recession, too many players and price transparency have all increased competition. Transparent pricing in particular places downward pressure on air travel fares, as smart consumers can find lower fares and ascertain the airlines' opportunity costs without using travel agencies (Granados, Gupta, & Kauffman, 2003). As a result, travel agencies are forced to mark down their pricing to compete with their suppliers.

Insufficient cash flow is another problem for travel agencies, as they initially pay their suppliers and are then allowed one to four weeks to sell the products. Airline tickets often entail high net costs. A travel agency with insufficient cash flow is thus likely to declare bankruptcy if it cannot sell its tickets.

Many travel agencies have closed down as a result of ineffective business strategy execution. The number of medium-to-small travel agencies that have closed in recent years illustrates their difficult financial challenges (Hong Kong Tourism Commission, 2011), ranging from an uncertain economic environment to suppliers no longer needing intermediaries.

Given this external environment, Hong Kong agencies' profit margins are shrinking. This problem requires an urgent solution to prevent higher unemployment and a decline in tax revenue for the government. Travel agencies may consider applying RM to increase their profits.

Numerous examples have demonstrated how well RM works in the hospitality industry (Dacko, 2004; Hanks, Gross, & Noland, 1992; Heo & Lee, 2009; Kimes & Singh, 2009; Marcus & Anderson, 2008; Sanchez & Satir, 2005; Sun, Jiao, & Tian, 2011). As a method for managing capacity profitability, RM has gained widespread acceptance in the airline and hotel industries, with both traditional (e.g. hotels and airlines) and nontraditional (e.g. restaurants and theme parks) RM industries using the method successfully.

Given their special features, travel agencies have the potential to incorporate RM practices into their businesses. Implementing RM in Hong Kong travel agencies will provide an opportunity for profit optimisation.

REQUIREMENTS FOR RM IN TRAVEL AGENCIES

The hotel industry maximises revenue per available room (RevPAR) by using RM analysis. The key factors in determining room revenue are average room rate and occupancy. Travel agencies could similarly calculate a performance metric by dividing customer revenue across different tourism products in different periods. Travel agencies could then focus on defining and measuring revenue per available tour product (RevPATP) to maximise the profit opportunities of each product. The key issues in determining tour product revenue are average expenditure per customer in a group and the occupancy level of preset group sizes within the overall product. For managing seat availability, RevPATP is a better indicator of the revenue generated by each product, along with the sales performance of the travel agency, than simply the total number of customers. RevPATP indicates the rate at which revenue is generated and captures the trade-off between expenditure and seat availability for a product or offering. If the number of customers signing up for a tour product or group increases as the average expenditure per customer decreases, a travel agency will achieve a lower or identical RevPATP. Conversely, if an agency can increase the average expenditure per customer (i.e. improve upon regular brochure pricing when selling to a price-elastic or price-insensitive customer), it can maintain a similar RevPATP with a slightly lower headcount. This leaves the travel agency with more seats, which can then be offered at various prices (such as early bird or special discounts) to capture price-inelastic or price-sensitive customers. Travel agencies need to understand how they can achieve a high-RevPATP rate instead of just increasing the number of customers.

Pricing strategies may vary according to the time of a reservation or the number of days booked. Once travel agencies understand their RevPATP patterns, they can develop strategies for dealing with high and low RevPATP periods. When RevPATP is low, tour managers can either attract more customers by increasing the number of purchases or use bundle strategies to increase customers' expenditures. Up-selling is another method for increasing customers' expenditures. During high-RevPATP periods, a tour manager might offer limited discount products or charge premium prices to maximise revenue.

RM – THE BASICS

The rationale of RM is to maximise expected revenue by selling the right product to the right customers. Airlines' traditional RM systems have lessons for hospitality organisations because they can forecast, overbook, control both seat inventory and pricing and provide details that elaborate on the characteristics of dynamic pricing. In the early 1970s, many airlines began offering restricted discount fare products, mixing discount and higher-profit passengers in the same aircraft to maximise total revenue (McGill & Van Ryzin, 1999).

Many scholars have reviewed the theory and practice of RM (Badinelli, 2000; Burgess & Bryant, 2001; Donaghy, McMahon, & McDowell, 1995; Heo & Lee, 2009; Kimes, 1989; Kimes, 2002; Kimes & Singh, 2009; Kimes & Wirtz, 2003, 2005; McGill & Van Ryzin, 1999). Kimes (1989) suggests that RM practices are applicable to a business in which the following conditions predominate:

a) capacity is relatively fixed;
b) demand can be separated into distinct market segments;
c) inventory is perishable;
d) the product is sold well in advance of consumption;
e) demand fluctuates substantially; and
f) marginal sales costs are low and marginal production costs are high.

According to Kimes (1989), airlines and hotels are traditional RM industries, whereas restaurants and spas are non-traditional RM industries.

RM can provide profit optimisation for both traditional and non-traditional industries. Travel agencies have characteristics of both traditional and non-traditional industries and could therefore successfully adopt RM. Hong Kong travel agencies, in particular, could take advantage of their special characteristics and use RM to create profit optimisation.

PROFIT OPTIMISATION STRATEGIES FOR HONG KONG TRAVEL AGENCIES

The practices of traditional RM industries such as airlines and hotels can be extended to non-traditional users such as restaurants, heritage sites, tourist attractions, ski resorts, golf clubs, cruise industries, resorts, casinos, theme parks and health care facilities. Travel agencies can be included in this list, as they have characteristics of both traditional and non-traditional RM users.

To implement an ideal RM strategy, travel agencies would need to be similar to traditional RM industries such as airlines and hotels (see Table 1). However, as travel agencies have some non-traditional characteristics, the successful application of RM in travel agencies requires the RM strategies to be modified (see Table 2).

PERISHABLE INVENTORY

The inventory of capacity-constrained service firms should be understood as the time in which a unit of capacity is available. Rather than counting the number of customers or calculating the average revenue per customer, managers should measure the revenue per an available time-based inventory unit.

Currently, travel agencies guarantee different suppliers that they will buy a large volume of seats or rooms within a block period (a month or a week), and this creates pressure to sell the products to their customers. To minimise unsold packages and products, tour managers should manage their time-based inventory by selling products to cover daily operating costs.

To achieve a better understanding of travel agencies' management practices, it is essential to discuss the current operation systems. In current practice, travel agencies offer discounts throughout the year for their

Table 1. Characteristics of Traditional RM Industries and Travel Agencies Characteristics.

Characteristics	Ideal Characteristics of RM Industries	Travel Agencies	Degree of Common Features
Perishable inventory	– *Inventory is perishable*	– *Inventory is perishable*	
Predictable demand	– *Significant variation in demand* – *Demand is quite predictable, high and low seasons, no-show rate and others*	– *Significant variation in demand* – *Demand is predictable, high and low seasons* – *No-shows rare due to full pre-payment before departure*	*Similarity*
Segmentable market	– *Market can be segmented* – *Significant differences in price elasticity by market segment*	– *Market can be segmented (e.g. demographic and buying behaviour)* – *Differences in price elasticity by market segment*	
Reservations made in advance	– *Service reserved by customers in different time periods* – *Uncertainty in actual use despite reservations creates the possibility of unsold seats*	– *Reservations made in advance* – *Limited last-minute reservations*	
Limited capacity	– *Capacity is fixed* – *Service providers have excess capacity at certain times and excess demand at other times* – *Overbooking used to compensate for no-shows*	– *Capacity relatively flexible* – *Excess demand during the high season, which can exceed limited capacity* – *Intermediary role; they do not own their products and rely on selling tourism products and services on behalf of hotels or airlines* – *Use of overbooking to increase capacity*	*Difference*
Appropriate cost and pricing structure	– *High fixed costs* – *Demand-based pricing*	– *Low-to-medium fixed costs* – *Cost-based pricing*	

products. However, the travel industry is characterised by perishable inventory and seasonal demand, and thus the timing of sales is important. Below are several suggestions for how travel agencies could control their inventories.

Table 2.   Suggested Practices for Profit Optimisation.

Travel Agencies	Current Operation System	Suggested Operation System
Perishable inventory	– Inventory is perishable – Travel agencies offer discounts throughout the year for their products	– Limit discounts during peak season, charge premium prices, offer discounts during off-season – Settle full payment before departure to reduce no-show rate – Manage perishable inventory, including full-risk and non-risk room agreements
Predictable demand	– Reservations according to public holidays or consumer needs	– Predict reservation period, duration of journey and typology of customers – Create promotional event to stimulate demand
Segmentable market	– Mostly mass-market products	– Apply demographic, psychographic and buying behaviour analyses to market segments and identify consumer preferences for a wide range of products – Use differential or niche marketing – Apply the non-post price method to target price-sensitive customers – Segment the market based on time-flexible travel plans (e.g. weekday or weekend pricing)
Reservations made in advance	– Pre-sales reservation system from retailer counters or through email	– Operate an online reservation system connected to the RM system – Use IT systems rather than email to confirm reservations to reduce waiting time for confirmations
Limited capacity	– Flexible capacity – Tourism products offered from different suppliers with contractual agreement	– Extend flexible capacity – Shift availability of certain products or services according to customer demand – Use overbooking to extend capacity and handle more inquiries
Appropriate cost and pricing structure	– Mostly cost-based pricing – Seasonal pricing promotion – Discount for specific target – Flat tariff rates throughout the year	– Time-based pricing (pre-fixed) – Demand-based dynamic pricing strategy (variable) – Destination package pricing along with destination life cycle – Design dynamic tariff rates for each quarter

Travel agencies should make use of complex strategies such as using low-demand seasons and weekdays to attract price-sensitive customers. During peak demand (e.g. Chinese New Year), discounts could be limited, as many holiday travellers are willing to pay premium prices. At such times, travel agencies could design higher-yield, higher-profit products to maximise revenue. The more restricted nature of demand during shoulder seasons limits the opportunities to charge premium prices but offers a chance to stimulate market demand through a variety of discounting practices. During low-demand periods, different products could be designed with special pricing and service upgrades, value-added services in packages and a focus on increasing customer satisfaction. A variable pricing strategy increases customers and thus generates more revenue.

Moreover, travel agencies could request full payment from customers to reduce cancellations and no-shows, or they could extend their payment credit from suppliers. Both of these techniques would reduce uncertainty and increase cash flow.

Travel agencies could also limit uncertainty and reduce spoilage through short-term RM strategies. Anderson and Xie (2010) summarised the optimisation models that the Canadian travel agency Sunquest Vacations uses to manage its inventory. The tour company manages room obligations using a method that minimises the number of rooms it purchases but cannot sell.

Using Hong Kong travel agencies as an example, suppose that a large travel agency provides full- and non-risk room agreements to serve a reservation request for eight rooms at Hotel A. This primary request can fill full-risk rooms, allowing the agency to simply replicate this process until all of the full-risk rooms in Hotel A are sold. Additional reservations can then be allocated to non-risk rooms in Hotels B or C. Non-risk rooms should not significantly alter spoilage. Full-risk rooms can cater primarily to group tour offers from glossy brochures (as most group tours reserved from brochures are assigned on the departure day), whereas non-risk rooms can cater to independent tour packages (as most independent tour packages come on short notice or during last-minute reservations). Non-risk room availability is subject to prior sales and continual changes, so using non-risk rooms to augment supply leaves full-risk rooms available as part of the supply, mixed with non-risk rooms to model the whole season simultaneously. Such effective control of service capacity requires the detailed tracking of booking histories and the development of room inventory control rules.

PREDICTABLE DEMAND

The demand for capacity-constrained firms in traditional RM industries balances customers who make reservations and those who walk in. The two forms of demand are managed with different strategies. Customers constitute an inventory from which managers can select the most profitable combinations. For travel agencies, the most profitable customers are those who can only travel during public holidays. Variation in demand is significant in travel agencies. Compared with traditional RM industries, no-show customers who have made full pre-payment before departure are rare in travel agencies.

Forecasting this demand and managing the generated revenue requires a manager to compile information on the percentage of reservations (e.g. reservations made by walk-in guests or through phone calls and emails), advance booking periods (e.g. number of days for advance reservations, particularly before a holiday), customers' desired time periods, probable service or holiday duration (e.g. number of days for the duration of the trip, percentage of short- and long-haul journeys) and when people are most likely to travel.

Travel agencies need to track their sales and continually monitor booking situations and the consistency of decisions in changing conditions. In current practice, reservations in travel agencies are based on availability during public holidays. Travel agencies could use graphical outputs to review the historical demand patterns of packages based on particular holidays and reservation volumes, and then use these patterns to plan promotions in non-peak or shoulder seasons.

Travel agencies should observe and predict historical patterns, advanced booking periods, journey durations and customer typology, and then offer the right products to the right customers. Moreover, to stimulate demand during slow periods, creative promotional events are an effective strategy for meeting customers' needs. 'Pull' strategies and promotions such as researched themes or event promotion can create consumer demand.

SEGMENTATION

The objective of RM is to increase revenue by adjusting prices to maximise capacity. A good RM system attracts price-sensitive and preventive consumers as a means of filling time slots that would otherwise be empty, while maximising time-sensitive and emergency segments of the market to increase average revenues (Berman, 2005). Many travel agencies currently exercise basic market segmentation, such as that based on the different perspectives of business and leisure travellers.

Travel agencies should use available data to differentiate between customers who are prepared to pay higher prices and those who are willing to alter their travel plans in exchange for lower prices. They should likewise design high-revenue products for peak seasons and offer product discounts during off-peak seasons.

When designing products, travel agencies could segment the market into small groups based on demographics, psychographics and buying behaviour. They could also offer discount policies for groups such as students, seniors and price-sensitive travellers.

Demographic applications of RM consider the family life cycle and customise products for market segments such as retired couples or honeymooners. Long-haul vacation packages could be provided for the budget-conscious, and information on family household income can be used to design various promotion packages. Psychographics based on consumer preferences (e.g. brand choice of hotel or airline), buying patterns and customisation of products can be used to provide customised features.

Anderson and Xie (2009) suggested that firms segment their customers using non-post price methods to reach price-sensitive customers. Travel agencies could adopt non-post price methods and make use of promotional tools such as targeted email offers or social media platforms for promotional messages and generating the promotion mix.

The application of flexibility or time flexibility could likewise be beneficial, with separate pricing offered to those who can travel on weekdays (from Monday to Thursday) and those who only travel on weekends (from Friday to Sunday). Hong Kong workers tend to take short breaks rather than long holidays; travel agencies could offer value to those who are willing to travel on weekdays.

Time flexibility could also widen market segments. For example, last-minute travel deals could be targeted at adventure-seeking students or careful planners seeking bargains to specific destinations. Business travellers often need to make travel plans at short notice. Agencies could thus promote last-minute travel to these customers, which would increase service demand and revenue.

RESERVATION MADE IN ADVANCE

Industries that practice RM use computerised reservation systems to forecast demand and calculate inventory. Many traditional RM industries use sophisticated pricing systems that interact with the reservation system and use techniques such as discounting early purchases, limiting early sales at a discounted price and overbooking (Kimes, 1989; Lieberman, 1993). A number of travel agencies use pre-sales systems from tour counters and others depend on email to manage reservations. IT systems can increase customers' convenience and satisfaction, as reservations no longer need to be processed over the counter and customers no longer need to wait for confirmation replies. In traditional RM industries, strategic systems could likewise adjust prices according to the number of early bookings and terminate reservations after the available capacity is exceeded. IT-based reservation systems provide information on customer demand and enable operators to set the best price for a given demand level at an appropriate time interval between the purchase and actual visit (Heo & Lee, 2009).

Travel agencies could operate online reservation systems connected to their RM systems. Records of booking patterns and a consumer database could be used to predict demand. Travel agencies could also forecast booking during crucial demand periods and come up with pricing adjustments.

Asking for full payment on confirmation of reservations could reduce the number of last-minute cancellations. Using websites to promote last-minute travel or extend promotions would help to move consumers through the different stages of the buying process (Kotler & Armstrong, 2001).

LIMITED CAPACITY

Defining limited capacity for travel agencies entails determining the number of available products (e.g. packages, hotel rooms and airline seats) and the volume of the suppliers' products that the agency can sell. Capacity in traditional RM industries is generally fixed over the short term and firms can change their capacity by adjusting the amount of available space or time.

Similar to other non-traditional RM industries, travel agencies have a service capacity that is not limited by physical constraints. As travel agencies are intermediaries, they have a special feature — a relatively flexible capacity — and can thus sell more seats or rooms during critical demand periods. However, allotment contracts constrain the volume (i.e. number of rooms and seats) they can sell at a special rate.

Some suppliers allow travel agencies to extend their capacity. In practice, travel agencies often deal with a large number of suppliers, such as hotel and airline sales representatives or large tour wholesalers. If overbooked, they can adopt the same method as other RM industries, suggesting that their customers use other suppliers. Leisure travellers often need to arrange their vacation plans and make reservations in advance, so a flexible capacity not only creates capacity use, but may help travel agencies increase profitability.

Thus, optimising flexible capacity could result in greater opportunities for travel agencies. Short-term flexible capacity is provided in agreements between travel agencies and suppliers, and the former could make use of their flexible capacity advantage by extending the various services offered during peak demand. Various contract agreements (full- and non-risk room agreements) and networks of different suppliers create varied advantages for travel agencies. Travel agencies can offer a wide variety of travel options to customers because, unlike airlines and hotels that cannot add more seats or rooms, travel agents are not limited by physical constraints. Based on customer demand, availability could be shifted to different tourism product suppliers. For example, if one hotel is fully booked, an effective manager offering many choices could offer customers a different hotel of the same standard and make use of full- and non-risk rooms to fulfil market demand during high season. This would reduce wasted rooms or seats, and the cost would be associated with items sold as part of packaged vacations.

APPROPRIATE COST AND PRICING STRUCTURE

Traditional RM industries have cost structures that feature relatively high fixed costs and fairly low variable costs. For example, hotels, airlines and other capacity-constrained industries must generate sufficient revenue to cover variable costs and offset at least a portion of fixed costs. The low variable costs associated with many capacity-constrained industries permit a certain pricing flexibility and provide operators with the option of reduction during low-demand times.

Compared to other industries, travel agencies have special cost structures and pricing strategies. The fixed costs of travel agencies are lower than those of traditional RM industries, as they do not own the products and do not need overbooking mechanisms that minimise the risk of empty seats or rooms. The price setting of a tourist package is predetermined by the company tariff. Annual tariffs are based on signed contract agreements from many suppliers plus a mark-up percentage, which for airline tickets and hotel rooms is usually 5−10%. Hong Kong travel agencies adopt typical cost-based pricing instead of dynamic pricing and use a bundling strategy (combining several products such as accommodations, airline tickets or sightseeing tours for sale as one packaged product), which allows them to hide the net cost of the packages. If this is done skilfully, demand can be stimulated and the overall contribution to revenue will increase significantly. The more products or items bundled in a package, the more profitable the package.

High-revenue products can be offered during peak season, whereas special prices can be offered in times of low demand. This technique not only reduces loss, it can lead to higher profits and improve brand image and customer loyalty, resulting in customer retention. Thus, travel agencies must decide which tourism products should be packaged together, and they should also know how to price and when to distribute the packages.

Most travel agencies use holiday and seasonal pricing promotions (Ingold, McMahon-Beattie, & Yeoman, 2000). However, the importance of time-based pricing strategies is often neglected. Time-based pricing is a type of offer or contract from a service provider or a commodity supplier in which the price depends on the time at which the service is provided or the commodity is delivered. Travel agencies' pricing should be based on the expected or observed change in the supply and demand balance during a certain period.

There is a distinct difference between the mindsets of travel agencies and their suppliers. Travel agencies obtain the lowest-priced contracts and then add a mark-up, believing that the delivery contract is fixed and can be relied on without exception, regardless of how good the business is for the said contract. This concept is the tour managers' idea of stability. Meanwhile, suppliers provide goods for marketers in search of contracts, guaranteeing them profitable sales up to certain agreed-on dates, at which time the contracts may be renewed or extended.

From the customer perspective, holiday tour package prices can constrain their budgets, but are often treated as a priority in planning personal or family expenditures. Thus, tourists generally choose not to spend money and time on alternative products and do not visit alternative destinations during their vacation.

Seasonal price banding and dynamic pricing strategies can be designed based on different customer buying behaviour and acceptance. One of the most common ways of setting holiday price differentials is seasonal banding, a typical practice of tour operator brochures that is familiar to all who purchase inclusive holidays in the form of price and departure date price matrices. Under seasonal price banding, tour operators provide brochures to all who purchase inclusive holidays, giving price and departure date price matrices. High-price strategies are used during peak seasons, and additional charges are levied on top of the tour fare or package price. Off-peak season packages offer reduced prices, and commonly offer discounts to specific target groups.

Dynamic pricing reflects the current supply-demand situation or makes differentiated offers for delivery of a commodity, depending on the date of delivery. The pricing set by travel agencies should be based on the demand and supply; that is, follow demand during special seasons or holidays and at other times offer different pricings.

Price setting in RM strategies involves establishing various price thresholds that reflect the assumptions of price-related differences in customers' buying behaviour, particularly with respect to seasonal preferences and responses to late or early booking reductions, which can be assessed by analysing the company's historical data.

CONCLUSIONS AND IMPLICATIONS

RM is a business strategy adopted by various industries to enhance profitability. RM can improve travel agencies' competitive stance and enhance profit maximisation. RM practitioners need to fully understand the concept and techniques and be willing to develop and promote the system among personnel at all levels within the travel agency. Obviously, much work is required to make managers in the industry aware of the concept of RM. The success of an RM implementation depends on the knowledge and skills of an organisation's managers. Travel agencies need to use information systems to support RM strategies. Practitioners should develop appropriate RM strategies as an effective management tool that will contribute to overall profitability and business growth.

REFERENCES

Airline Business. (2000). A reed business publication, Jane Levere, Changing Roles, October, pp. 48–76.

Anderson, C., & Xie, X. (2009). Room-risk management at Sunquest vacations. *Cornell Hospitality Quarterly*, 50(3), 314–324.

Anderson, C., & Xie, X. (2010). Improving hospitality industry sales: Twenty-five years of revenue management. *Cornell Hospitality Quarterly*, 51(1), 53–67.

Badinelli, R. (2000). An optimal, dynamic policy for hotel yield management. *European Journal of Operational Research, 121,* 467–503.

Barnett, M., & Standing, C. (2000). Repositioning travel agencies on the internet. *Journal of Vacation Marketing, 7*(2), 143–152.

Berman, B. (2005). Applying yield management pricing to your service business. *Business Horizons, 48,* 169–179.

Burgess, C., & Bryant, K. (2001). Revenue management: The contribution of the finance function to profitability. *International Journal of Contemporary Hospitality Management, 13*(3), 144–150.

Dacko, S. (2004). Marketing strategies for last-minute travel and tourism: Profitability and revenue management implications. *Journal of Travel & Tourism Marketing, 16*(2), 7–19.

Donaghy, K., McMahon, C., & McDowell, D. (1995). Yield management: An overview. *International Journal of Hospitality Management, 14,* 139–150.

Granados, N., Gupta, A., & Kauffman, R. J. (2003). *Orbitz, online travel agents and market structure changes in the presence of technology-driven market transparency.* Working paper #03-20, MIS Research Center, Carlson School of Management, University of Minnesota.

Hanks, R., Noland, P., & Cross, R. (1992). Discounting in the hotel industry: A new approach. *The Cornell Hotel and Restaurant Administration Quarterly, 33,* 15–23.

Heo, Y. C., & Lee, S. (2009). Application of revenue management practices to the theme park industry. *International Journal of Hospitality Management, 28,* 446–453.

Hong Kong Tourism Commission Fact Sheet: Tourism arrival information. (2011, July 28). Retrieved from http://www.gov.hk/en/about/abouthk/factsheets/docs/tourism.pdf

Information Service Department. (2012). Hong Kong special administrative region. Retrieved on March 15, 2012.

Ingold, A., McMahon-Beattie, & Yeoman., I. (2000). *Yield management strategies for the service industries* (2nd ed.). London: Continuum.

Jancey, S., Mitchell, I., & Slamet, P. (1995). The meaning and management of yield in hotels. *Progress in Tourism and Hospitality Management, 7*(4), 23–26.

Kimes, M. G. (2011). An option-based revenue management procedure for strategic airline alliances. *European Journal of Operational Research, 215,* 459–469.

Kimes, S. (2002). Perceived fairness of yield management. *Cornell Hotel and Restaurant Administration Quarterly,* 21–30.

Kimes, S. E., & Singh, S. (2009). Spa revenue management. *Cornell Hospitality Quarterly, 50,* 82–85.

Kimes, S. E. (1989). Yield management: A tool for capacity-considered service firms. *Journal of Operations Management, 8,* 348–363.

Kimes, S. E., & Wirtz, J. (2003). Has revenue management become acceptable? *Journal of Service Research, 6*(2), 125–135.

Kotler, P., & Armstrong, J. (2001). *Principals of marketing* (9th ed.). Upper Saddle River, NJ: Prentice Hall.

Liberman, S., & Yechiall, H. S. (1993). On the hotel overbooking problems. *Management Science, 24,* 1117–1126.

Marcus, B., & Anderson, C. (2008). Revenue management for low cost providers. *European Journal of Operational Research, 188,* 258–272.

McGill, J. I., & Van Ryzin, G. J. (1999). Revenue management: Research overview and prospects. *Transportation Science, 33,* 233–256.

Sanchez, J. F., & Satir, A. (2005). Hotel yield management using different reservation models. *International journal of Contemporary Hospitality Management, 17*(2), 136–146.

Sharpley, R. (2004). *The tourism business: An introduction* (2nd ed.). Sunderland: Business Education Publishers.

Sun, X., Jiao, Y., & Tian, P. (2011). Marketing research and revenue optimization for the cruise industry. *A Concise Review, 3*, 746–755.

PART II
HOSPITALITY MANAGEMENT

CHAPTER 8

DIFFUSION PATTERNS IN LOYALTY PROGRAMS

Pedro Pimpão, Antónia Correia, João Duque and Carlos Zorrinho

ABSTRACT

This chapter aims to assess how effective loyalty programs are in contributing to retaining guests for hotels. The effectiveness is measured by means of a Bass model which allows the measurement of the diffusion patterns of adopters within potential adopters. The data used to perform this model allow the depiction of the effect of geographical localization over a time frame of three years. Results suggest that the loyalty card's acceptance was measured from the internal and external parameters, based on the concept of diffusion theory. The results indicated a need for innovation of the loyalty program from 2019. Due to the existence of several hotels with different typologies in different countries, a segmentation of clients by nationalities is suggested with a "waterfall" strategy being placed in the hotel chain loyalty program.

Keywords: Diffusion theory; diffusion processes; Bass model; customer relationship management; hotel loyalty programs

Tourism and Hospitality Management
Advances in Culture, Tourism and Hospitality Research, Volume 12, 115–126
Copyright © 2016 by Emerald Group Publishing Limited
All rights of reproduction in any form reserved
ISSN: 1871-3173/doi:10.1108/S1871-317320160000012009

INTRODUCTION

Developments in modeling, computing, and communication strategies during recent decades have provided the ingredients which allow marketing models to improve decision-making in modern organizations. The ultimate aim of loyalty programs is to increase reservations and enact word of mouth (WOM), the most effective and inexpensive marketing strategy.

These topics are covered by diffusion theory, which is the understanding of the spread of innovation from the perspective of communication and adopter (user) perceptions and interactions (Peres, Muller, & Mahajan, 2010). This theory has been tested with the Bass model (Lilien, Rangaswamy, & De Bruyn, 2012) and is solely concerned with demand size (Jain, Mahajan, & Muller, 1991). Over the years, the Bass model has been improved to accommodate the main moderate effects on diffusion patterns, mainly through the parameters p and q. These parameters constitute the diffusion of innovation and imitation respectively (representing WOM effects) (Pae & Lehman, 2003; Peres et al., 2010).

Most loyalty programs are based on a card which offers the client a number of benefits that may increase as the number of reservations grows. The effectiveness of these cards are stored in a customer relationship management (CRM) program and randomly assessed. To revert this tendency, this research uses CRM database to assess diffusion patterns, and uses an *Initiative:pt* Program to assess the WOM communication diffusion. These two databases include clients from one of Portugal's biggest and best-known hotel chains worldwide.

Diffusion patterns of hotel clients are assessed through a hotel chain loyalty program based on a CRM system and through enquiries made at all airports of Portugal and based on the *Initiative:pt* Program. The data comprise 377,864 card holders for the former and 1,270 enquiries (i.e., referring to every person who has stayed at that hotel group) for the latter. The Bass model was performed to analyze and predict hotels' sales, being a competitive loyalty diffusion tool.

This study aims to contribute to an understanding of how diffusion patterns (e.g., a new loyalty program at a hotel chain) affect the acquisition and use of loyalty cards. Furthermore, this may contribute to bringing diffusion theory and its processes to discussion, as well as the main advantages of testing this through the Bass model, as a quantitative method to assess the diffusion model.

Finally, this study attempts to add significantly to the body of tourism and hospitality areas, testing empirically, with the Bass model, the link between diffusion theory through the CRM systems and loyalty programs at hotels. A very large database is used to analyze behavioral and geographical measures across the different adopters' nationalities and different kinds of hotels of the Group.

THEORETICAL CONSIDERATIONS

The diffusion perspective was introduced into consumer behavior literature in the mid-1960s and it represents the strength of the communications effects, such as flow of information, products, and services (Gatignon & Robertson, 1985; Mahajan, Muller, & Bass, 1990). The term "diffusion" involves the communication channels with users' interactions, through the understanding of the spread of innovations – a view increasingly supported in diffusion theory (Peres et al., 2010).

Over the years, diffusion theory has often been used to model the first-purchase sales growth of a new product or service over time and space (Mahajan & Muller, 1979; Mahajan, Muller, & Bass, 1995). The clarity of a need for a new product or service is first shown by the adoptions of a few innovators who, in turn, influence others to adopt it, this behavior being called personal influence (Gatignon & Robertson, 1985). It is a basic underlying component of diffusion theory and diffusion models and has, mostly, a shape of verbal influence or interpersonal communication (WOM) (Libai, Muller, & Peres, 2009; Mahajan et al., 1990; Peres et al., 2010). This "interaction" between adopters (users) and non-adopters (non-users) is posited to account for the shape and rapid growth stage in the diffusion process (Gatignon & Robertson, 1985; Schmittlein & Mahajan, 1982).

With respect to diffusion processes, the literature differentiates the rate of diffusion, the pattern of diffusion, and the potential penetration level as the three dimensions (Gatignon & Robertson, 1985). The rate of diffusion reflects the speed at which sales occur over time (Van den Bulte, 2002) and represents the intensity of diffusion of that product or service. The pattern of diffusion concerns the shape of the diffusion curve (s-shaped) (Gatignon & Robertson, 1985). This diffusion dimension relates the time interval between the time service or product introduction and the time of a potential reformulation of that service or product. The potential penetration level is a separate dimension indicating the size of the potential market and is related to all of the interpersonal or personal influences among users and non-users (Peres et al., 2010).

Despite the diffusion approach being originally intended for durable goods, nowadays is widely used in the services market (Libai et al., 2009). The diffusion processes provide a clear view that for modeling services there is a need to incorporate CRM in that diffusion process/framework (Peres et al., 2010). However, linking diffusion processes in services, such as hotel loyalty programs, with CRM systems, has been neglected. Forecasting diffusion processes (i.e., forecasting market potentials and sales growth patterns) are crucial for planning marketing programs (Pae & Lehman, 2003). However, they have to be empirically validated, because there are difficulties in observing individual behavior at the brand level (Parker & Gatignon, 1994). The greater the sensitivity of the marketing program to the changing characteristics of segments at different stages of the diffusion process, the faster the rate of diffusion and the greater the penetration level (Gatignon & Robertson, 1985).

The CRM, highly popular (long-term) relationship theory is easy to develop and execute (in system) and provides a simple, detailed assessment of the importance of various components of user knowledge and the diffusion of that knowledge (Mahajan et al., 1990). An awareness of this modeling of diffusion represents the level of spread of an innovation. Thus, the purpose of a diffusion model is to depict the successive increase in the number of adopters (users) and predict the continued development (in a long-term view) of a diffusion process already in progress (Landsman & Givon, 2010; Mahajan & Muller, 1979).

The best-known and most widely used diffusion model of first-purchase demand of new product acceptance in marketing is that of Bass (1969). Due to its modeling requirements, the Bass model is a quantitative diffusion model focusing on aggregated data, representing the market penetration of a new process, product, or technology (Lilien, Rangaswamy, & Den Bulte, 2000). The Bass model provides a framework for guessing the long-term sales behavior of a product based on early sales data (Dodds, 1973; Lilien et al., 2000; Schmittlein & Mahajan, 1982). One of the advantages of the Bass model is that it permits a forecast of a long-term penetration pattern, measuring the timing of adoption of an innovation, the timing of a turndown in sales, and the timing of subsequent developments (Dodds, 1973; Lilien et al., 2000).

Moreover, the Bass model can be thought of as a two-stage communication diffusion model (Jain et al., 1991; Mahajan & Muller, 1979). It represents the strength of WOM from potential adopters to adopters (Krishnan, Bass, & Kumar, 2000) and assumes that potential adopters are influenced by two means of communication: mass media and WOM

(Mahajan et al., 1990). However, Rogers (1983) suggests that, although mass media communication (i.e., external influence) is more important during the early stages of an innovations' implementation, it is the internal influence (i.e., WOM) which dominates the later sales. In this sense, a key feature of this model is that its "embeds" a contagion process to characterize the spread of WOM between those who have adopted the innovation and those who have not yet adopted (Lilien et al., 2012). WOM is an internal influence and can be incorporated into the Bass model by specifying the coefficient of internal influence as systematically varying over time as a function of penetration level (Mahajan et al., 1990). Thus, this contagion or imitation process of WOM contributes to the underlying behavioral theory in the Bass model for new product acceptance (Mahajan & Muller, 1979).

In this sense, this discussion underscores the importance of measuring patterns of users already using a loyalty card from a diffusion perspective within a contagion process. It also encourages the use of the Bass model in a service context, such as a hotel chain loyalty program.

METHOD

Model formulation is defined in the key behavioral and mathematical assumptions of the Bass model: (i) over the period of three years there are m initial reservations in the loyalty program and there are no repeat purchases; (ii) the behavioral forces are represented by parameters p, q, and m (Dodds, 1973; Mahajan et al., 1995). In our work, we follow Bass model statement of Jain et al. (1991), Pae and Lehman (2003), and Lilien et al. (2012):

$$\frac{\mathrm{d}N(t)}{\mathrm{d}t} = p[m - N(t)] + \frac{q}{m}N(t)[m - N(t)] \tag{1}$$

where $N(t)$ is the cumulative number of adopters (users) at time t with two or more reservations; m is the total population of potential adopters who have one or less reservations; p is the coefficient of innovation and represents the fraction of unmet potential users that adopt in each period (i.e., the number of reservations by card divided by total population of adopters and potential adopters) (Pae & Lehman, 2003; Peres et al., 2010); and q is the coefficient of imitation or coefficient of conformity (i.e., the intention to recommend) (Gatignon & Robertson, 1985; Peres et al., 2010) since its effects increase as more people adopt, thus representing effects such as WOM (Pae & Lehman, 2003).

In recent years, a number of estimation procedures have been suggested to estimate the parameters p, q, and m of the Bass model. The main question is which estimation procedures should be used and how. There are several estimation methods such as ordinary least squares estimation (initiated by Bass, 1969), maximum likelihood estimation (introduced by Schmittlein & Mahajan, 1982) nonlinear least square (NLS) estimation (Srinivasan & Mason, 1986), among others. For this study, we use the NLS estimation to estimate parameter values (m, p, q) due to several advantages. The NLS helps to minimize the sum of squared errors, it is widely used for forecasting purposes with at least four observations of $N(t)$, and provides the best predictive validity for the Bass model (Lilien et al., 2012; Schmittlein & Mahajan, 1982).

The data were provided by CRM systems from the hotel chain loyalty program and by the *Initiative:pt* Program from questionnaires administered in all Portuguese airports. Although only three data points are utilized to estimate these parameters, the study, in order to calibrate the Bass model, concentrates on two different data for the values of p, q and m. The parameters m and p are provided by CRM systems for a period of three years (2011, 2012, and 2013) with a total of 377,864 cards issued and refers to every guest or customer who adopts a new loyalty card. The parameter q is provided by the *Initiative:pt* Program for a period of one year (2011) with a total of 1,270 enquiries and refers to every person who has stayed with that hotel group.

For the sake of validity of parameter q, since the data are provided by another source, we compare ages from the *Initiative:pt* Program (with 1,270 respondents) and the CRM systems (with 9,750 clients) in the same year (2011).

Table 1 shows that ages do not differ significantly from each other. This evidence is very important for the adoption of data available for estimation.

Table 1. Validation of Parameter q.

Ages	Initiative:pt (%)	Loyalty Program (%)
30–40	16.2	19.3
41–50	20.8	22.6
51–60	25.1	22.5
61–75	21.6	22.7

In this sense, the three unknown parameters are estimated from real data using the solver tool embedded within Excel developed by Sundar (2006, retrieved on www.faculty.washington.edu/sundar). This software was built to forecast sales and forecasts are very sensitive to estimated WOM effects. As such, assessing the most reliable determinants of WOM is critical to apply the Bass model.

FINDINGS

This study focuses on the diffusion patterns of a hotel chain loyalty program in order to estimate the three parameters' values (m, p, q). It also examines the relation between the speed of diffusion, as well as the diffusion process by market segment (i.e., by hotel's typology and hotel's country origin).

Turning our attention to the parameter values, Table 2 shows a higher value, which indicates that the rate or speed of diffusion of this loyalty program had a slow start (i.e., it takes longer to realize sales growth for the innovation, but accelerates after a while) (Lilien et al., 2012; Van den Bulte, 2002).

When $q > p$, the plot has an inverted U-shape (see Fig. 1) showing its pattern of diffusion of this product. This evidence indicates that a higher value of q means a less heterogeneous population and higher maximum penetration level (Gatignon & Robertson, 1985). This means that loyalty program has the potential to have more adopters at different hotels of the Group supported by the strength of WOM for product acceptance. Therefore, predicting total adopters (users) or sales is crucial for the sake of the program. In this way, Fig. 1 shows this evolution in time from the year 2010 (year 0) to the year 2022, by presenting the total of adopters and cumulative total of adopters.

Table 2. Simulation of Parameters M, N, p, and q.

Parameter	Value
M	244.436
N	41.807
p	0.008
q	0.704

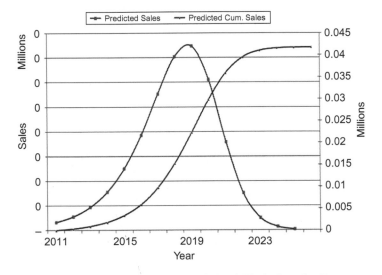

Fig. 1.   Forecast of the Diffusion of Hotel Chain Loyalty Program.

In this sense, Fig. 1 represents the forecast of the hotel chain loyalty program. It follows Table 1 confirming the "low speediness" of accepting the program. However, it shows the existence of a turndown at the year 2019. Before reaching that point (two or three years before), the hotel chain should modify or innovate its loyalty program. It is important to consider the country effect given past experiences with a product, such as the loyalty card since 2011, in order to explain and to continue to have higher values of penetration level (Talukdar, Sudhir, & Ainslie, 2002). The country effect is also crucial to evaluate attractiveness of markets; specifically this effect disappears from the loyalty program from 2019.

Another important issue concerns the market segment of the loyalty program's diffusion. The intensity of diffusion among adopters (users) of some nationalities and between different typology of hotels is shown in Table 3.

Table 3 shows that for values of *p* by hotel typology (four and five stars) means different results in the six nationalities presented. Adopters from Great Britain, Norway, and Sweden indicated having a quicker diffusion (i.e., acceptance) in five-star hotels than in four-star hotels. Adopters from Portugal, Spain, and Ireland indicated the opposite. These results show how well some brands grow in relation to other brands of the hotel chain in terms of country of origin (Krishnan et al., 2000).

Table 3. Simulation of Parameter p by Hotel's Typology and Client's Nationalities.

Country	p (4 Stars)	p (5 Stars)	p Total
Great Britain	0.30	0.50	0.79
Norway	0.30	0.48	0.78
Sweden	0.31	0.45	0.76
Portugal	0.16	0.15	0.31
Spain	0.23	0.17	0.40
Ireland	0.54	0.31	0.85

Note: Accumulated data from 2011 to 2013.

Table 4. Diffusion Evolution by Hotel's Localization.

Year	Loyalty Program has Started (%)	2012−2013 Evolution (%)
Portugal	1.380	49
Europe	1.685	105
Brazil	1.491	576
Other America	4.250	249
Central America	−	6.400

In terms of total values of p by country's origin, Table 3 shows that a higher value of p corresponds to countries with higher purchasing power per capita (Van den Bulte, 2002). This is the case for all, including Portugal for example, which has a lower value of p and a lower gross national product (GNP) per capita. When p and purchasing power per capita are higher, it makes it easier to adopt new services or products immediately (Van den Bulte, 2002).

The hotel's typology and country's origin findings highlight the importance of the product's effects (i.e., past experiences with different nationalities explaining the coefficients of external and internal influence) (Talukdar et al., 2002). These effects help to explain the influence of parameters p and q on the diffusion of the loyalty card.

In order to differentiate the country's origin influence from adopters (users) and hotels, Table 4 shows the effects of hotel localization on the diffusion process.

Table 4 also shows the "loyalty program has started," which means the growth rate between p 2012 and p 2011, and the same meaning for the "2012–2013 evolution," between p 2013 and p 2012. Thus, the results in Table 4 show that the hotel Central America, which introduced the loyalty program later, has increased more than others, indicating a lead-lag effect (Peres et al., 2010). This effect indicates countries which introduce a given innovation later show a faster diffusion process and a shorter time to takeoff (Peres et al., 2010). Due to these results, it is suggested that the hotel chain should enter all of its markets sequentially (i.e., a "waterfall" strategy) (Peres et al., 2010). Because of the higher maximum penetration levels, the hotel chain should increase the number of adopters in each hotel which has already the program implemented. It is shown that almost all different hotels which belong to the hotel chain are located in countries with costs and risks and a low competitive pressure, which means a higher lead-lag effect. In this sense, results indicate that the hotel chain needs marketing actions in order to achieve faster penetration to secure a quick investment return.

CONCLUSION AND IMPLICATIONS

Diffusion processes should be an important subject of study for both academicians and managers of the tourism and hospitality industry. A wide range of retail activities, including a loyalty program, generate various types of diffusion consequences. Such studies could range from forecasting the development of a hotel base around a new location under different launch strategies to tracking the WOM networking process.

The present work related the Bass model, intended originally for durable goods, nowadays widely used in services market, to a hotel chain loyalty program. This model gives us a conceptually appealing and mathematically solid structure of how a new loyalty card diffuses through a target population of adopters, used for long-term forecasting.

Furthermore, the Bass model gives consistent results in order to implement a "strategic necessity." First, Bass model analyzes the speed at which sales occur. Results show a higher value of q, indicating a slow start with acceleration after awhile. Second, the shape of the diffusion curve is analyzed. Due to its inverted U-shape, it is estimated that the year 2019 is the turndown point, meaning a necessity for marketing actions and a strategic planning for the loyalty program. Third, the study focuses also on the user's behavior according to their country of origin and the hotel's typology. However, this analysis is restricted to parameter p. Results show that, for example, a British client, who stays at a five-star hotel, is more likely to adopt a loyalty card than another British client who stays at a four-star hotel. And the diffusion of a loyalty card is quicker among clients belonging to a country with a higher GNP per capita. Fourth, the study also points out the relation between user behavior and hotel localization. Results indicate that hotels which introduce the loyalty program later have a faster diffusion process, meaning a lead-leg effect.

In this sense, these results lead to important implications about more effective launch strategies for this loyalty program. This study provides us the suggestion to implement and develop long-term relationship measures based on a "waterfall" strategy. This strategy should be conceptualized more multidimensionally, where repeat purchase is the key. The hotel chain loyalty program needs higher penetration and this is attained by intensifying the speed of a WOM networking strategy.

Although results show a higher WOM, the sample procedure adopted was restricted to 2011, due to inclusion of *Initiative:pt* Program to calculate the parameter q. In this sense, future research should focus on a thorough analysis of how and why these effects arose, and a survey of data and interviews should contribute to enriching the figures that these methods unveil.

REFERENCES

Bass, F. (1969). A new product growth for model consumer durables. *Journal of Management Science, 15*(5), 215–227.

Dodds, W. (1973). An application of the Bass model in long-term new product forecasting. *Journal of Marketing Research, 10*(3), 308–311.

Gatignon, H., & Robertson, T. (1985). A proportional inventory for new diffusion research. *Journal of Consumer Research, 11*(4), 849–867.

Jain, D., Mahajan, V., & Muller, E. (1991). Innovation diffusion in the presence of supply restrictions. *Journal of the Academy of Marketing Science, 10*(1), 83–90.

Krishnan, T., Bass, F., & Kumar, V. (2000). Impact of a late entrant on the diffusion of a new product/service. *Journal of Marketing Research, 37*(2), 269–278.

Landsman, V., & Givon, M. (2010). The diffusion of a new service: Combining service consideration and brand choice. *Journal of Quantitative Marketing and Economics, 8*(1), 91–121.

Libai, B., Muller, E., & Peres, R. (2009). The diffusion of services. *Journal of Marketing Research, 46*(2), 163–175.

Lilien, G., Rangaswamy, A., & Den Bulte, C. (2000). Diffusion models: Managerial applications and software. In V. Mahajan, E. Muller, & Y. Wind (Eds.), *New-product diffusion models* (pp. 295–311). Boston, MA: Kluwer Academic Publishers.

Lilien, G., Rangaswamy, A., & De Bruyn, C. (2012). *Principles of marketing engineering*. Oxford: Trafford Publishing.

Mahajan, V., & Muller, E. (1979). Innovation diffusion and new product growth models in marketing. *Journal of Marketing, 43*(4), 55−68.

Mahajan, V., Muller, E., & Bass, F. (1990). New product diffusion models in marketing: A review and directions for research. *Journal of Marketing, 54*(1), 1−26.

Mahajan, V., Muller, E., & Bass, F. (1995). Diffusion of new products: Empirical generalizations and managerial uses. *Journal of the Academy of Marketing Science, 14*(3), 1−10.

Pae, J., & Lehman, D. (2003). Multigeneration innovation diffusion: The impact of the intergeneration time. *Journal of the Academy of Marketing Science, 31*(1), 36−45.

Parker, P., & Gatignon, H. (1994). Specifying competitive effects in diffusion models: An empirical analysis. *International Journal of Research in Marketing, 11*(1), 17−39.

Peres, R., Muller, E., & Mahajan, V. (2010). Innovation diffusion and new product growth models: A critical review and research directions. *International Journal of Research in Marketing, 27*(2), 91−106.

Rogers, E. (1983). *Diffusion of innovations*. New York, NY: The Free Press.

Schmittlein, D., & Mahajan, V. (1982). Maximum likelihood estimation for an innovation diffusion model of new product acceptance. *Journal of the Academy of Marketing Science, 1*(1), 57−78.

Srinivasan, V., & Mason, C. (1986). Nonlinear least squares estimation of new product diffusion models. *Journal of the Academy of Marketing Science, 5*(2), 169−178.

Talukdar, D., Sudhir, K., & Ainslie, A. (2002). Investigating new product diffusion across Products and countries. *Journal of the Academy of Marketing Science, 21*(1), 97−114.

Van den Bulte, C. (2002). Want to know how diffusion speed varies across countries and products? Try Using a Bass Model. *PDMA Visions, 26*(4), 12−15.

CHAPTER 9

SURPRISE, HOSPITALITY, AND CUSTOMER DELIGHT IN THE CONTEXT OF HOTEL SERVICES

Ahmad Azmi M. Ariffin and Noor Balkhis Omar

ABSTRACT

The main purpose of this chapter is to investigate whether hotel hospitality mediates and/or moderates the relationships between surprise experience and customer delight in the context of hotel services. This study, involving 300 Malaysian and non-Malaysian hotel guests, employs questionnaire surveys as the main data collection method. The results indicate that there is a strong and positive relationship between surprise and customer delight, and hotel hospitality mediates and also moderates the abovementioned direct relationship.

Keywords: Customer delight; surprise; hospitality; hotel marketing

INTRODUCTION

Research on the consequences of the construct of "surprise service experience" in the context of tourism in general and hotel marketing in specific is still very scarce. Customer delights is very critical in hotel industry as

Tourism and Hospitality Management
Advances in Culture, Tourism and Hospitality Research, Volume 12, 127–142
Copyright © 2016 by Emerald Group Publishing Limited
All rights of reproduction in any form reserved
ISSN: 1871-3173/doi:10.1108/S1871-317320160000012010

evidences have showed that hotels that outperform in delighting guests are often the most successful. Previous research has shown that surprise is one of the main determinants of customer delight. Apart from customer delight, hospitality is also unquestionably one of the most important factor in hotel services, particularly in creating memorable experience for the guests (Ariffin, Nameghi, & Zakaria, 2013).

As the service industry becomes ever more competitive, customers have become smarter about their purchase decisions and more demanding in their search for service providers (Devlin, Gwynne, & Ennew, 2002). Furthermore, the traditional goal to satisfy customer does not seem relevant anymore and also does not seem to be sufficient to ensure customer loyalty. Only those firms that move from a traditional philosophy of merely satisfying their customers to a philosophy that is supported by appropriate strategies, which is delighting their customers, will be successful in this context (Oliver, Rust, & Varki, 1997).

Pine and Gilmore (1999) argue that service providers should not only provide products and services, but also stage "experiences" to add value to their customers. The most important strategy in creating memorable experiences and customer delight is to provide surprise to the customer (Hetzel, 2002; Pine & Gilmore, 1999; Schmitt, 1999; Vanhamme, 2008). Surprise happens when people encounter unexpected or expecting otherwise (occurring imprecisely) products or services (Ekman & Friesen, 1982; Izard, 1977; Scherer, 1984; Vanhamme & Snelders, 2001). Previous studies' results have shown that by surprising customers, companies can also delight them (e.g., Finn, 2005; Oliver et al., 1997; Vanhamme & Snelders, 2003).

Hotels are increasing their investments to improve hospitality and the perceived value for guests so as to achieve better customer satisfaction and loyalty, thus resulting in better relationships with each customer (Jones, Mak, & Sim, 2007). Generally, customers' evaluations on service encounters are based on their basic hospitality interactions with the service employees. The interaction between the service employees and customers, commonly referred to as the service encounter, is a crucial part of the service delivery process as its elements greatly impact customers' evaluations of service consumption experiences (Soloman, Suprenant, Czepiel, & Gutman, 1985).

Thus, the main objective of this study is not only to confirm on the relationship between surprise and customer delight in the context of hotel services, but also to investigate the moderating and the mediating effects of hospitality on the relationship between surprise and customer delight.

LITERATURE REVIEW

Hospitality

Hospitality in an organizational setting is a specific kind of relationship between two parties, that is, a host and a guest (Ariffin, 2013). In this relationship, the host understands what would give satisfaction to the guest and enhances his or her comfort, pleasure and well-being, and delivers it generously and perfectly in face to face interactions, with respect, and tactfulness. Hospitality can be described as concerns by host for the well-being of guests. It also implies a selfless commitment to the meeting of the physiological and emotional needs of the guests.

Basically, the study of hospitality as a human behavior essentially involves the association between the host and the guest. Unlike most service industries, it is the manner in which the hospitality employees provide the service, as opposed to the service itself which is critical to the customer's overall enjoyment of the product or "experience" being purchased. According to Lashley and Morrisson (2000), they noted that hospitality essentially is a relationship based on hosts and guests, and it is the host and guest relationship that is the key distinguishing characteristic of hospitality from which several other dimensions emerge.

Lashley and Morrisson (2000) also contended that hospitality requires the guest to feel that his host is being hospitable through his display of generosity, a desire to please, and a genuine regard for him as an individual. Hotel hospitality is therefore not only about the host providing accommodation but also about entertaining or taking care of the guest's psychological needs (Ariffin & Maghzi, 2012).

Hemmington (2007) described hospitality based on five main factors, namely generosity, lots of little surprises, host—guest relationship, theater and performance, as well as safety and security. Basically, the host should be motivated by the desire to entertain his guest rather than by profit-seeking objectives alone (Lashley, 2008). Since hospitality is emphasizing on entertaining, theatrical experiences must offer "lots of little surprises" to create excitement. Customers generally evaluate hospitality experiences based on the emotional dimension rather than the physical aspects of the services.

A study by Lashley, Morrisson, and Randall (2005) on "memorable meals" found that emotional aspects had a bigger impact than the quality of the food in creating memorable dining experiences. It is the quality of the interaction between the waiters and guests, as well as the restaurant ambience that develops the emotional value. Thus, the extent of guest satisfaction or delight is dependent on such dining experiences, rather than the food being served (Lashley, 2008).

Surprise

Surprise is seduced by either unexpected or mis-expected products, services, or attributions (Ekman & Friesen, 1982; Scherer, 1984). The former means fuzzy and not clearly defined expectations about products, services, or attributions, and the latter means accurate expectations about products, services, or attributions that do not happen (Vanhamme & Snelders, 2001). More specifically, surprise is induced by a "schema discrepancy" (Meyer, Reisenzein, & Schutzwohl, 1997; Reisenzein, 2000). A schema can be regarded as private, usually informal, inarticulate, unconsidered theory about the essence of objects, situations, and events (Meyer et al., 1997; Rumelhart, 1984). Individuals constantly check if their schemas are consistent with the inputs coming from the surrounding environment. As long as there is a difference between inputs and schema is detected, surprise is induced (Meyer et al., 1997; Vanhamme & Snelders, 2003).

After the evaluation of the schema discrepancy, individuals immediately assess whether the experience is pleasant or unpleasant. That is, surprise is often followed by another emotion that colors it from neutral into either a positive or negative emotion. When it is followed by a positive emotion (e.g., joy), it becomes positive, whereas, when it is followed by a negative emotion (e.g., anger), it turns negative (Ekman & Friesen, 1982; Meyer, Niepel, Rudolph, & Schützwohl, 1994; Vanhamme & Snelders, 2001). This explains why previous researchers have studied positive or pleasant surprise and negative or unpleasant surprise.

Delight

The concept of customer delight started developing in the 1990s, emerging in literature through the discussion of effective (Westbrook, 1987) and experimental (Holbrook & Hirschman, 1982) dimensions of consumption. In Plutchik's theory, delight is a mixture of joy and surprise, conceptually similar to Westbrook and Oliver's (1991) customer behavior dimension "pleasant surprise."

Customer delight can be defined as the reaction that customers have when they experience a product or service that not only satisfies, but also provides an unanticipated level of value or satisfaction (Chandler, 1989). Based upon this conceptualization, customer delight is related to but distinct from customer satisfaction. While customer satisfaction is widely viewed as the result of exceeding one's expectations, most existing studies indicate that customer delight requires that the customer receives a positive surprise beyond his/her expectations (e.g., Arnold, Reynolds, Ponder, & Lueg, 2005; Berman, 2005; Oliver et al., 1997; Rust & Oliver, 2000).

The value of merely satisfying customers has been questioned. It is increasingly argued that what is really important to intentions, future behavior, and customer loyalty is the emotional response to the experience (Schlossberg, 1993; Schneider & Bowen, 1999). While satisfying customers is considered as a proper way to increase customer loyalty, previous studies found that customers who were completely satisfied were more likely to be loyal than customers who said they were satisfied (Kumar, Olshavsky, & King, 2001). Satisfied customers do not necessarily get excited with a firm; they are merely at ease. Delighted customers on the other hand have greater appreciation for the firm and its services (Paul, 2000). According to Torres and Kline (2006), the condition of being satisfied is not strong enough to hold customers in a highly competitive environment.

METHODOLOGY

This study is fundamentally descriptive to explain the influences of hospitality on the relationship that existed between hotel's surprise service and customers' delight. Questionnaire survey was employed as the main method of data collection by using structured form. The measurements for all the three main variables were adapted from well-established scale and therefore there were no issues on validity and reliability. In view of time and cost constraints and also because of the large population, a convenient sampling method is used to collect the data. A total of 300 respondents were targeted for this study.

The sample size should be considered adequate only for an exploratory analysis and a larger sample would be needed to validate the study (Bejou, 1998). This study employs both judgmental/convenient sampling. Judgmental sampling in the context of this research means that the respondents should have had experiences staying in any hotels. Data were mainly analyzed using regression analysis.

RESULTS

Hospitality as Mediating Variable between Surprise and
Customer Delight

In step 1 (Table 1), the influence of surprise is highly significant and positively associated with "Customer Delight" with coefficient of 0.587 ($p < 0.01$). The overall model is sufficient given a significant value of F-statistic. R-squared indicates that 53.9% of the effect on hospitality is explained by the surprise element in hotel services.

In step 2, the influence of surprise is highly significant and positively associated with "hospitableness" with coefficient value of 0.472 ($p < 0.01$). R-squared indicates that 50.10% of the effect on hospitality is explained by the surprise element in hotel services. The result supports a direct relationship between surprise and hospitality. The result also suggests that the higher amount of the surprise service experience, the higher is the "hospitableness" of the hotel services provided.

In step 3, the influence of hospitality is highly significant and positively associated with "Customer Delight" with coefficient of 0.656 ($p < 0.01$). R-squared indicates that 38.6% of the effect on hospitality is explained by the surprise element in hotel services. The result supports a direct relationship between hospitality and customer delight. The result also suggests that the better hospitability provided by hotel services are able to enhance the customer delight.

In step 4, the influence of hospitality and surprise are both highly significant and positively associated with "Customer Delight" with coefficient of 0.656 ($p < 0.01$). The overall model is sufficient given a significant value of F-statistic. R-squared indicates that 56% of the effect on hospitality is explained by the surprise element in hotel services.

Hospitality as Moderating Variable between Surprise and
Customer Delight

Table 2 describes the result of the moderating effect of hospitability between "surprise" and "Customer Delight." The result shows that the interaction variable of hospitality × surprise is highly significant and positively associated with "Customer Delight" given the coefficient of 0.0313 ($p < .01$). R-squared indicates that 59.2% of the effect on "Customer Delight" is explained by the moderating effect of hospitality. The result

Table 1. Mediating Effect of Hospitality.

Variables	Coefficient	S.E.	*t*-stat	*p*-Value
Step 1: DV: Customer Delight				
(Constant)	2.0315***	0.218	9.328	0.00
Surprise	0.5875***	0.055	10.710	0.00
F-stat	114.713***			
R-squared	0.539			
Step 2: DV: Hospitality				
Customer Delight	2.314***	0.215	10.783	0.00
Surprise	0.5361***	0.054	9.920	0.00
F-stat	98.416***			
R-squared	0.501			
Step 3: DV: Customer Delight				
Customer Delight	1.4114***	0.371	3.805	0.00
Surprise	0.6564***	0.084	7.854	0.00
F-stat	61.679***			
R-squared	0.386			
Step 4: DV: Customer Delight				
Customer Delight	1.5334***	0.316	4.848	0.00
Surprise	0.4721***	0.076	6.189	0.00
Hospitality	0.2152***	0.101	2.137	0.04
F-stat	61.73			

Note: Significance *** at the 0.01 level

Table 2. Moderating Effect of Hospitality.

Variables	Coefficient	S.E.	*t*-stat	*p*-value
DV: Customer Delight				
(Constant)	2.048	0.125	16.345	0.00
Surprise	0.440	0.068	6.448	0.00
Hospitality × Surprise	0.031	0.011	2.873	0.00
F-stat	215.717***			
R-squared	59.20%			

Note: Significance *** at the 0.01 level

provides the evidence that the effect between surprise and delights is moderated by hospitability.

The overall results indicated that hospitality can act as both moderator and mediator in the relationship between surprise and customer delight in the context of hotel services. It is however not the intention of this study to compare the results of the two analyses.

DISCUSSION

The ultimate aim of hospitality is to achieve extremely high level of customer delight and loyalty. As expected, the results of the multiple regressions on the effect of hospitality on satisfaction shows a significantly strong positive relationship ($\beta = -0.47$, $p = 0.001$). The result shows that there is a positive relationship between surprise service experience and hospitableness of the hotel services provided. The result in Table 1 supports a direct relationship between surprise and hospitality. The result suggests that the higher amount of the surprise service experience, the higher is the "hospitableness" of the hotel services provided.

The findings which supports the issues relating to hospitality provision in the commercial sector relates to the hospitality authenticity provided. Dominici and Guzzo (2010) describe that hotel guest satisfaction is largely hooked on the quality of service offered in the hotel industry. Review of literature indicated that hospitality is one of the enhancing services that can contribute substantially to the high relationship quality. The degree to which customer satisfaction or "customer value creation" is mainly determined by the way of interaction between employees and guests take place. The reciprocal long-term relationship between guests and the hotel is becoming increasingly crucial due to the highly positive correlation between guests' overall satisfaction levels and the possibility of their repeat visits to the same hotel (Choi & Chu, 2001).

Based on the findings also, surprise is the most influential factor in explaining customer delight followed by hospitality. It is supported by Jones et al. (2007) who state that hotels are increasing their investments to improve service quality and the perceived value for guests so as to achieve better customer satisfaction and loyalty, thus resulting in better relationships with each customer. Relationship quality has a remarkable positive effect on hotel guests' behavior because it creates positive word of mouth and increments repeated guest rates (Kim, Han, & Lee, 2001). In a competitive hospitality industry which offers homogeneous services, individual hoteliers must be able to satisfy customers better than their counterparts (Choi & Chu, 2001).

The hospitality industry, in particular, being friendly to people is a value-added part of the product that hosts provide. Most of the hotel managers believe that the friendliness and good cheer that their hotel employees provide are strongly related to customer satisfaction and increased customer commitment, and loyalty, and therefore, affect bottom lines. In addition, Kotler, Bowen, and Makens (2006) also defined hospitality industry like all the above but added entertainment for the travelers. Additionally, hospitality industry is the manner in which the hospitality employee provides the service as opposed to the service itself which is critical to the customer's overall enjoyment of the product or "experience" that is being purchased.

The Relationship between Surprise Service Experience and Customer Delight in the Context of Hotel Services

Based on the results of the analysis, it is found that there is strong relationship between surprise service experience and customer delight ($r = 0.762$). From the findings of this study, all the business that offers any services to the guests should put in extra efforts to boost interaction between their employees and guests. According to Torres and Kline (2006) delight entails a stronger emotion and a different physiological state than satisfaction. Delighted customers are those whose expectations have been exceeded. The hotel has gone beyond what it needed to do in order to satisfy them and provide the guest with an experience pleasurable and distinctive enough to arouse the emotion of delight.

When the self-esteem needs of our customers are satisfied, they make them feel better about themselves and about their stay in a particular hotel. Thus customers will be delighted as a function of the fulfillment of this high-order need. Satisfaction is an "overall customer attitude towards a service provider," or an emotional reaction to the difference between what customer anticipate and what they receive (Zineldin, 2000), regarding the fulfillment of some need, goal, or desire. For most products or services, aspects of performance can be objectively assessed.

The findings on the relationship of surprise and customer delight also demonstrate how both these variables are as a single variable. The interaction significantly gives stronger effects toward customer delight as compared to surprise as individual variable. Customer delight can be defined as the reaction that customers have when they experience a product or service that not only satisfies, but also provides an unanticipated level of value or satisfaction (Chandler, 1989).

Based upon this conceptualization, customer delight is related to but distinct from customer satisfaction. While customer satisfaction is widely viewed as the result of exceeding one's expectations, most existing studies indicate that customer delight requires the customer to receive a positive surprise beyond his/her expectations (e.g., Arnold et al., 2005; Berman, 2005; Oliver et al., 1997; Rust & Oliver, 2000).

Thus, delighting customers have been proposed as a way to increase customer loyalty towards a firm (Kumar et al., 2001). It was suggested that firms should move from satisfaction to delight in an effort to stand loyal customers and profitable operations (Torres & Kline, 2006). According to Patterson (1997), customer delight involves going beyond satisfaction to delivering what can be best described as a pleasurable experience for the client. Delight therefore entails a stronger emotion and a different physiological state than satisfaction.

Surprise is also characterized as a syndrome of reactions. In other words, when facing surprise, individuals will have a specific pattern of reactions at subjective (e.g., subjective feeling, surprise exclamation), physiological (e.g., changes in the respiration rates), and behavioral levels (e.g., specific facial expression [mainly eyebrows raising and eyes widening], interruption of ongoing activities, focusing on the surprising stimulus) (Meyer et al., 1997; Reisenzein & Studtmann, 2007; Vanhamme & Snelders, 2001).

From a theoretical perspective, the results of this study provide evidence that the surprise service experience is valid and measureable construct that has a strong association with the customer delight. Data clearly indicate that a surprise component is more robustly correlated to customer delight. Hence, it can be concluded from these results that surprise is an essential service experience components of the delight. This important finding reinforces Plutchik's (1980) original conceptualization of the delight construct and appears to refute any recent momentum toward the contention the surprise is not a necessary component of the construct.

From a managerial lens, providing elements of delightful surprise has a greater impact on repurchase intent and positive word of mouth. Is it possible to provide an element of positive surprise each time a customer visits? In the case of enterprises that serve customers on a frequent basis, the answer is probably no. However, in a tourism paradigm where encounters are typically infrequent we infer the answer is yes, and is evidenced by the commitment made via benchmark organizations in our industry to service quality (Crotts, Dickson, & Ford, 2005). Fuller, Matzler, and Faullant (2006), for example, contend that opportunities to delight guests in tourism venue can most readily relate to facets of customer service and fostering a sense of destination's originality.

Moreover, the findings that support this hypothesis is the research by Pine and Gilmore (1999) who had argued that service providers should not only provide products and services, but also stage "experiences" to add value to customers. The utmost goal of a service companies especially hotels to provide a complete service that renders the customers experiences more meaningful and memorable. The most important strategy in creating memorable experiences and customer delight is to provide surprise to the customer (Hetzel, 2002; Pine & Gilmore, 1999; Schmitt, 1999; Vanhamme, 2008). Surprise must be combined with joy (e.g., Plutchik, 1980).

Hospitality Moderates the Relationship between Surprise and Customer Delight

The result shows that the interaction variable of Hospitality × Surprise is highly significant and positively associated with "Customer Delight" given a coefficient value of 0.0313 ($p < 0.01$). The overall model is adequate given a significant value of F-statistic. R-squared is 59.2% which indicates that 59.2% of the effect on "Customer Delight" is explained by the moderating effect of "surprise service experience" and hospitality, and "surprise service experience."

The result supports the hypothesis that the effect between "surprise service experience" and "customer delights" is moderated by hospitability. It is anticipated that hospitality moderates the relationship between surprise and customer delight. Consistent to forecast, the results of multiple regressions with interaction effects found statistical supports for moderating effects of hospitality on the relationship between surprise and customer delight.

The hospitality industry is often associated with the tourism industry but most people relate it to hotels and restaurants (Powers & Barrows, 2006). Interestingly, the Macmillan Dictionary (2010) provides two distinct but related definitions of hospitality. The first one defines hospitality as "friendly and generous behavior towards visitors and guests, intended to make them feel welcome," while the second definition looks at hospitality as "food, drink, and entertainment given to customers by company or organization." The latter definition is apparently more specific than the more former in terms of the types of service provisions. The dictionary also offered a definition for "corporate hospitality" (which can be associated with commercial hospitality) as "entertainment provided by companies for their customers, for example, at major sports events, in order to get more business.

Furthermore, based on the findings by Jones et al. (2007), hotels are pumping up their investments to improve hospitality and the perceived value for guests so as to achieve better customer satisfaction and loyalty, thus resulting in better relationships with each customer to increase their level of delight. Moreover, hotel managements are always aware of the importance of continuously striving to improve the quality of the interactions in order to increase their customer delight. Generally, customers' evaluations on service encounters are based on their nature of interactions with service employees such as surprise service experience. The interaction between the service employees and customers, commonly referred to as the service encounter, is a critical part of the service delivery process because its elements greatly impact customers' evaluations of service consumption experiences (Soloman et al., 1985).

Hospitality Mediates the Relationship between Surprise and
Customer Delight

Based on the results of regression analysis, the influence of "surprise service experience" (surprise) is highly significant and positively associated with "customer delight" with given coefficient value of 0.587 ($p < 0.01$). Thus, the influence of "surprise service experience" (surprise) is highly significant and positively associated with "hospitableness" (hospitality) with a given coefficient value of 0.472 ($p < 0.01$) for surprise and coefficient value of 0.215 ($p < 0.05$) for variable hospitality. Besides, the result supports a direct relationship between surprise and hospitality. The result suggests that the higher amount of the surprise service experience, the higher is the "hospitableness" of the hotel services provided.

The influence of "hospitableness" (hospitality) is highly significant and positively related to "customer delight" given a coefficient value of 0.656 ($p < 0.01$). The result supports a direct relationship between hospitality and customer delight. The results imply that the better hospitability provided by hotel services, the more they are able to enhance the customer delight. Moreover, the influence of "hospitableness" (hospitality) and surprise are both highly significant and positively associated with "customer delight" given a coefficient value of 0.656 ($p < 0.01$). Therefore, it is anticipated that hospitality mediates the relationship between surprise and customer delight.

Consistent to earlier predictions, the results of multiple regressions with interaction effects found statistical supports for mediating effects of hospitality on the relationship between surprise and customer delight.

Hospitality in an organizational setting is a specific kind of relationship between individuals, that is, a host and a guest. In this relationship, the host understands what would give satisfaction to the guest and enhances his or her comfort and well-being, and delivers it generously and perfectly in face to face interactions, with respect, and tactfulness.

Alternately, hospitality can be described as friendly and generous reception and entertainment of guests or strangers (Oxford Dictionary of Current English, 1993). According to Rust and Oliver (1994), they defined satisfaction as the "customer's fulfillment response," which is an evaluation as well as an emotion-based response to a service. It is an indication of the customer's belief on the probability of a service leading to positive feeling. While Cronin, Brady, and Hult (2000) assessed that service satisfaction's items include interest, enjoyment, surprise, anger, wise choice, and doing the right thing.

CONCLUSION AND IMPLICATIONS

The influence of surprise service experience on customer delight in the context of hotel industry is strengthened by offering hospitable services to the guests. In other words, the interaction between surprising service and hospitality would substantially enhance the guest experiences with the hotel services.

On the other hand, hospitality can also act as a consequence variable for surprise. The more unexpected (surprise) the service experience, the more hospitable the service as perceived by the guests. This is in line with the conceptualization of hospitality which generally aims to generate memorable experience. In order to be memorable, offering surprising service (in a positive fashion) is among the element that is required. Subsequently, the more hospitable the service, the more delighted are the guests with the hotel services.

Hotels should find innovative ways to improve hospitality as the construct is influencing customer delight in both situations as a mediator and a moderator. Surprising service experiences can be provided by understanding the standards (procedures) of hotel service required by the guests and then offer them the enhanced standards instead. Thus, continuous market study and creativity are extremely important to provide inputs for hotel marketing strategies in today's world.

REFERENCES

Ariffin, A. A. M. (2013). Generic dimensionality of hospitality in the hotel industry: A host–guest relationship perspective. *International Journal of Hospitality Management, 35,* 171–179.

Ariffin, A. A. M., & Maghzi, A. (2012). A preliminary study on customer expectations of hotel hospitality: Influences of personal and hotel factors. *International Journal of Hospitality Management, 31*(1), 191–198.

Ariffin, A. A. M., Nameghi, E. N., & Zakaria, N. I. (2013). The effect of hospitableness and servicescape on guest satisfaction in the hotel industry. *Canadian Journal of Administrative Sciences/Revue Canadienne des Sciences de l'Administration, 30*(2), 127–137.

Arnold, M. J., Reynolds, K. E., Ponder, N., & Lueg, J. E. (2005). Customer delight in a retail context: Investigating delightful and terrible shopping experiences. *Journal of Business Research, 58*(8), 1132–1145.

Bejou, D. (1998). Relationship marketing: Evolution, present state and future. *Psychology & Marketing, 144*(8), 727–735.

Berman, B. (2005). How to delight your customers. *California Management Review, 48*(1), 129–151.

Chandler, C. C. (1989). Specific retroactive interference in modified recognition tests: Evidence for an unknown cause of interference. *Journal of Experimental Psychology: Learning, Memory and Cognition, 15,* 256–265.

Choi, T. Y., & Chu, R. (2001). Determinants of hotel guests, satisfaction and repeat patronage in Hong Kong hotel industry. *International Journal of Hospitality Management, 20,* 277–297.

Cronin, J. J., Brady, M. K., & Hult, G. T. M. (2000). Assessing the effects of quality, value, and customer satisfaction on consumer behavioral intentions in service environments. *Journal of Retailing, 76*(2), 193–218.

Crotts, J. C., Dickson, D. R., & Ford, R. C. (2005). Aligning organizational processes with mission: The case of service excellence. *The Academy of Management Executive, 19*(3), 54–58.

Devlin, J. F., Gwynne, A. L., & Ennew, C. T. (2002). The antecedents of service expectations. *The Service Industries Journal, 22*(4), 117–152.

Dominici, G., & Guzzo, R. (2010). Customer satisfaction in the hotel industry: A case study from Sicily. *International Journal of Marketing Studies, 2*(2), 3–12.

Ekman, P., & Friesen, W. V. (1982). Felt, false and miserable smiles. *Journal of Non-verbal Behavior, 6*(4), 238–252.

Finn, A. (2005). Reassessing the foundations of customer delight. *Journal of Service Research, 8*(2), 103–116.

Fuller, J., Matzler, K., & Faullant, R. (2006). Asymmetric effects in customer satisfaction. *Annals of Tourism Research, 33*(4), 1159–1163.

Hemmington, N. (2007). From service to experience: Understanding and defining the hospitality business. *The Service Industries Journal, 27*(6), 35–50.

Hetzel, P. (2002). *Planète conso: Marketing expérientiel et nouveaux univers de consommation.* Paris: Editions d'Organisation.

Holbrook, M. B., & Hirschman, E. C. (1982). The experiential aspects of consumption: Consumer fantasies, feelings, and fun. *Journal of Consumer Research, 9*(2), 132–140.

Hospitality. (1993). *Oxford Dictionary of Current English* (Vols. 1–2). Additional Series. Oxford: Oxford University Press.

Hospitality. (2010). *Macmillan Dictionary.* Retrieved from http://www.macmillandictionary. com/dictionary/british/hospitality. Accessed on August 5, 2010.

Izard, C. E. (1977). *Human emotions.* New York, NY: Plenum.

Jones, D. L., Mak, B., & Sim, J. (2007). A new look at the antecedents and consequences of relationship quality in the hotel service environment. *Services Marketing Quarterly, 28*(3), 15–31.

Kim, W. G., Han, J. S., & Lee, E. (2001). Effects of relationship marketing on repeat purchase and word of mouth. *Journal of Hospitality & Tourism Research, 25*(3), 272–288.

Kotler, P., Bowen, J. T., & Makens, J. C. (2006). *Marketing for hospitality and tourism.* London: Pearson Prentice-Hall.

Kumar, A., Olshavsky, R. W., & King, M. F. (2001). Exploring alternative antecedents of customer delight. *Journal of Consumer Satisfaction Dissatisfaction and Complaining Behavior, 14*, 14–26.

Lashley, C. (2008). Studying hospitality: Insight from social science. *Scandinavian Journal of Hospitality and tourism, 8*(1), 69–84.

Lashley, C., Morrisson, A., & Randall, S. (2005). More than a service encounter? Insights into the emotions of hospitality through special meal occasions. *Journal of Hospitality and Tourism Management, 12*(1), 80–92.

Lashley, C., & Morrisson, M. (2000). *In search of hospitality: Theoretical perspective and debates.* Oxford: Butterworth Heinemann.

Meyer, W. U., Niepel, M., Rudolph, U., & Schützwohl, A. (1994). An experimental analysis of surprise. *Cognition and Emotion, 5*, 295–311.

Meyer, W. U., Reisenzein, R., & Schutzwohl, A. (1997). Towards a process analysis of emotions: The case of surprise. *Motivation and Emotion, 21*, 251–274.

Oliver, R. L., Rust, R., & Varki, S. (1997). Customer delight: Foundations, findings, and managerial insight. *Journal of Retailing, 73*, 311–336.

Patterson, K. (1997). Delighted clients are loyal clients. *Rough Notes, 140*(3), 221–234.

Paul, J. (2000). Are you delighting your customers? *Non-profit World, 18*(5), 34–36.

Pine II, J., & Gilmore, J. H. (1999). Welcome to the experience economy. *Harvard Business Review, 76*(July), 97–105.

Plutchik, R. (1980). *Emotion: A psych evolutionary synthesis.* New York, NY: Harper & Row.

Power, T. F., & Barrow, C. W. (2006). *Introduction to the hospitality industry* (Vol. 1). New York, NY: John Wiley.

Reisenzein, R. (2000). Exploring the strength of association between the components of emotion syndromes: The case of surprise. *Cognition and Emotion, 14*, 1–38.

Reisenzein, R., & Studtmann, M. (2007). On the expression and experience of surprise: No evidence for facial feedback, but evidence for a reverse self-inference effect. *Emotion, 7*, 612–627.

Rumelhart, D. E. (1984). Schemata and the cognitive system. In R. S. Wyer & T. K. Srull (Eds.), *Handbook of social cognition* (Vol. 1, pp. 161−188). Hillsdale, NY: Lawrence Erlbaum Associates.

Rust, R. T., & Oliver, R. L. (1994). *Service quality: New directions in theory and practice* (pp.1−19). Thousand Oaks, CA: Sage.

Rust, R. T., & Oliver, R. L. (2000). Should we delight the customer? *Journal of the Academy of Marketing Science, 28*, 86−94.

Scherer, K. R. (1984). Toward a concept of "modal emotions". *The nature of emotion: Fundamental questions* (pp. 25−31). New York, NY: Oxford University Press.

Schlossberg, H. (1993). Departing exec says customer satisfaction is a continuous process. *Marketing News,* 27 (April 26), 8.

Schmitt, B. H. (1999). *Experiential marketing: How to get customers to sense, feel, think, Act, and relate to your company and brands.* New York, NY: The Free Press.

Schneider, B., & Bowen, D. E. (1999). Understanding customer delight and outrage. *Sloan Management Review, 41,* 35−46.

Soloman, M. R., Suprenant, C., Czepiel, J. A., & Gutman, E. G. (1985). A role theory perspective on dyadic interactions: The service encounter. *Journal of Marketing, 49,* 99−111.

Torres, E. N., & Kline, S. (2006). From satisfaction to delight: A model for the hotel industry. *International Journal of Contemporary Hospitality Management, 18*(4), 290−301.

Vanhamme, J. (2008). The surprise-delight relationship revisited in the management of experience. *Recherche et Applications en Marketing, 23*(3), 113−140.

Vanhamme, J., & Snelders, D. (2001). The role of surprise in satisfaction judgments. *Journal of Consumer Satisfaction, Dissatisfaction and Complaining Behavior, 14,* 27−45.

Vanhamme, J., & Snelders, D. (2003). What if you surprise your customers ... Will they be more satisfied? Findings from a pilot experiment. *Advances in Consumer Research, 30,* 48−55.

Westbrook, A. R., & Oliver, R. L. (1991). The dimensionality of consumption emotion patterns and consumer satisfaction. *Journal of Consumer Research, 18*(1), 84−91.

Westbrook, R. A. (1987). Product/consumption-based affective responses and postpurchase processes. *Journal of Marketing Research,* 258−270.

Zineldin, M. (2000). Beyond relationship marketing: Technological ship marketing. *Marketing Intelligence & Planning, 18*(1), 9−23.

CHAPTER 10

TRANSFERABILITY OF ASIAN PARADIGM IN HOSPITALITY MANAGEMENT TO NON-ASIAN COUNTRIES

Athena Lele Chen and Kaye Chon

ABSTRACT

The Asian paradigm is more than just a demonstration of visually impactful behaviors and practices by hospitality establishments that can be explained by their different Asian cultural backgrounds and reinforced by training; it is focused on the customer, leveraging of the commercial environment while highlighting, not hiding, cultural and destination differences to give people more reasons to visit and repeatedly use their properties. This chapter examines to evaluate transferability of Asian paradigm in hospitality management concepts to non-Asian countries; what and how Asian paradigm in hospitality management can be transferred. For the detailed level on examination and discussion of transferability of Asian concepts, the chapter includes case of Shangri-La Hotels and Resorts for operators' point of view.

Keywords: Asian paradigm; hospitality management; transferability

Tourism and Hospitality Management
Advances in Culture, Tourism and Hospitality Research, Volume 12, 143–157
Copyright © 2016 by Emerald Group Publishing Limited
All rights of reproduction in any form reserved
ISSN: 1871-3173/doi:10.1108/S1871-317320160000012011

INTRODUCTION

Asia's hospitality and tourism industry is well-known for providing out-standing service (Wan & Chon, 2010). In recent years, many Asian hotel brands famous for their high-end service have been expanding their net-work and penetrating markets outside their Asian roots by establishing themselves in Europe and beyond (Kolesnikov-Jessop, 2010).

A number of Asian hotel brands have become global benchmarks in their own right. A look at the 2014 Forbes five-star list (Forbes Travel Guide 2014 Star Award Winners, 2014), which shows that 18 out of 97 five-star hotels and 14 out of 42 five-star spas are of brands of Asian ori-gin. A closer look will show that out of the 18 five-star hotels from Asia, 10 are from Mandarin Oriental, 5 from the Peninsula group, 2 from Shangri-La, and 1 from an independent Asian brand. Based on the percentage of total hotels that are in operation in these hotel groups, the accolade is even more amazing: 37% of Mandarin Oriental hotels and 50% of all Peninsula hotels in the world are rated as five-star by Forbes. This Asia-based top hotel brands have been initiated in South East Asia first and successfully expanded to other parts of the world such as North Americas and Middle East. Among the four-star list, other Asian brands that have also achieved global recognition include Aman, Raffles, and the Langham.

More and more Western hotel brands have adopted practices from Asian paradigm in hospitality management to position as top-class leaders in the hospitality industry. What is the secret to their success? What are the lessons for hotel developers and operators? This chapter aims to evaluate transferability of Asian paradigm in hospitality management concepts from Asia to non-Asian countries. Besides, it will be delivered on what and how Asian paradigm can be transferred in hospitality management. This chapter attempts to answer these questions from an inductive analysis of one Asia-based hotel brand — Shangri-La Hotels and Resorts (hereinafter Shangri-La) to draw some preliminary conclusions for further study.

THEORETICAL CONSIDERATIONS

According to Lashley (2008), hospitality is a human activity. It involves a host—guest relationship (King, 1995). Hospitality has been studied from the three perspectives of "social," "private," and "commercial" (Lashley, 2000) and published literature on the subject support the point that hospitality is social, and is about "people" serving other "people." Wan and Chon (2010) quoting Derrida (2002) asserted that "hospitality is culture itself" and there is an obligation for the host to ensure the well-being of the guest. Lashley (2008) asserted that it is culture and religion. This implies that any study of hospitality must necessarily involve a study of culture and its impacts.

WHAT IS CULTURE?

Regarding our understanding of culture: "a collective phenomenon, shared with people who live or lived within the same social environment, it is consists of the unwritten rules of the social game." It is the collective programming of the mind that distinguishes the members of one group or category of people from others (Hofstede, Hofstede, & Minkov, 2010). The author attempted to dive deeper to develop our definition of the Asian paradigm of hospitality management and deduce what gave rise to the movement. If the European paradigm is all about practice, while the American paradigm is all about concepts, analytics, and theories of management, then what is the Asian paradigm?

WHAT IS THE ASIAN PARADIGM?

The author wants to indicate what is so special about this period of hospitality management that has given birth to a number of legendary hospitality companies originating from Asia in the last 15 years including the likes of Shangri-La, Banyan Tree, Peninsula, Mandarin Oriental, etc. The author also attempts to compare the developing trend of some hospitality properties from Europe and America, like Ritz-Carlton, Four Seasons, Holiday Inn, Hilton, Sheraton, Best Western, etc.

When talking about the difference between different countries, the difference of cultural values is always a vital factor. Hofstede's Five Cultural Dimensions are widely used to understand the workplace values around the world, including power distance, individualism, masculinity, uncertainty avoidance index, and long-term orientation (Hofstede's Cultural Dimensions, 1996−2012). The following figures list out American and some European countries' cultural values:

From Fig. 1, it may indicate that generally people in America show more individualism. In service industry like the hospitality industry, it

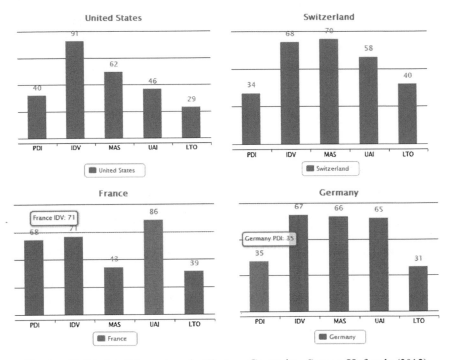

Fig. 1. Hofstede's Dimensions in Western Countries. *Source*: Hofstede (2012).

indicates that American people and companies are mostly merit or evidence based on promotions and awards. Therefore, individual staffs are more interactive and more outgoing. They are searching to get various opportunities and information. Given that American culture is short-term oriented, it indicates that the companies and individual are more focused on quick service and quick result. Compared with America, European countries have different styles. One thing in common is the relatively high uncertainty avoidance index. It implies that teaching and trainings are more deductive. In management structure, rules and security are welcome and if lacking, it creates stress. Thus, for hotel industry the service delivery, management, and operation may be relatively slow and inconvenient.

When the *New York Times* published an article in 1909 with the title "American hotels lead in many things — but the European are more home-like" (New York Times, 1909), the author has not known this may still be the case after 100 years. In the article, American hotels are outstanding because of the conveniences they delivered to their guests. On the other hand, European hotels are more focused on a homelike approach, which creates an environment to make someone feel at his or her own house.

For Asia, the culture values are significantly different from that of Western world as shown in Fig. 2.

Compared to the Western world, Asians are more future oriented and get high LTO (long-term oriented) score. In this culture, relationships are ordered by status and the order is observed. Persistence and perseverance are normal. In hospitality industry in Asia, people are used to working in heavy schedules. Relationship development like loyal customers is always the key. During our stays in various Asian hotels, warm service and emotional connection are always impressed. Hotels always want to create a long-term relationship with us. Emotional and memorable experiences are always delivered by various ways.

The same as Kolesnikov-Jessop (2010) describes Asia's integrated approach to caring their guest. He believes "Asian brands seem to grasp more profoundly than their Western counterparts is a more holistic

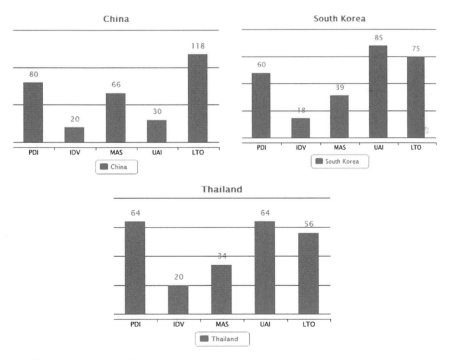

Fig. 2. Hofstede's Dimensions in Asian Countries. *Source*: Hofstede (2012).

approach to a guest's stay, from remembering names to dealing with the smallest details." Asian is a collective culture. In-group considerations affect hiring and promotions of hotels. Relationships with colleagues are cooperative for in-groups. Team work and team spirit building in hotels are essentially important. This is because various hotel departments need to work together to deliver a good service to customers. Therefore, the sense of "we are in the same group" is the key for Asian hoteliers to focus on.

In addition, top facilities are always highly rated in customer experience as emphasized by Kolesnikov-Jessop (2010). Asian hospitality industry is the balance of cultural elements in services and they use more emotional and intangible words such as intimate, spirit, romance, etc. While Western hospitality industry focuses on professional practice and management skills and they use more tangible words for promoting their business.

Tourists always would like to gaze something different (Urry, 1990). The uniqueness and otherness is always the key for tourism and hospitality industry. Thus, cultural differences and destination uniqueness has been showcased during our visitation. The atmosphere in hotels gives us a feeling of we are in the best part of the region.

THE DEVELOPMENT OF ASIA HOSPITALITY

Hospitality shows the desire of the host to make guests happy and to see that their needs are satisfied (King, 1995; Lashley, 2008; Wan & Chon, 2010) and Asian hospitality fully demonstrates that. An analysis of key players and the economic background to the development of the Asian hotel industry was done to see how their impact and influence have resulted in a service style that is much more customer-focused and service oriented.

Owners

Traditional top-class Asian hotel owners take their obligations as hosts seriously and companies such as Shangri-La have their roots in their owners' desire to create "paradise on earth" for their guests. Taking into consideration the importance of maintaining "face" and the need to cultivate *guanxi* in a social environment that aims at achieving harmony, it is not surprising that a lot of Asian hotels have become showcases of their owners' wealth and achievements while creating a platform for more business opportunities for them with local communities and authorities. As a result, many top-class Asian hotels were designed and outfitted lavishly to create impressions of opulence, raising design and decoration standards in the region. Such hotels were created for owners to be able to invite both local and foreign guests to "their home"; hence they usually offer the best of the best in hardware and software.

As employers, Asian owners by and large enjoy high power distances (Hofstede, 2001), which could come from their Confucius upbringing. With respect to staff, they are generally paternalistic and caring. While they may not offer the highest salaries, they tend to offer more stability in pay and benefits. In many parts of Asia, even the lowest ranked staff can enjoy fixed monthly salaries and an annual bonus that is a prerogative of the owner, and is normally based on the overall performance of the company rather than individual achievement. This kind of pay and benefit system is well accepted by the staff, reflecting their collective mentality according to Hofstede's cultural dimensions. Asian owners also demonstrated their long-term orientation when many of them refrained from laying off staff despite suffering temporary operational losses during the days of SARS in 2003.

Consequently, under the influence of this type of ownership, many hotel companies show a strong sense of social obligation and involvement with their local communities by taking part in many local initiatives. Such as Shangri-La, they have unified all initiatives within five key areas of CSR (Corporate Social Responsibility) namely, Environment, Health & Safety, Employees, Supply Chain, and Stakeholder Relations under the umbrella brand of "Sustainability." This campaign strives to properly educate its stakeholders, inspire and engage its employees, enjoin its business partners, and align with the local community initiatives so that CSR can be used as a more significant tool towards development (Shangri-La, 2014).

Staff

Asian staffs are strongly influenced by Asian religion and philosophies such as Buddhism and Confucianism. They tend to be more collective, have a longer term orientation and tolerate a higher power distance. As a result, Asian staffs tend to be more respectful, obedient, cooperative, and to adhere to team work, while comparing with Western staff.

It has also been pointed out that Asians in service industries tend to exercise good emotional controlling (Lashley, 2008), maintaining harmony and giving rise to the perception of seamless and selfless service.

Guests

In the early days of hotel industry development in Asia, most of the guests patronizing the highly acclaimed hotels of Mandarin Oriental, Peninsula, and Shangri-La were from long haul overseas markets. Compared to a lot of the local people in Asia and in particular to Asian hotel staff, these guests from more developed countries were wealthier and had more position power. Not only did these guests represent authority figures to be served well, but in the days when foreign language capabilities were not as strong, good service would have required very close attention to detail by hotel staff in order to ensure smooth operations and to avoid mistakes.

These travelers also had impact on the types of products and services provided by hotels in Asia. Language barriers and hygiene concerns would prevent many foreigners from dining in local Asian restaurants. Hence traditional hotels in Asia tend to have large food and beverage operations and run multiple restaurants on property to cater to hotel guests' dining needs. Of course these outlets would also cater to wealthy locals who would like to impress their dining guests so fine-dining in hotels was very much in demand.

Management

Due to historic interaction with very capable and competent foreigners, almost top-class Asian hotels willing to initiate the hiring and usage of foreign talent − for a better mix of expertise and diversity. This makes them better equipped to absorb the best of other cultures, be more accommodating of differences between different types of people and able to deal with different types of guests. A lot of hotel owners open a hotel because they want to be a gracious host and they want to provide guests the best of best service.

Unlike Western hospitality, which employs franchising or offers management contracts, a lot of the hotels in Asian markets are owned by large family groups. In many Asian hotels, the annual bonus is based on overall performance instead of individual performance reflecting the collectivism mentality in Asia. Asian hospitality possesses unique destinations which attract novelty seekers including an exposure of traditions, customs, religion, ceremonies, rituals and architecture, landscaping, and so on. Asian companies are very open to tapping overseas talent to ensure the quality of their delivery and to maintain an international outlook.

Government and Public

In many Asian cities, hotels have a major role to play in terms of job creation. Luxury hotels also have the tendency to become the social hub for the local communities. As a result, governments and the public are usually supportive of hotels and show it by providing investment incentives and patronage. As prestigious venues for entertainment and events, iconic hotels would become the centers of attraction and pride of communities. In many locales, authorities and the general public will work closely with hotels to resolve infrastructure or labor issues. At the same time, there is an expectation of reciprocity from the locals in that hotels are expected to "give back" to community. Hotels are also expected to support their staff to observe local cultures and religions and maintain harmony with the societies that they are in.

Business Environment in Asia

To appreciate the full picture of Asian hospitality development, the reality of the economic environment and trade development in Asia must be taken into consideration. The business environment in the early days of hotel development in Asia was such that most of the travelers to Asia were senior executives on business or merchandisers on buying trips. They came from places with high living standards and price levels. In comparison, Asia's relatively low price levels made it very affordable for these overseas guests. The abundant supply of labor at low cost in relation to average achieved room rates made it possible for hotels in Asia to operate with very high staff to room ratios, which enables Asian companies to provide an attentive service to guests. Due to the slowing growth in Europe and North America and the Olympic Games in Beijing in 2008 a lot of powerful hotel chains started targeting Asia and China in particular. Names such as Regent, Ritz-Carlton, Sheraton, and others imposed a huge pressure on the local hotels bringing with them their higher Western standards, practices and expectations.

Asia's low labor costs were really tempting for them. Moreover, they boosted hotel gross profits immensely (Shangri-La Paper, 2014).

METHOD

The name Shangri-La was inspired by James Hilton's legendary novel "Lost Horizon." A tranquil haven in the mountains of Tibet, Shangri-La casts a spell on all who resided there. Today, Shangri-La stands as a synonym for paradise, and even though mythical in origin, the name perfectly encapsulates the genuine serenity and service for which Shangri-La have come to be recognized (Peterson, 2005). The Shangri-La group believes in the unique characteristics encapsulated by Asian hospitality, which shapes its philosophy "Shangri-La Hospitality from a caring family," which differentiates this Chinese hotel group from other Western competitors.

Shangri-La Asia Ltd. is the Asian region's leading and fastest-growing luxury hotel group. The company, part of Malaysia's Kuok Group, operates 83 hotels throughout Asia. The Shangri-La story began in 1971 with the first deluxe hotel in Singapore.

The early 2000s proved a difficult period for the company, however. The global drop-off in tourist and business travel following the terrorist attacks against the United States in 2001 was further exacerbated by the SARS epidemic in much of Asia both in 2002 and 2003 (Peterson, 2005).

Fortunately, Mainland China remained central to Shangri-La's growth plans. In 2005, for example, the company announced that it planned to build 15 new hotels in that country before 2010. Shangri-La already has 55 hotels and resorts in Mainland China, and 23 new hotels and resorts are pre-opening until September 2012. At the same time, Shangri-La, by then the largest luxury hotel operator based in the Asian region, had set its sight on building a global brand, announcing plans to enter Europe and North America during the decade as well. Finally, Shangri-La enters North America with Shangri-La Hotel, Vancouver, in 2009. In the spring of the same year, Shangri-La Hotel, Tokyo, opens the first Shangri-La hotel in Japan.

Shangri-La Paris was one of the most hotly anticipated of new hotels in Paris, a sumptuous and sophisticated property that opened its doors back in December 2010, just across the Seine from the Eiffel Tower. This is the first Shangri-La in Europe; the former palace in which it is situated is actually a historic building dating back to 1896. The opening of Shangri-La Paris is a higher attainment of transferability in Shangri-La style Asian paradigm.

On May 11, 2013, Istanbul welcomes its newest luxury hotel with the opening of the Shangri-La Bosphorus, Istanbul. The opulent 186-room hotel is the second in Europe for Shangri-La. Shangri-La brought its inimitable Asian "hospitality from the heart" to Paris in 2010 to rave reviews and now adds Istanbul to its growing list of international gateway cities (Shangri-La, 2014).

Back in February 2005, the company announced its first European property, a 30-year lease contract for a hotel in the London Bridge Tower development, scheduled for completion in 2009. In 2014, Shangri-La finally reached an even higher level of attainment, when it launched a new luxury hotel inside the spire of The Shard. The uniquely Asian view of service at Shangri-La in London also embodies the core values of respect, helpfulness, courtesy, sincerity, and humility. These qualities have been the cornerstone of the Shangri-La's success (Shangri-La, 2014).

FINDINGS

As Shangri-La expands significantly outside its traditional Asian homeland, the groups' philosophy is to enrich cultures rather than dilute or pollute them. The author believes global hotel players are responsible for expanding peoples' cultural horizons; they have an obligation to introduce people to other customs and cultures within reason.

The countries in Europe and North America which Shangri-La targeted for its expansion have specific features; they cannot be easily compared with the Asian ones. One of their characteristic features is the more expensive labor markets which prevents the hotel from maintaining high staff-to-guest ratio, which has never been a problem before when they were in Asian countries. While adapting to the cultural differences in new non-Asian markets, Shangri-La faced the great challenge in Asian brand transferring. The challenges for Shangri-La here are to adapt to the new markets, to ensure its guests superior customer service, to train local people into its distinctive Asian culture, and to ensure them a proper payment, and to preserve its own signature, in other words, to translate Shangri-La quality and service standards to new hotels in new markets. These challenges are two-fold: on the one hand they result from the external factors, which are the new cultures and economic situation of the countries, and on the other hand they stem from factors depending entirely on the company itself (Shangri-La Paper, 2014).

This case study uses the example of Shangri-La expanding into its first hotel in Paris, France. Some challenges identified by the management of Shangri-La in the beginning days of entering the European market are mentioned here.

"My working process is more Asian. In Paris, it was tough. Asians have the positive attitude and they'll always try. In France, they will try to find a way not to do it. Service and pleasing somebody are noble jobs in Asia" (Enriquez, 2013). The management applied the Shangri-La philosophy of hiring staffers with the right mindset. The hotel favored young people with less experience but could easily be trained the Shangri-La Way. Every employee carries a booklet which states its core values, philosophy, mission, vision, and guiding principles. These are inculcated in all the Shangri-La properties worldwide. To distinguish Shangri-La Paris from the other hotels, it focused on serving guests with more warmth and sincerity (Enriquez, 2013).

Another challenge is that Shangri-La needs to keep working on promoting the name and the brand in very specific markets that are often in Paris: the US market, the Russian market, and the Brazilian market. These are three important markets in Paris and they do not have a Shangri-La in those countries. Hence, their challenge is to be as visible to them as possible by doing sales calls and promoting themselves. It was also important to have the right positioning and the right rates right from the beginning, then they would be accepted by the market (Elephant Lifestyle, 2014).

Shangri-La Hotel, Paris, opened at the end of 2010 on 17 December, and the hotel occupancy grew month after month. In January 2011, they were close to full every day and 25–28% of the customers are return guest. Right from the beginning, they were able to place room rates amongst the top two or three in town and keep it like that throughout the year while occupancy was growing (Elephant Lifestyle, 2014). "Performance of the Shangri-La Hotel, Paris improved significantly, registering an increase in occupancy and RevPAR (Revenue Per Available Room) of 27 percentage points and 58%, respectively" (Shangri-La Asia Limited Annual Report, 2012). "The operating performance of the Group's recently opened hotels in Paris has shown remarkable turnaround and these hotels have established an enviable reputation for the brand with impeccable product and service standards. The Group remains cautiously optimistic about the operating performance of its hotel portfolio for 2013" (Shangri-La Asia Limited Annual Report, 2012).

"The Shangri-La Hotel, Paris recorded a decrease in occupancy of 7 percentage points to 70% and a decrease in RevPAR (Revenue Per Available

Room) of 6% as a result of the increase in total room inventory after the completion of the extension to the hotel by 20 rooms in early June 2013. ATR increased by 2% to US$1,320" (Shangri-La Asia Limited Annual Report, 2013). Two years after its opening, Shangri-La Paris has been touted as one of the best luxury hotels in Paris not only for its glorious interiors, amenities, and Michelin-starred restaurants but also for its genuine hospitality (Enriquez, 2013).

CONCLUSION AND IMPLICATIONS

For the combination of guests, staffs, and companies' points of view, the case of Shangri-La is a good example of global expansion through the transfer of Asian hospitality management culture to non-Asian countries. Their core values are show of respect, helpfulness, courtesy, sincerity, and humility. The management team shows the strong leadership on the innovation strategy and has established unique corporate culture. Shangri-La takes the best of the east and west in terms of management, practices, talent, and expertise, then uses innovation, design, and distinctive service styles with attentive service and strong cultural flavors to deliver world class service. The underlying principle is the creation of customer delight to achieve world renowned quality and superior financial performance. Iconic hotel brands laying down their roots overseas must strike a balance between creating home and away, the familiar and the exotic. It is important to export some Asian flavors into the European hotels as much as adapting to the local culture (Enriquez, 2013).

Going by Shangri-La group wisdom, many rules of the diplomatic world seem to apply to hotel groups who transmute their DNA into another country or continent: local respect, strong cultural references, and open minds (Enriquez, 2013). To increase the transferability of Asian hotel chain into Western market could be done by understanding new customers and delivering hotel chain concepts to guests. Shangri-La's success is a good example. But challenges are still affecting Asian hotels to establish their properties in non-Asian countries. Customer taste and their behaviors may simply become challenges for Asian hotel chains.

The example tells us that the Asian paradigm is more than just a demonstration of visually impactful behaviors and practices that can be explained by their different Asian cultural backgrounds and reinforced by training; but it is a savvy way of doing business by focusing on the customer, leveraging on the commercial environment while highlighting, not hiding, cultural and destination-based differences to give people more reasons to visit and repeatedly use their properties. It can be seen that much can be learnt from the Asian paradigm of doing businesses on how to not only create but also sustain service quality excellence with a difference. In summary, the author found that the key to the success includes in order achieving brand differentiation.

REFERENCES

Elephant Lifestyle. (2014). *Elephant lifestyle meets Alain Borgers, General Manager, Shangri-La Paris*. Retrieved from http://www.elephantlifestyle.com/elephant-lifestyle-meets-alain-borges-general-manager-shangri-la-paris_73.html. Accessed on June 23, 2014.

Enriquez, M. C. (2013). *Hotelier keeps Shangri-La in top shape*. Retrieved from http://business.inquirer.net/151629/hotelier-keeps-shangri-la-in-top-shape. Accessed on June 23, 2014.

Forbes Travel Guide 2014 Star Award Winners. (2014). Retrieved from http://www.startle.com/about/awardwinners. Accessed on June 23, 2014.

Hofstede, G. (2001). *Culture's consequences: comparing values, behaviors, institutions and organizations across nations* (2nd ed.). London: Sage.

Hofstede, G., Hofstede, G. J., & Minkov, M. (2010). *Cultures and organizations: Software of the mind* (3rd ed.). New York, NY: McGraw-Hill.

Hofstede's Cultural Dimensions. (1996−2012). *Mind tools*. Retrieved from www.mindtools.com/pages/article/newLDR_66.htm#np. Accessed on April 06, 2012.

King, C. (1995). What is hospitality? *International Journal of Hospitality Management*, *14*(3−4), 219−234.

Kolesnikov-Jessop, S. (2010, January 23). *Asian hotel brands make the journey to Europe*. The New York Times. Singapore.

Lashley, C. (2000). In search of hospitality: Towards a theoretical framework. *International Journal of Hospitality Management*, *19*, 3−15.

Lashley, C. (2008). Studying hospitality: Insights from social sciences. *Scandinavian Journal of Hospitality and Tourism*, *8*(1), 69−84.

New York Times. (1909). American hotels lead in many things − But the European are more homelike; So says Louis Adlon, Proprietor of Newest Berlin Hostelry, Who is here picking up "Points" in Hotels, May 9. Retrieved from http://query.nytimes.com/gst/abstract.html?res = F0061EF63F5D12738DDDA00894DD405B898CF1D3. Accessed on September 03, 2012.

Peterson, J. P. (2005). *International directory of company histories* (Vol. 71). Detriot, MI: St. James Press.

Shangri-La Asia Limited Annual Report. (2012). Retrieved from http://quicktake.morningstar.com/stocknet/secdocuments.aspx?symbol = shaly. Accessed on June 23, 2014.

Shangri-La Asia Limited Annual Report. (2013). Retrieved from http://quicktake.morningstar.com/stocknet/secdocuments.aspx?symbol = shaly. Accessed on June 23, 2014.

Shangri-La Hotel and Resorts (hereinafter Shangri-La). (2014). Retrieved from http://www.shangri-la.com. Accessed on June 23, 2014.

Shangri-La Paper. (2014). Retrieved from http://www.academia.edu/7032911/Shangri-La_ paper. Accessed on September 23, 2014.

Urry, J. (1990). *The tourist gaze*. London: Sage.

Wan, S., & Chon, K. (2010). Asianess — An emerging concept in hospitality management. Asia-Pacific CHRIE (pp. 175–186). Phuket: The 8th APacCHRIE Conference 2010.

CHAPTER 11

THE DEVELOPMENT OF HOSPITALITY INDUSTRY IN KRAKOW: HISTORICAL PERSPECTIVE

Robert Pawlusiński and Magdalena Kubal

ABSTRACT

The growing importance of Krakow as the tourist destination in Eastern Europe has inspired changes in its hospitality industry as early as in the mid-nineteenth century. This chapter addresses the following questions — how has the hospitality industry developed during this period? Where did it concentrate? How did the hospitality offer expanded, and was the nature of the competition between owners? Due to the limited availability of historical statistical information on the service industry, the data for this study was derived from guide books, diaries, calendars, and newspapers ("Chronicle of Cracow") throughout 1848–1939. The authors have examined about 30,500 volumes from which a selection of relevant information and press advertisements was made. Through the examination of historical press announcements for more than 90 years, the authors were able to reproduce the direct location of the hospitality industry objects, their changes of location, the

Tourism and Hospitality Management
Advances in Culture, Tourism and Hospitality Research, Volume 12, 159–171
Copyright © 2016 by Emerald Group Publishing Limited
All rights of reproduction in any form reserved
ISSN: 1871-3173/doi:10.1108/S1871-317320160000012012

identity of owners, the profile of provided services, and the economic and spatial transformations of the hospitality industry in Krakow.

Keywords: Hotel industry; history of tourism; historical geography; Krakow

INTRODUCTION

Cities have attracted crowds of visitors both as places of concentration of population and the location of trade, service, and manufacturing since the ancient times. In the Middle Ages it was the political, administrative, commercial, and religious functions that played the important role for the development of European cities and for the influx of visitors; since the end of the Middle Ages the academic function, associated with the formation of universities, also played its role. Since the Renaissance, European cities (again as in the ancient times) have become the main centers of cultural and artistic life of the countries. The interest in the legacy of ancient Italy, artistic and cultural life of the France becomes the growth factor for so-called Grand Tour.

Further changes in the development of European cities in terms of their tourism development have been brought by the era of industrialization in Europe, dating back to the beginning of the nineteenth century. The evolving industrial activity in the cities and the emergence and development of the rail transport network have created new driving forces for the influx of people to cities, including also people, who today we would call tourists. Since the mid-nineteenth century the first travel agencies have appeared. Although they were geared toward the organization of leisure time for urban residents, quite fast they also started developing their services toward tourists by organizing them an offer with cognitive or entertainment character. The above stages of development of the tourist centers largely reflected the state and directions of development of accommodation and catering facilities.

The beginnings of hospitality in modern Europe date back to the early Middle Ages. The process of servicing guests was first developed by the monasteries, which under the edict of Charles the Great (ninth century) were obliged to provide accommodation for pilgrims. In later centuries this activity in the monasteries has become more of a commercial nature. With the development of commercial travels, diplomats, and students' travels, the city inns and taverns have appeared. Their importance has been suggested by the creation of medieval Europe special guilds, affiliating of innkeepers and owners of inns in many cities. Functional and organizational arrangement of taverns in Europe changed in the late eighteenth and nineteenth centuries, along with the intensification of journeys. This applies especially to the cities that become more and more important tourism destinations. There is a substantial change taking place within the hotel industry. The contemporary taverns began to convert into hotels, the newly-built hotel facilities. This involved the increase of the standard of services and increased the capacity of reception of the tourists, in response to the market needs.

Since the nineteenth century, the development of hotel industry has been moving towards separation of hotels with high quality accommodation offer, from the other facilities, that provided services for less wealthy travelers. Hotels were located not only within the city centers, but also in the vicinity of railway stations, which were becoming important points in the city. Luxury hotels have become "the business cards" of their cities. The most famous city hotels built in the nineteenth century were: Hotel Grand in Paris (50s of the nineteenth century), Keiserhoff in Berlin (1874). Since the end of the nineteenth century, European hotel industry has been developing rapidly. The level of this development, however, has been uneven especially in spatial terms.

With this chapter, the authors attempt to answer the following questions: (1) How did the hotel and catering industry in Krakow took its shape in the first years of the tourist development of the city? (2) How did the hospitality industry develop during this period? (3) Where did it concentrate? (4) How did the hospitality offer expand? (5) What was the nature of the competition between owners? The complicated political situation in the nineteenth century and the beginning of twentieth century, the lack of statistical reporting prevents the correct diagnosis of shaping the hotel and catering industry in Krakow, in this first period of the tourist development of the city. Due to the limited availability of statistical information on the state of development of the service industry, the starting materials for the study were guide books, diaries, calendars, and newspapers; the latter proved a particularly rich source with a column entitled "Chronicle of Cracow."

KRAKOW AS A TOURIST CENTER

Krakow has long tourism traditions. The city, as the former Polish capital, has, since the medieval times, been an important political, cultural, and religious center, and therefore a destination of many different social groups from Poland and abroad (Pawlusiński & Kubal, 2011). The tourist development of the city began on a large scale in the mid-nineteenth century (Warszyńska, 1992). At that time independent Poland did not exist, because for 123 years (1795–1918) it remained under the control of the three neighboring forces: Habsburg monarchy, Russia, and Prussia. Political freedoms within the Habsburg monarchy (to which Krakow officially belonged) contributed significantly to the city's cultural revival and the rebirth of the Polish tradition.

Krakow had weak connection with the railway systems of Austria and other parts of Poland (which stayed under the control of Russia and Prussia) in the nineteenth century, due to the peripheral location on the north end of the Habsburg Empire. As a result of the absence of a resource base for the industry, it did not develop as an industrial center. The political freedom was the main factor for changes in the city, which helped to spur artistic, cultural, scientific activities of the city. Its aim was to preserve Polish cultural values. During that time a university functioned in the city (its origins date back to the fourteenth century) which educated in Polish language (that was not possible in other lands of partitioned Poland). During this time, important scientific and cultural institutions started to develop, numerous theaters and museums started to operate. This resulted in the new trends of literature and art developing in Krakow at the end of the nineteenth century – the so-called Young Poland (in Polish: Młoda Polska).

Significant spatial and economic development of the city took place at the beginning of the twentieth century, especially after the independence of Poland in 1918 (after World War I). The population of Krakow between 1900 and 1930 has more than tripled, from 80 thousand to more than 250 thousand. The so-called interwar period (1919–1939) was the time of Krakow's great development, which stimulated rapid tourist boom. These times, however, were characterized by a slow loss of importance of the city, in contrast to Warsaw, which, as the capital of an independent state, became the center of political, scientific, cultural, and economic life of the country.

The city in the mid-nineteenth century was the target of patriotic arrivals and became the center of Polish culture, the so-called "Spiritual capital of the country." In addition to the arrival of aristocracy, the world famous scientific and artistic people, Krakow began to attract, in the nineteenth century, a new group of people, from the middle and poor social classes. Poles scattered throughout the area of the three partitions made sentimental travels to the former capital, the burial place of Polish kings. The city became famous for numerous museums, theater, and patriotic initiatives, focusing on stimulating national consciousness. Krakow obtained a connection with the railway system of Prussia (1847) and Vienna and Warsaw, which resulted in rapid artistic and cultural revival of Krakow.

The growing importance of Krakow as the tourist destination has also brought changes in its hospitality industry. The old taverns, which formed the basis of accommodation of the city, began to be transformed into hotels — some of them still exist today, operating not only as accommodation, but also as a historical monument of Krakow's hospitality industry. There has been a gradual development — not only quantitative, but also qualitative — in the city: clearly differentiating districts, around which grew expensive hotels for the rich clientele and neighborhoods with taverns for merchants and traders. Although the outbreak of World War I slowed the development of tourism, up to the outbreak of World War II in 1939, the city was the most visited tourist destination in the country. Every year Krakow was visited by about 125 thousand tourists, of which about six thousand were foreigners (Warszyńska, 1996).

Krakow, as the conservative center, the city in which the clerical career and stable life was highly esteemed, was marked by the rhythm of the celebration of religious and patriotic events. It was therefore ideal for the birth of rebellion among the young artists and the bourgeois society. A rapid adaptation of the western ideas of modernism, decadence, Nietzsche or Schopenhauer philosophy has been observed. In urban life the new, modern, bohemian artistic cafes appeared, where young people, with the accompaniment of coffee and alcohol, could spend long nights on the discussions. Painters used to gather in a cafe Michalik and Sauer, and actors in the café Janikowski. The main meeting place was the premises of Turliński — Paon.

In the twentieth century, the city of Krakow grew into a tourist resort of international fame, attracting mass tourism. Currently Krakow is visited by about 9 million tourists, of which 28% are foreigners.

THE USE OF DATA SOURCES FOR TOURISM STUDIES

Tourism, as an interdisciplinary and multidimensional phenomenon, is of the interest to various disciplines (see Kowalczyk, 2000; Warszyńska & Jackowski, 1978). Studies on tourism are multifaceted and include both studies of a comprehensive character and those focusing on narrow problems (see Kowalczyk, 2000; Warszyńska & Jackowski, 1978). Also the spatial scale of studies varies from local studies, by about regions, countries, and studies which cover the whole world, as well as different dimensions of time: the state of past, present, and potential future developments. The most important research issues of tourism geography include: space travel and tourism, relations between tourism and other socioeconomic functions, tourism in the functional structure of the socioeconomic space, and human being as the subject of tourism (see Warszyńska, 1986).

Research, related to the history of tourism, has been conducted not only by the historians but also by the geographers (see Kowalczyk, 2000; Warszyńska & Jackowski, 1978). Analysis of the spatial aspects of the tourism development in the past requires a comprehensive study. Interesting facts were concluded by Towner (1996) in a publication: *An historical geography of recreation and tourism in the western world.* Towner (1996) indicates that the studies must include "three main geographical components: the visitor-generating area forming the center of demand, the visitor destination area forming the center of supply, and two linked by the third component of transport and communication."

The fundamental problem of geographical research associated with the analysis of historical phenomena is rather limited sources of information. Geographical studies attempt to exploit new sources of information, especially about the evolution of social and economic phenomena in geographical space in a historical context. For example, the landscape researchers analyzed was the records contained in painting, literature, film, music (e.g., Bański, 2011; Bartnik, 2009; Carles, Barrino, & de Lucio, 1999; Mackenzie & Fiona, 2006; Holzer, 1978; Jeffus & Aramini, 2008; Kaufmann, 2004; Morris, 2005; Olwig, 1987; Orłowska, 2002; Towner, 1996; Waterman, 2000) as well in historical sources: the press or the urban annals (see Raska, Klimes, & Dubisar, 2013). This brought new developments to the research on cultural landscape (e.g., see Kaufmann, 2004; Orłowska, 2002) and the natural environment or the space in which a person lives and works. Tourist guide books were also used as the source of information in historical research, in the field of tourism geography; their closer investigation allowed to gain deeper knowledge of the spaces and places explored by tourists. The local press, especially the part relating to advertisements and a list of entities operating in the city, was less frequently used in geographical research.

Studies, related to the history of tourism, are conducted with the use of methods of historical geography and history of tourism. Both fields deal with the past of the tourist phenomena in time and space. Historical geography is one of the fundamental disciplines of geographical sciences, which stands between geography and history. Pursuing a reconstruction of the events that took place in the past, geographers examine, inter alia, the changes in the function and the space of towns and villages, including the tourist function of the town over the centuries (Jackowski, 2004).

Historical geography uses retrogressive and genetic methods, history of tourism deals with a critical analysis of historical sources (Ślusarczyk, 2003). As Ślusarczyk indicates (2003), historical sources relating to tourism are the psychophysical and social remnants, which are products of human labor, and thus participate in the development of societies, souped by the ability of reflecting this process.

The most common historical sources of research used by the history of tourism are: biographies, autobiographies, travel correspondence, diaries, and travel reports (books, epistolographic descriptions, memoirs strict sense, poetry); brand publications: guides, brochures, handouts, and promotional printed list of patients and tourists. These are the direct source of information. Indirectly, to obtain the largest possible spectrum of historical information, geographers also rely on encyclopedias, dictionaries, travel books, legislative sources, commemoratives, accommodations, financial, accounting documents, accommodation and dining facilities' inventories, official statutes, timetables, pricing of services, brochures, and leaflets (see Ślusarczyk, 2003).

Tourist guides are used quite often, as the source of information in historical research in the field of tourism geography. They allow to determine the extent of the space, explored by tourists (e.g., Bieniarzówna & Małecki, 1979, 1984, 1997; Migała, 2005; Warszyńska, 1968, 1992, 1996). Local press is used less frequently in geographical research, especially the part related to the advertising and announcements list of entities, operating in the city.

The research on the history of tourism in Krakow, especially in its early phase, is scarce. There are many more sources concerning the period after the World War II and present times. Nevertheless there are still some rare sources that covered these topics (e.g., Kulesza, 2001; Kuźniarski, 2001; Pawlusiński & Kubal, 2011; Warszyńska, 1968, 1992, 1996). The developments of Krakow's hotel base have been included in volumes devoted to the general history of Krakow (e.g., Bieniarzówna & Małecki, 1979, 1984, 1997) and in publications about the history of Polish hospitality (e.g., Błądek, Tulibacki, 2003a, 2003b; Kowalczyk, 1967; Kulesza, 2001; Matczak, 2004; Pustoła, 1986).

METHOD

In this study, the authors follow in the footsteps of geography researchers using the text as their source of analysis: newspaper advertisements, both advertising and accounting for the events of social, political, and scientific utility. These texts often provide not only geographical information but also more complex knowledge of the social structure or differences in spatial characteristics of the regions. In addition to the advertising function, they also tell us about the city and therefore provide a particularly interesting documentation of the geographical space. Classified newspaper advertisements from archive newspapers have particular value because they can facilitate the analysis and comparison of the state of geographical space and Krakow's hospitality industry at the turn of the century. It should be noted that this methodological choices are not consistent with the assumptions of mainstream cultural geography, which refers to newspaper advertisements not as an object of study, but as a source of information and knowledge in geographical research.

The study used mainly local newspapers issued in this period in Krakow, whereas nationwide and macro-regional newspapers were not searched in detail, assuming their lower "sensitivity" to local events. It is the only source of information, which in addition to tourist guide books (appearing irregularly) provides an overview of the status of the city in such a long period of time. So far, no scientific studies on tourism in Krakow have been made, based on the local press. A wide time range of archive sources was used to collect information about hotel and catering industry on the study areas. The oldest data source used (newspaper issue) comes from 1848 whereas the youngest is from 1939. The range of datasets represents the availability of the written sources, especially newspapers. All the written sources, which were screened, are located in the local regional archive of Malopolska Digital Library. The archive sources for Krakow are predominantly written in Polish, but some of them, especially from the oldest issues, were written in German.

Authors analyzed the contents of the daily newspaper: *Czas* [*The Time*] (daily; years 1848–1939), *Djabeł* [*The Devil*] (1869, 1871–1906, and from 1911), and *Chwila* [*The Moment*] (preserved only selected numbers from the years 1863 and 1864). These newspapers were chosen for two reasons. First, they contain an advertisement section and second, there was a section of the local chronicle, "Chronicle of Cracow," included in most of the volumes. In the search for sources of information we have examined about 30,500 copies of the material from which the selection of information and press advertisements was made. Tested advertisements and print advertisements, appearing in local Krakow's newspapers in the years 1848–1939 have a different shape and volume. For the geographer it is important that this message contains information about the location, which, in many cases, is read not by the address but colorful description of the location. Through the examination of announcements and advertisements for more than 90 years, we were able to reproduce not only the direct location of the object, but the changes of location, the owners, the profile of provided services and the economic and spatial transformations of hospitality industry in Krakow, in time and space.

FINDINGS

The consulted empirical material covering almost one century demonstrated that since the mid-nineteenth century, there have been significant changes in Krakow hotel industry. How did the changes look like? These changes were of spatial and qualitative character.

First, by the mid-nineteenth century, a network of taverns rapidly developed in the city. These were houses of relatively low quality, mostly wooden, bunk, offering only modest accommodation, food and shelter for horses, possessing limited capacity of reception area, allowing accommodation for up to 10 people each. Interestingly, there are two zones of concentration of these objects, which formed the north-south axis within the medieval city (the Market Square and the main roads, at the gates of the city) and outside the old city walls – especially in the area of Kleparz which was then a separate city and served as trade and economic area. Location of taverns on Kleparz also stemmed from the old tradition of closing the gates at night, which functioned at the beginning of the nineteenth century. Hence, those who came to Krakow after dusk could spend the night only on Kleparz.

Secondly, in the mid-nineteenth century, some of the taverns in the center began to transform into hotels, with a higher standard and greater capacity. The oldest hotels are: Hotel pod Białą Różą (1799), Pod Różą (1801), hotel Saski (1812), hotel Drezdeński (1814). These last two hotels exist up to the present, in the same locations, in the Sławkowska Street, within the medieval city center. All of these hotels have started their activities as taverns. In 1850, in Krakow there were 13 hotels and up to 167 taverns. The entire city complex had a population more than 30 thousand residents.

At the end of the nineteenth century, the emergence of Krakow's low-cost accommodation facilities was observed, intended for students arriving at the Jagiellonian University to study. These facilities were located in the vicinity of the university buildings in the western and north-western part of Krakow. These were the B&B's, dormitories, and private rooms, run by landlords or tenants, intended for long-term rental. These facilities also offered, but on a smaller scale, the rooms of lower standards than the hotels and also for short-term rental. Around these objects domestic kitchens were created; these offered full board, under the name of "home cooking," and also the dinners for students. These were unusual restaurants and catering facilities, offering low-cost meals.

However, by the late nineteenth century there was a drastic decrease in the number of taverns, especially in area of the medieval city. They were replaced by the hotel facilities.

The railway connection, via Galician Rail to Vienna and Warsaw, boosted the development of the hotel base, in the years 1847–1850. During this period three new hotels in the vicinity of the train station were created. In the early years of the twentieth century there was about 20 hotels and only a few taverns, especially in the area of Kleparz.

At the turn of the nineteenth and early twentieth century there was a number of coffee houses and cafes, which reflected the influences of Habsburg monarchy, and mirrored the character of the city of Vienna. These facilities were located mainly in the old town, especially in the hotels. From the very beginning, these cafes were the meeting place of the local bohemian artists. Analogically to the Viennese establishments these cafes became popular meeting places for drinking coffee and hot chocolate. These drinks were served not only in cafes, but also in pastry shops, restaurants, and grocery trades. The pastry shops became popular since the mid-nineteenth century and were created within the medieval city center. In this period of time the cultural life of the city took place in trendy cafes, pastry shops, and restaurants. Overall in the early twentieth century, in Krakow there were several catering facilities: cafes, many of which got high reputation and a rich artistic program. It is worth to mention that the development of Krakow's hospitality industry was closely associated with Vienna – one of the leading hotels in Krakow was ruled by a member of the Sacher family from Vienna.

An interesting phenomenon in Krakow catering premises was breakfast dinning. Thanks to the information contained in local newspapers of Krakow, authors were able to reconstruct the history of these places and the history of dining options that have evolved from the objects for indigent customers to the restaurant. An example is the Krakow restaurant Antoni Hawełka at the Market Square. The first object of the proprietor was created in 1876; it was a colonial store "Under the Palm," located first in the Palace "Under Krzysztofory," 35 Market Square, where the activity was expanded to catering service – the so-called "handelek śniadankowy" [English: breakfast market]. This typical term functioned in the 90s of nineteenth century in Krakow. It meant something between a buffet and a cheap restaurant. Hawełka was the supplier of the Royal Court of Greece. He received the honorary title of emperor Suppliers Manor. Descendants of Hawełka, moving operations to another location, formed in 1913 the restaurant "Hawełka."

After the end of World War I, Krakow's hotel industry experienced a period of collapse, which was associated with the global economic crisis. In 1927 in Krakow there were less than 10 accommodation facilities with a total capacity of 500 beds. After 1935, however, Krakow experienced a revival. What is interesting: new hotels were formed not so dynamically as the facilities for social tourism. In 1939 in Krakow there were 16 hotels and B&B's (700 beds) and a couple of large accommodation facilities for youth and tourism group (a total of over 1,000 beds). The area where these facilities were located expanded a lot in the 30s of twentieth century.

CONCLUSION AND IMPLICATIONS

Announcements and advertisements, published in local newspapers, have a high potential for obtaining good quality historical data about hotels and tourism facilities in Krakow. Interpretation of newspaper advertisements provided a unique opportunity to gain extensive knowledge of the spatial structure of cities, their neighborhoods and individual buildings, stages of districts development, and economic restructuring. The content, which mainly provides the reader with historical facts, is a form of recording location in the geographic space in the past and supplies factual information.

While the collected material allowed for the reconstruction of the spatial structure of the Krakow hotel market and its transformation at the turn of the century, it does not tell the complete and exhaustive story. In the years 1848–1939 in Krakow, there were a number of small buildings with low standard of accommodation, with a small capacity reception or opened only for one or two seasons. Many facilities did not advertise promotional campaigns in the local press — at least about few objects we know only from the chronicle information of the city, because they have become a stage for criminal or social events. Many facilities simply could not afford to carry advertising campaigns in the local press. In order to research these more in depth complementary study could be carried out examining tax records, containing information about the economic activities, run by residents of the city. However, due to the city's history and membership of Krakow in the Austrian partition, obtaining such information is almost impossible.

Sources, such as personal correspondence, narrative sources (e.g., chronicles), official economic records, and other governmental records, newspapers, drawings, and other scientific sources, can be used complementarily to the information gathered from the newspapers of Krakow. Of these sources, local newspapers have shown the greatest potential to provide relevant and comprehensive information. The data we currently collected allow recreating the atmosphere of the city and the hospitality market in Krakow at the turn of the twentieth century. The thorough investigation of many of these facts and their interpretation as embedded in the context of a specific, concrete historical reality (political, cultural, social, or economic), combined with visualization (e.g., map), enables a broader view of social relations, business methods, and results in a greater knowledge of the development of tourist activity in the city from the turn of the twentieth century.

REFERENCES

Bański, J. (2011). Dzieło sztuki jako źródło wiedzy w badaniach geograficznych. *Przegląd Geograficzny, 83*(2), 233–250.

Bartnik, R. (2009). *Portret miasta. Lublin w malarstwie, rysunku i grafice* (pp. 1618–1939). Lublin: Muzeum Lubelskie.

Bieniarzówna, J., & Małecki, J. M. (Eds.). (1979). *Dzieje Krakowa, t. 3, Kraków w latach 1796–1918*. Kraków: Wydawnictwo Literackie.

Bieniarzówna, J., & Małecki, J. M. (Eds.). (1984). *Dzieje Krakowa, t. 2, Kraków w wiekach XVI – XVIII*. Kraków: Wydawnictwo Literackie.

Bieniarzówna, J., & Małecki, J. M. (Eds.). (1997). *Dzieje Krakowa, t. 2, Kraków w latach 1918–1939*. Kraków: Wydawnictwo Literackie.

Błądek, Z., & Tulibacki, T. (2003a). *Dzieje krajowego hotelarstwa: Od zajazdu do współczesności: fakty, obiekty, ludzie* (p. 277). Poznań, Warszawa: Albus.

Błądek, Z., & Tulibacki, T. (2003b). *Hotele w polsce* (p. 79). Warszawa: Wyższa Szkoła Turystyki i Hotelarstwa.

Carles, J. L., Barrino, I. L., & de Lucio, J. V. (1999). Sound influence on landscape values. *Landscape and Urban Planning, 4*(4), 191–200.

Holzer, J. (1978). Świat zdeformowany. Dzieło literatury XX wieku jako źródło historyczne. In Z. Stefanowska & J. Sławiński (Eds.), *Dzieło literackie jako źródło historyczne* (p. 336). Warszawa: Czytelnik.

Jackowski, A. (Ed.). (2004). *Encyklopedia szkolna, Geografia*. Kraków: Zielona Sowa.

Jeffus, S., & Aramini, J. (2008). *Geography through art*. Nancy, KY: Geography Matters.

Kaufmann, T. (2004). *Toward a geography of art*. Chicago, IL: University of Chicago Press.

Kowalczyk, A. (2000). *Geografia turyzmu* (p. 288). Warszawa: Wydawnictwo Naukowe PWN.

Kowalczyk, J. (1967). *Hotelarstwo warszawskie wczoraj i dziś*, Ruch Turystyczny: Monografie, Szkoła Główna Planowania i Statystyki. Zakład Prawnych i Ekonomicznych Zagadnień Turystyki, 4, Warszawa.

Kulesza, M. (2001). Gastronomia i Hotelarstwo w miastach polskich drugiej połowy XVIII wieku, *Turyzm 11(2)*. Łódź: Wydawnictwo Uniwersytetu Łódzkiego.

Kuźniarski, A. (2001). Śladami krakowskiego hotelarstwa. *Folia Turistica, 10.*

Mackenzie, A., & Fiona, D. (2006). "Against the tide": placing visual art in the Highlands and Islands, Scotland', social and cultural geography. *Special Issue on Geographies of Art and the Environment*, 7(6), 965—985.

Matczak, A. (Ed.). (2004). *Lokalizacja hoteli w krajowych metropoliach Europy Środkowo-Wschodniej*. Łódź: Łódzkie Towarzystwo Naukowe.

Migała, M. (2005). Znaczenie przewodników, wydawnictw literackich i korespondencji w popularyzacji uzdrowisk i turystyki na Śląsku w XIX i pierwszej połowie XX wieku. In W. Mynarski (Ed.), *Wybrane zagadnienia z turystyki i rekreacji* (pp. 125—135). Opole.

Morris, E. (2005). The cultural geographies of abstract expressionism: Painters, critics, dealers and the production of an Atlantic Art. *Social and Cultural Geography*, 6(3), 421—437.

Olwig, K. (1987). Art and the art of communicating geographical knowledge: The case of Pieter Brueghel. *Journal of Geography*, 86(2), 47—51.

Orłowska, E. (Ed.). (2002). *Kultura jako przedmiot badań geograficznych (1 and 2), PTG.* Wrocław: Uniwersytet Wrocławski.

Pawlusiński, R., & Kubal, M. (2011). Tradycje turystyczne Krakowa. In M. Mika (Ed.), *Kraków jako ośrodek turystyczny* (pp. 35—55). Krakow: IGiGP UJ.

Pustoła, J. (1986). *Kierunki rozwoju hotelarstwa w Polsce międzywojennej, Instytut Turystyki, 202.*

Raska, P., Klimes, J., & Dubisar, J. (2013). Using local archive sources to reconstruct historical landslide occurrence in selected urban regions of the Czech Republic: Examples from regions with different historical development, *Land Degradation & Development*, 46, 142—157. Accessed on November 10, 2013.

Ślusarczyk, J. (2003). Historia turystyki. In R. Winiarski (Ed.), *Nauki o turystyce, studia i monografie* (Vol. 7, pp. 67—84). Krakow.

Towner, J. (1996). *An historical geography of recreation and tourism in the western world* (pp. 1540—1940). Chichester: Wiley.

Warszyńska, J. (1968). Kraków jako ośrodek turystyczny. *Folia Geographica, Series Geographica — Oeconomica, 1.*

Warszyńska, J. (1986). Problemy badawcze geografii turyzmu. *Folia Geographica, Series Geographica — Oeconomica, 19.*

Warszyńska, J. (1992). Cracow as the centre of tourist traffic. *Turyzm, 1.*

Warszyńska, J. (1996). Kraków jako ośrodek ruchu turystycznego. *Folia Geographica, Series Geographica — Oeconomica, 27—28*, 255—278.

Warszyńska, J., & Jackowski, A. (1978). *Podstawy geografii turyzmu*. Warszawa: Wydawnictwo Naukowe PWN.

Waterman, E. (2000). Sound escape: Sonic geography remembered and imagined. *Cultural Geographies*, 7(1), 112—115.

CHAPTER 12

DIVERSIFICATION OF HOTELS IN A SINGLE-ASSET TOURISM CITY

Hilal Erkuş-Öztürk

ABSTRACT

The importance of diversification and innovation in strengthening of global competitiveness has been emphasized in both tourism and local development literature. The aim of this chapter is to define the factors (company type, company size, intra-industry investments, collaboration with other companies, and associations) that influence the product- and service-diversification of hotels. This chapter addresses the diversification and innovation strategies of hotels, not only in the light of tourism literature, but also of local development literature, and it provides empirical evidence based on a company-level survey. The findings of the study show that company type, company size, sector-specific knowledge (intra-industry investments and experience of hotel workers), and collaboration with other companies and institutions matter for product- and service-diversification of hotels.

Keywords: Diversification; innovation; company size; collaboration; sector-specific knowledge

Tourism and Hospitality Management
Advances in Culture, Tourism and Hospitality Research, Volume 12, 173–185
Copyright © 2016 by Emerald Group Publishing Limited
All rights of reproduction in any form reserved
ISSN: 1871-3173/doi:10.1108/S1871-317320160000012013

INTRODUCTION

In the volatile economic conditions imposed by globalization, "being different" is the only way to cope with competition (Porter, 1990). Innovation and product diversification are increasingly said to be indispensable factors not only for the survival of companies but also for the development of a region because they strengthen competitiveness and long-term economic growth (Sørensen, 2007). Innovation and diversification are equally crucial factors for tourism companies and tourism places to promote their competitive advantage. As the tourism market is highly fragile and risky (it is volatile, full of quality uncertainties of consumers, and ever changing life styles of consumers), tourism companies are forced to be innovative and to diversify their goods and services.

Over the last two decades, it has been stressed again and again in tourism literature that the era of fordist mass-tourism is over now and has been followed up by market differentiation (the growth of niche markets) that goes hand in hand with flexibly specialized production. As in all consumer markets, niche markets in tourism create a feeling of exclusiveness and offers opportunities to tourists to distinguish themselves in class- and status position. And ever more tourism entrepreneurs have entered and/or created niche markets in tourism in order to keep out of the price-fighters markets in mass-tourism. There is more competition on quality than on price in niche markets. However, the assets on which the competitive advantages of tourist places are based are highly variegated, and can range from one dominant asset such as sea-sun-sand tourism to a broad mix of different assets. It is claimed that in the long-term single-asset tourism places seem to be more vulnerable than multi-asset ones (Terhorst & Erkuş Öztürk, 2012).

The competitive advantage of multi-asset tourism places is based on a combination of historical identity and other assets. The competitive advantage of Florence, Siena, and other Tuscan cities is based on a mix of historical identity, beautiful landscape of the surrounding countryside, and high-quality food and wines, and that of Amsterdam on a mix of historical identity, a highly varied land-use, museums, and a libertarian atmosphere (fun, soft drugs, and sex). And the variety of assets on which the competitive advantage of world cities like New York, London, and Paris is based is even much broader. In those cities gentrifiers, business people, and tourists support such a wide range of urban amenities, ranging from symbolic landmarks, movie multiplexes, superstores, exclusive shops, a huge variety of restaurants and pubs, museums, symphony orchestras, opera houses, jazz and pop-music clubs, professional sports, bohemian life styles to a dynamic urban atmosphere in general, that ever more tourists are attracted (Terhorst & Erkuş Öztürk, 2012).

Apart from the importance of multi-asset cities, "monopolies of place" are also very important for tourism entrepreneurs by offering good opportunities to innovation and differentiation in niche markets that make competition monopolistic and enables firms to keep out of price-fighters markets. Tourism entrepreneurs who first exploit such an asset are real innovators in a Schumpeterian sense because they make a "new combination" that no one did before. In other words, tourism entrepreneurs who first exploit a natural tourism place, even if that place has only one single asset to attract tourists, are the first innovators in that place. But their monopoly position is only temporary because imitators attracted by excess profits made by the innovator, enter the market. Consequently, a process of homogenization takes place in which the excess profits of the first innovator are being eroded. This process of homogenization is characterized by an ever stronger competition by price rather than by quality. And some firms (think of franchise hotels) perform much better under these market conditions than do others. This process of homogenization, however, does not end in a static equilibrium in which no actor has an interest to change his or her position. As both Braudel and Schumpeter have argued, no capitalist wants to operate in fully competitive markets because that is not where the biggest profits are made. They are made in monopolies or oligopolies. That is why the spur for economic change is not market competition but how to keep out of such competition. Thus the process of homogenization stimulates tourism entrepreneurs to escape from fully competitive markets by innovating, that is, by offering new tourism services and/or opening up new niche markets in different places of the city (Erkuş Öztürk & Terhorst, 2012).

The growth of tourism in single-asset cities is highly fragile because it is based on so-called localization economies (instead of urbanization economies) (Polèse, 2009; Sheng & Tsui, 2009). In addition, the development of tourism places follows the same life cycle as "Tourism Area Life Cycles" (Butler, 2011) which implies that it is not until the stagnation phase of the life cycle that tourism entrepreneurs become interested in diversification and pro-active strategies.

According to the tourism area life cycle model, it is during the growth phase of a tourism place that astute potential developers seek new locations with lower costs, untouched resources, and greater opportunities for expansion (Butler, 2011, p. 5). In addition, if the carrying capacity of a resort threatens to be exceeded, the relative appeal of the resort decreases and becomes less competitive, as is reflected in a decline of visitors (Butler, 2011). It is not until then that new solutions to attract the tourists are searched that, when found, would again guarantee the attractiveness for a certain time. In most resorts, however, it is only when decline, or initially stagnation, occurs that much attention is paid to pro-active planning and development rather than reactive measures (Butler, 2011, p. 7).

However, if these pro-active planning strategies are applied to tourism cities, then it stimulates diversification of that sector. For instance, the success of Las Vegas relies on continued renovation, replacement, and addition of its attractions which is based on the crucial role of appropriate interventions by major developers and their collaboration with and support from local and state administrations (Butler, 2011, p. 9). Recent local development literature has also pointed out the importance of collaboration/networking between institutions (Belussi, 1996; Tödtling, 1994) and interfirm relationships (Camagni, 1991) which are defined as factors of knowledge transfer between companies that induce creative diversified projects and innovations.

It is stated that the more an economy is diversified, the more knowledge spillovers are generated through local interfirm relations in related industries that enable firms to tap new (tacit) knowledge (Boschma & Iammarino, 2009; Frenken, Van Oort, & Verburg, 2007). It is claimed in the regional geography literature that the relation between companies which have a close cognitive distance (Noteboom, 2000) in local economic activities is a necessary precondition to innovation and, therefore competitive advantage (Cooke, 2007). Thus in a situation of "related variety" there exists a relationship, a relatedness (Lazzeretti, Capone, & Cinti, 2010), among industrial sectors and economic activities in terms of (effective and potential) competences, innovations, and transfers of knowledge. The main advantage of "related industries" is the higher capacity to absorb innovations from neighboring sectors. So, whether or not the situation is the same for hotels is examined in this chapter. To what extent do they develop diversified products to become more competitive and how do they handle homogenization tendencies and the fragile nature of single-asset tourism cities?

It is doubtful whether a high urban tourism growth in a single-asset tourism city implies an ever stronger specialization and, therefore, a locked-in process of path-dependent urban economic development. In this chapter, contrary to above-mentioned arguments that multi-asset cities have better opportunities to diversification and differentiation in niche markets (Florida, 2002; Jacobs, 1969, 1984), it is claimed that even in single-asset tourism places a growth of tourism, by time, stimulates tourism actors to diversify their products and overcome the stagnation phase of the tourism area life cycle.

In this chapter, the opportunities of the single-asset tourism city, Antalya, to diversify its tourism products will be explored by focusing on hotels as one of the main agents of tourism. Thus the question is tried to be answered whether or not tourism growth in a single-asset city stimulates hotels to diversify their products and to become more innovative. If the answer is positive, then the factors (such as company type, company size, intra-industry investments, and collaboration with other companies) influencing product and service diversification/innovation will be examined. Studies are still far from revealing the factors that influence diversification/innovation in tourism. Therefore, this chapter will take these arguments one step further by combining and exploring the relationship between firm size/type, interfirm collaboration, intra-industry investments as an indicator of the influence of related variety and innovation/product diversification of hotels.

In this context, three questions are put forward in this study to identify the level of diversification of hotels. Does the level of diversification/innovation change according to the size of tourism companies? To what extent does collaboration with other hotels and membership of business associations matter for diversification of hotels? And do investments and employment in the hotel industry matter for product diversification and innovation of hotels?

METHOD

Antalya tourism city (Turkey) is selected as a case-study area not only because of its dominant role in the country's tourism (it attracts yearly more than 10 million tourists in recent years) as a single-asset tourism city, but also because of its diversification tendency based on a statistic analysis. After having evaluated the results of a quantitative analysis on sectoral diversification, the factors that influence the diversification of hotels will be explored by analyzing primary data taken from in-depth interviews with hotels. To define the sample for making face-to-face interviews with hotels, the unit of analysis and the data universe were defined firstly. A total of 66 hotels were found in the city center of Antalya with varying sizes and types such as 5,4,3,2-star hotels and boutique hotels. A 50% sampling is applied (95% confidence level) while making face-to-face interviews with all types of hotels. While choosing the samples for each type of hotel category, an equal distribution was tried to be made on the coastal location of hotels.

Face-to-face interviews were designed on three groups of questions. The first group tries to reveal the company type and size-related questions, the second group tries to find out the relation between interfirm collaboration as well as membership of business associations and their contribution to diversified, innovative products, and the last group of questions is based on defining types and numbers of diversified products and services. The interviews were completed between January and March 2014. Based on the data we got from different types of hotels, primary evaluations were made on the basis of a simple share-based cross-tabulation technique which is the well-known exploratory data analysis technique for showing similarities and differences among variables. While evaluating the level of innovation (soft innovation) and diversified products and services, the number of different products and services offered to tourists which are not served in other hotels (like special small gifts to tourists in their birthdays, honeymoons, national holidays, surprise gifts and services in the rooms, special and organic meal services and organic bath equipment into their rooms, tree planting especially for repeaters in the garden of hotel, private call buttons for services, technological applications in rooms, tables and sport activities, private personnel for each floor, Michelin-Star chef meals, molecular cooking, etc.) are taken as indicator of the level of diversification/innovation.

FINDINGS

In this section, firstly, the level of innovation/diversification in hotels of Antalya is explored by examining whether or not hotels in a single-asset city diversify their products and become more diversified in terms of product and services. Secondly, the factors (such as company size, intra-industry investments, collaboration with other companies and membership of associations that influence product and service diversification/innovation) are evaluated on the basis of the questions mentioned above.

First of all, only 47% of the hotels in Antalya seem to supply innovative/diversified products and services. However, the degree of innovation/diversification varies with type of hotels. When the diversification/innovation level of hotels is cross-tabulated with type of hotels, a high innovation/diversification in product and services is mainly seen in 5-star hotels — 70% of the 5-star hotels innovate/diversify and 60% of 5-star hotels are innovative at the highest level. Boutique hotels are the second important group that is innovative at the highest level compared to other hotel types. Boutique hotels have some products and services that show both a high innovation level (12.5%) and a low innovation level (25%). However, 3,4-star hotels have not realized any high innovation in their products and services, and most of them are not innovative in products and services at all (their non-innovation varies between 40% and 80%). They have some products and services covering low innovation varying between 20% and 60%.

One of the main questions of this study is whether the level of diversification/innovation varies with the size of hotels? According to the findings, it seems that there is a strong connection between the size of hotels and innovative products and services. A 100% of high innovation in products and services is only seen in big hotels — 67% of small hotels, 17% of medium-sized hotels, and 16% of big hotels have not realized any innovation in products and services (Table 1).

Except boutique hotels, the shares of diversified products of small companies and hotels are low when compared to medium- and large-sized tourism companies. It seems, according to the findings, that hotels which are big and have 5 stars tend to have a high level of innovation and diversification of their products and services. This finding for hotels is in line with discussions in local development literature, and in line with some previous tourism studies on hotels. According to Erkuş-Öztürk (2010), due to an increased uncertainty in the sector and an ever more critical demand of consumers, big hotels in Antalya have been stimulated to be more creative to attract tourists.

Regarding the second question on the relation between collaboration with related companies and membership of associations on the one hand and degree of diversified projects of tourism companies on the other, a

Table 1. Company Size and Diversification/Innovation Level.

Number of Diversification & Innovation in Products & Services	Small-Sized Hotels	Medium-Sized Hotels	Big-Sized Hotels	Grand Total
No innovation	12 (67%)	3 (17%)	3 (16%)	18
Low innovation (1−2)	5 (43%)	1 (14%)	5 (43%)	7
Medium innovation (3−4)	2 (67%)	1 (33%)	0 (0%)	3
High innovation (5−8)	0 (0%)	0 (0%)	6 (100%)	6
Grand total	19 (56%)	5 (15%)	10 (29%)	34

Note: Low innovation: 1−2 innovations in hotels; Medium innovation: 3−4 innovations; and High innovation: 3−8 innovations.

cross-tabulation table has been made. With respect to the relation between number of collaborative projects realized with member associations and innovative product/service development, the most innovative/diversifying hotels are the ones that are members of collaborative tourism associations. Especially 57% of the highest diversified product hotels have a minimum of 3−4 memberships to these collaborative tourism associations and the remaining 43% of them have a minimum of 1−2 memberships to them. However, hotels which have a low level of membership to those collaborative associations (varying between 3 and 4 associations) have no innovative/diversified products at the highest level (minimum 3−8 diversified products). Hotels that are not member of any of these collaborative tourism associations do not have highly diversified innovative products and services. They have only a low level (22%) of innovative/diversified product development (Table 2). It seems that the level of innovative product development is associated with the level of membership to collaborative tourism associations for hotels. This finding is also in line with what has been claimed in previous local development and tourism studies.

To evaluate the relation between innovation/diversification and the existence of collaboration with other companies, hotels which show collaboration with other companies could also be taken as a good indicator to evaluate the contribution of collaboration to diversified product and service development. According to the findings, 89% of hotels which collaborate with other companies have both a high and a low level of innovation in their services and products − 68% of the hotels which do not collaborate with other companies have no innovative product or service development. These findings show that collaboration between hotels is an important

Table 2. Collaboration with Associations and Diversification/ Innovation Level.

Diversified Innovative Tourist Product or Service	No Membership to Associations	Low (1−2) Membership to Associations	High (3−8) Memberships to Associations	Grand Total
No innovation	3 (17%)	15 (83%)	0 (0%)	18 (100%)
Low innovation	2 (22%)	6 (67%)	1 (11%)	9 (100%)
High innovation	0 (0%)	3 (43%)	4 (57%)	7 (100%)
Grand total	5 (15%)	24 (71%)	5 (14%)	34 (100%)

Note: Low innovation: 1−3 innovations in hotels and High innovation: 3−8 innovations.

factor for evaluating the correlation with innovation and diversification. These findings verify the claim of Tödtling and Kaufmann (2001) and Erkuş-Öztürk (2010) on company size, collaboration, and innovation.

The last question defined in this study is on the relation between intra-industry knowledge-spillovers and its relation with diversification of hotels. Investments in the hotel sector and hotel employment are evaluated as an indicator of intra-industry knowledge-spillovers. In this context, first, intra-industry investments and its association with diversified product development is analyzed. Owning another hotel is taken as an indicator of an intra-industry investment. When the relation between investments in hotels and innovative product development is evaluated, a strong association between innovative product/service development and hotel investments is seen. It seems that 65% of all hotels (29% at the lowest level of innovation, 36% at the highest level of innovation) which have made an investment in that sector (having other hotels), have developed innovative products and services − 65% of hotels which own no other hotels have not developed new products and services. According to the first findings, it can be stated that hotels that are investing within the sector tend to develop more innovative and diversified services and products compared to the hotels without intra-industry investments (Table 3).

With respect to the debate on knowledge spillovers and their influence on innovation, the background of hotel workers is analyzed below. So, the question to what extent the background of hotel workers influencing for innovative product development is explored. Firstly, a high (3−8 innovative products) and a low (1−3 innovative products) level of innovation/diversification are distinguished on basis of the data. Then, the level of intra-industry movement of workers is defined on the basis of three scales,

Table 3. Having Other Hotel Investment and Diversification/Innovation Level.

Innovative/Diversified Products for Tourists	No Other Hotel	Having Other Hotel	Grand Total
No innovation	13 (65%)	5 (36%)	18 (53%)
Low innovation	5 (25%)	4 (29%)	9 (26%)
High innovation	2 (10%)	5 (36%)	7 (21%)
Grand total	20 (100%)	14 (100%)	34 (100%)

Note: Low innovation: 1−3 innovations in hotels and High innovation: 3−8 innovations.

namely a large number of workers coming from other hotels, a medium number of workers coming from other hotels, and a small number of workers coming from other hotels.

The findings show an association between a high diversification and a large number of workers who worked in other hotels before. The most innovative hotels are the ones that employ most workers who were employed by other hotels before. In total, hotels which have high and medium level of innovation in their products and services are the ones that employ workers, 50–100% of whom worked in another hotel before (Table 4). A 70% of hotels that employ a large number of workers who worked in other hotels before have developed innovative products and services. Most of the hotels which employ workers who worked outside the hotel industry before have not developed innovative/diversified products and services.

These findings clearly show the influence of intra-industry knowledge-spillovers and a short cognitive distance in producing innovative services in the tourism sector, specifically in hotels. This is in line with what is seen in many other sectors discussed in the local economic development literature (Boschma & Iammarino, 2009; Cooke, 2007; Frenken et al., 2007; Noteboom, 2000).

CONCLUSION AND IMPLICATIONS

As competitiveness of cities and companies has become increasingly crucial in the global economy, diversification and innovation are taken as key solutions to the development strategies of cities and companies. They are

Table 4. Within Sector Worker and Diversification/Innovation Level.

Level of Within Sector Employment	No Innovation/ Diversification	Low Innovation/ Diversification	High Innovation/ Diversification	Grand Total
No	5 (28%)	2 (22%)	0 (0%)	7 (21%)
Low	3 (16%)	0 (0%)	0 (0%)	5 (15%)
Medium	5 (28%)	2 (22%)	1 (14%)	6 (18%)
High	5 (28%)	5 (56%)	6 (86%)	16 (47%)
Grand total	18 (100%)	9 (100%)	7 (100%)	34 (100%)

Notes: High: 80–100% workers coming from hotels; Medium: 60–80% workers coming from hotels; Low: 1–50% workers coming from hotels, No: none of the workers coming from hotels.
Low innovation: 1–3 innovations in hotels and High innovation: 3–8 innovations.

especially very crucial to tourism cities and tourism destinations in reducing their economic fragility, in coping with the stagnation phase of tourism area life cycles, and a possible negative impact of localization economies. Defining diversification levels, types and factors that influence diversification of tourism companies and destinations becomes very crucial against the background of an ever exacerbating competitiveness in the global economy. Due to the risk of falling into a strong homogenization – the main pitfall of tourism places and companies – defining diversification levels and innovation strategies, especially for tourism places which serve standardized all-inclusive services is very important. For this reason, Antalya mass-tourism city is taken as a case-study area to define diversification tendencies of hotels dominated by tour operators and an all-inclusive system of service provision. The current system in Antalya stimulates hotels of varying sizes and types to copy the diversification strategies of big tour-operator oriented hotels which, in time, leads to homogenization and is a risky development in the long term. However, the counter strategies of hotels that really want to distinguish themselves from others should be carefully analyzed to make them more competitive in the tourism market.

Given this aim, hotels in Antalya city center were interviewed. The findings, first, show that their diversification and innovative product- and service-development varies with their size, type, collaboration with other hotels and member tourism associations, and intra-industry investments and knowledge of workers as a result of intra-industry job hopping. Especially big, 5-star hotels show a clear tendency to diversify their products and services compared to the others in the city. This is also seen even in some 5-star hotels located in the city center. Indeed, it is logical that big companies have the financial means to try something new. In the tourism case, the bigger the hotel, the larger the amount of money spent on its growth strategy to diversify its services. Growth of hotels is realized through a diversification of services.

Secondly, the findings show that hotels that collaborate with other hotels and are member of tourism associations diversify their products and services more than others do. This collaboration is generally seen in hotels around the Aksu-Kundu tourism zone which show a high rate of membership of tourism associations. Collaboration between hotels is stimulated by being located in the same zone. The same applies to collaboration between hotels and tourism associations located around the Lara-Kundu zone. However, hotels in the city center hardly collaborate. This could be related with their spatial segregation from the tourism zone as well as the supply of tourism services by other institutions in the city center.

Thirdly, hotels that benefit more from intra-industry knowledge-spillovers tend to produce more diversified, innovative products than other hotels. This is clearly seen in hotels which have invested in other hotels: it indicates that they have a lot of knowledge of the sector. Moreover, this is also seen in the background of workers in those hotels. If hotel workers have built up working experience in other hotels, they increase the success of hotels in innovating and diversifying its services and products.

Although the factors that contribute to diversification of hotels are important and are examined in this study, other factors influencing the diversification in tourism sector should also be discussed, broadly explained and empirically tested for different tourism companies. Factors influencing diversification in tourism places should also be analyzed at the city sectoral level comparatively to find a solution to the discussion in the literature on how to handle fragility of tourism places.

ACKNOWLEDGMENT

The author thanks the Scientific Council of Turkey (TUBITAK) for funding this research (Project No:112K443) on Economic Diversification and Homogenization in Tourism Cities: The Case of Antalya.

REFERENCES

Belussi, F. (1996). Local systems, industrial districts and institutional networks: Towards a new evolutionary paradigm of industrial economics. *European Planning Studies,* *4*(1), 5−26.

Boschma, R., & Iammarino, S. (2009). Related, trade linkages, and regional growth in Italy. *Economic Geography, 85*(3), 289−311.

Butler, R. W. (2011). *Tourism area life cycles, contemporary tourism reviews.* Oxford: Goodfellow Publishers Ltd.

Camagni, R. (1991). Local milieu, uncertainty and innovation networks: Towards a new dynamic theory of economic space. In R. Camagni (Ed.), *Innovation networks* (pp. 121−144). London: Belhaven.

Cooke, P. (2007). To construct regional advantage from innovation systems first build policy platforms. *European Planning Studies, 15*(2), 179−194.

Erkuş-Öztürk, H. (2010). The significance of networking and company size in the level of creativeness of tourism companies: Antalya case. *European Planning Studies*, *18*(8), 1247−1266.

Erkuş Öztürk, H., & Terhorst, P. (2012). Urban tourism as a generator of economic diversification? In Regional Studies Association Research Network Conference on Tourism, Regional Development and Public Policy, Knowledge Dynamics in the Diversification of Mass Tourism: Challenges for European and Mediterranean Destinations, Antalya, Turkey, 25−27 January.

Florida, R. (2002). *The rise of the creative class and how it's transforming work, leisure and everyday Life*. New York, NY: Basic Books.

Frenken, K., Van Oort, F. G., & Verburg, T. (2007). Related variety, unrelated variety and regional economic growth. *Regional Studies*, *41*(5), 685−697.

Jacobs, J. (1969). *The economy of cities*. New York, NY: Random House.

Jacobs, J. (1984). *Cities and the wealth of nations − Principles of economic life*. New York, NY: Random House.

Kaufmann, A., & Tödtling, F. (2001). Science-industry interaction in the process of innovation: The importance of boundary-crossing between systems. *Research Policy*, *30*(5), 791–804.

Lazzeretti, L., Capone, F., & Cinti, T. (2010). The regional development platform and "related variety": Some evidence from art and food in Tuscany. *European Planning Studies*, *18*(1), 27–45.

Noteboom, B. (2000). *Learning and innovation in organizations and economies*. Oxford: Oxford University Press.

Polèse, M. (2009). *The wealth and poverty of regions: Why cities matter*. Chicago, IL: University of Chicago Press.

Porter, M. (1990). *The competitive advantage of nations*. London: Macmillan.

Sheng, L., & Tsui, Y. M. (2009). Casino booms and local politics: The city of Macao. *Cities*, *26*(2), 67−73.

Sørensen, F. (2007). The geographies of social networks and innovation in tourism. *Tourism Geographies*, *9*(1), 22−48.

Terhorst, P., & Erkuş Öztürk, H. (2012). Economic diversification in a multi-asset and a single-asset tourism places: Amsterdam and Antalya compared. Regional Studies Association's European Conference on Networked regions and cities in times of fragmentation: Developing smart, sustainable and inclusive places, Delft, Netherlands, 13−16 May.

Tödtling, F. (1994). The uneven landscape of innovation poles: Local embeddedness and global networks. In A. Amin & N. Thrift (Eds.), *Globalisation, institutions and regional development in Europe* (pp. 68−90). Oxford: Oxford University Press.

CHAPTER 13

THE BRANDED CONTENT IN THE BALEARIC HOTEL CHAINS

Ángela Aguiló Lemoine,
Maria Antonia García Sastre and
Margarita Alemany Hormaeche

ABSTRACT

The purpose of this chapter is to emphasize the importance that the branded content has acquired when it comes to increasing the companies' brand knowledge in general, and particularly, the hotel chains, analyzing the implantation of this strategy in the Ushuaïa Ibiza Beach Hotel. The methodology applied is the content analysis, studying the presence of the hotel from Ibiza in Facebook and Twitter although mainly studying which are the contents published by Ushuaïa Beach Hotel that generate a bigger engagement with its target audience. The sample period goes for one year, from January 2012 to January 2013. The results show that its key to success is to publish contents that seduce its audience involving it voluntarily and taking part in it.

Keywords: Prosumer; brand awareness; marketing strategy; engagement

Tourism and Hospitality Management
Advances in Culture, Tourism and Hospitality Research, Volume 12, 187–196
Copyright © 2016 by Emerald Group Publishing Limited
All rights of reproduction in any form reserved
ISSN: 1871-3173/doi:10.1108/S1871-317320160000012014

INTRODUCTION

In developed countries, attention has become a scarce commodity. Nowadays there are a lot of users that surf the Net and search for information on mobile devices at the same time that they watch television or they are connected to Internet at any moment or any place. This issue has caused consumers to be considered as multitask viewers and that companies have more difficulty to raise them.

New communication channels on the net have changed the model of understanding marketing and communication. The Internet and social media have favored more interactivity and more fluency in the conversations between people. The user is not only an advertising message receptor, thanks to the ability to generate content in the 2.0 web, any person is able to be a prosumer (Sheehan, 2012); that is people not only consume information, but they also create it. In this sense, excess of information and the ease of accessing it has brought out that information competes with each other, from which has emerged the concept of attention economy.

Additionally, the crisis of conventional media and traditional publicity as well as audience fragmentation has caused more difficulty for companies in raising their target audience, which is more demanding and informed every time (Aguado, 2008). A report published by the consultant Infoadex (2014) points out that publicity inversion in the traditional media (television, newspapers, radios, magazines, ...) has decreased to less than half between 2007 and 2013.

Nevertheless the fall of traditional media is balanced with a high rise on the Net with an increase of 86%.

A significant fact is that in 2007 the Internet had a 6% market share and was on the sixth position after television, radios, etc., whereas in 2013 it had a 21% market share, only overcome by television.

In addition, since 2011 the participation of mobile technology as a part of the Internet with an important growth year after year is significant, although it will be good to see its evolution in the next few years.

On the other hand, many online advertisements are disturbing and annoying for the user, so they deteriorate the surfing experience. The Internet user only wants to read news or visualize a video, therefore one uses all the ways to avoid publicity. In this way, a lot of online publicity is a copy of the television model.

According to a report made in February 2014 by Rhythm NewMedia about the publicity in online videos, only a 31% of users would accept this kind of advertisement as long as they could see quality content for free.

A total of 13.5% stated that they would accept disappointment, a 24.3% would accept it occasionally, while a 31.4% would not accept. Therefore, many companies end up setting online campaigns with unidirectional messages that generate more annoyance than sales to the Internet user.

THEORETICAL CONSIDERATIONS

Since the emergence of the Internet, companies have had to focus on redefining their marketing strategies; they have to change the communication code of their brands to raise the final consumer since information saturation has reduced the efficacy of their advertising messages. Now users are more informed, therefore they are more demanding with the brands.

The paid media is still important for companies but it is the least reliable for consumers. Own media, and mostly, earned media, have gained importance when it comes to impacting final consumers.

Currently companies look for new ways to generate engagement with their audience. Nowadays companies want to build solid, strong, reciprocal, permanent, and long-lasting relations between their brands and their consumers with the aim of achieving more brand awareness.

On a globalized economy, individuals do not buy brands for their reasonable attributes, but for the experiences (Pine & Gilmore, 1999), and consequently for the emotions. When an individual buys a product or a service, he/she gets a tangible good or a combination of intangible activities respectively. Nevertheless, when the consumer gets an experience, what he/she really gets is the pleasure of unforgettable events that will last for a long time.

Currently, it is important for companies and their brands to offer experiences to individuals in order to get users involved in the company and to be not only clients, but also brand fans.

Companies, aware of how difficult is to reach their target audience, have decided to come forward in their experiential marketing strategies applying branded content techniques with the aim of positioning themselves in the consumer's mind (Regueira Mourente, 2012).

Branding allows companies to differentiate between them and in this process they highlight the importance of not only the products and services that they offer, but also the perceptions, sensations, and emotions that their consumers can reach. In this way the companies' core idea is to achieve an engagement with their target audience (Brakus, Schmitt, & Zarantonello, 2009), since the engagement leads to consumer trust and loyalty.

Companies can establish this link not only through offers, but also through experiences or linking the brand directly to hobbies. The audience chooses brands that define their personal identity and reflect the position that they take up in the society (Vallet Saavedra, 2006).

The web 2.0 and social media development has positioned, more than ever, the user in a privileged situation as he/she acts in a collaborative, participative, and interactive way, and he/she can viralize brand content (Maciá & Gosende, 2011). Nowadays consumers trust what a user says or does about a brand rather than what a brand says about itself. So in the current context the consumer is an ambassador of the own brand through the gained media.

Accordingly, companies are developing new marketing strategies: instead of searching strictly publicity impact, companies try to get their own consumers to spread the brand values. Companies have to empathize with their audience offering them offline and online experiences, that is, to listen to the audience valuation and wishes, showing that their opinions are important.

More and more companies are aware of the active role that users have at the time to increase their reputation. Nowadays consumers are the ones that take the initiative when consuming advertising contents. One of the exponents of this new marketing strategy to increase the brand fame is the branded content, a strategy where companies generate a relevant content for the consumer with the aim to reinforce the brand values without using a publicity speech.

The last purpose of the branded content is to create an emotional link in a direct but non-invasive way between brands and consumers. This content generation is any entertainment content, information or education that is done without direct messages encouraging purchase.

METHOD

Currently there are a few scientific investigations related to branded content. In fact, most of the contributions are rather recent and they come from the corporate sector, especially from marketing professionals.

Going in-depth analyzing the concept and the practices of the branded content, it is opportune to apply the case method as a learning method based on experience, in real and complex situations in a context that brings the researcher closer to the business environment.

An ideal analysis context to set goals in this research is to describe the corporate practice linked to branded content contrasted with theoretical communication models.

This research shows the implementation level linked to the brand in relation to the main touristic market in the Balearic Islands, that is, the hotel industry had 423,282 hotel beds in 2013. According to the "top 10" ranking by Hosteltur in 2013, 6 out of 10 Spanish hotel chains with more International presence are from the Balearic Islands.

This research has required a detailed analysis of the different brand strategies that the main hotel groups are carrying out in the Balearic Islands as well as a search of their presence in the digital environment. In the connectivity era, brands also have to consolidate themselves in the digital market.

However, the present chapter just focuses on Ushuaïa Ibiza Beach Hotel case that is an example of best practice for its branded content strategy to create engagement with its target market through its own media and earned media.

The content analysis is the basis of the methodology. Although this methodology is usually used as a quantitative research technique, it is also used as a qualitative technique. The sample period is one year, from January 2012 to January 2013.

FINDINGS

Main hotel chains have already assumed that in order to be competitive, it is important to focus their effort on creating links with the users' community that follows them, as we can see in the rankings that analyze the number of followers and fans in Twitter and Facebook in 2013.

The Palladium Hotel Group is a paradigmatic case. Tables 1 shows as in Facebook the hotel chain was on fourth place in 2012 with 22,746 fans and went up to the second place in 2013 with 356,113 fans, that is an increase of a 1465.6%. Table 2 shows that in Twitter it moved from the second place in 2012 with 45,499 followers to first in 2013 with 112,103 followers, that is an increase of a 146.4%.

In both cases, the hotel chain has increased spectacularly the number of followers in Facebook and Twitter, making a total of 478,216 followers in 2013. In this sense, after analyzing in detail the different brands that

Table 1.   Balearic Island Hotel Chains Ranking as for Number of Followers on Facebook.

Hotel Chain	Facebook			
	Fans 2012	Fans 2013	Ranking Facebook 2012	Ranking Facebook 2013
Meliá Hotels International	538.241	808.637	1	1
Palladium Hotel Group	22.746	356.113	4	2
Riu Hotels & Resorts	144.215	282.913	2	3
Iberostar Hotels & Resorts	67.049	135.006	3	4
Barceló Hotels & Resorts	14.984	94.414	6	5
Grupo Piñero	19.636	47.852	5	6

Source: Adapted from Revista Hosteltur (2013).

Table 2.   Balearic Island Hotel Chains Ranking as for Number of Followers on Twitter.

Hotel Chain	Twitter			
	Followers 2012	Followers 2013	Ranking Twitter 2012	Ranking Twitter 2013
Palladium Hotel Group	45.499	112.103	2	1
Barceló Hotels & Resorts	57.005	108.591	1	2
Meliá Hotels International	11.991	22.372	3	3
Riu Hotels & Resorts	8.742	17.914	4	4
Iberostar Hotels & Resorts	7.652	15.062	5	5
Grupo Piñero	1.136	2.794	6	6

Source: Adapted from Revista Hosteltur (2013).

the company has in Twitter and Facebook, 368,500 followers belong only to its brand Ushuaïa Ibiza Beach Hotel.

Ushuaïa Ibiza Beach Hotel belongs to Palladium Hotel Group, from the Empresas Matutes Group and it is a new touristic product pioneer in the Balearic Islands as it has incorporated the concept of theme as an argument to redefine the Ibiza's Hotel offer. The hotel combines in an innovative way touristic accommodation and leisure through an offer based on experiences oriented to a high purchasing power public, lover of electronic music, and latest digital trends.

Since its opening in 2011, Ushuaïa Ibiza Beach Hotel has become an inflection point in the social media management of the Palladium Hotel Group. Social media is not only a sales channel, but also a customer service channel and a way to get loyal customers.

Additionally, new technologies and the strategic use of social media have allowed the "Ushuaïa experience" to be brought up, linked to electronic music, to the online world. Consequently, the hotel has achieved a strong emotional link with its followers whom, through social media, spread the hotel contents thereby increasing its renown and taking part in the construction of a strong brand.

As we pointed out before, branded content is any content relevant to entertainment, information, or education that companies and their brands do with the aim of reinforcing their brand values without using an advertising discourse.

This strategy favors an engagement with its public; it makes loyal customers so it makes them users of their products and services. In this sense, Ushuaïa Ibiza Beach Hotel has specialized in creating branded content associated to entertainment, thanks to electronic music and "lifestyle Ushuaïa," a lifestyle linked to luxury.

At present videos are the star content on the Internet. Videos achieve an important number of viewers, likes, and retweets and their images last in the follower's brain, thanks to their capacity to recall experiences. Also it is a content that can be shared in the different social media.

In relation to this kind of contents, Ushuaïa Ibiza Beach Hotel is specialist at creating interest in its followers' community in the previous days of its events: the brand creates regularly teasers of the next parties and after-movies with a summary of the best moments of a live party. In this way, the brand converts a short live product into a lasting product.

Ushuaïa Ibiza Beach Hotel has an own channel in Youtube with 83 videos and around 6,000 subscribers that receive a notice every time that the hotel uploads new contents. With this strategy, the brand strengthens a link with its followers as the videos allow to remember experiences.

It should be pointed out that after writing in Youtube the words "Ushuaia Ibiza" appears about 171,000 results. Therefore, the brand followers have uploaded the most of the videos and they collaborate spreading the brand values.

Ushuaïa Ibiza Beach Hotel not only generates business through accommodation, but also it obtains benefit from its events' experiences. An Ushuaïa Ibiza Beach Hotel admirer wants more than an entry for the next party or offers to stay in the hotel, he/she wants to know all that is taking place in the hotel backstage, that is the reason the brand shares photos of the staff, gogos shows, aftermovies making offs, etc. on Facebook, Twitter, and Instagram.

On the other hand, as a hotel linked to electronic music, Ushuaïa Ibiza Beach Hotel is on Mixcloud, a social platform specially addressed to DJs and music producers. As it is a market niche very specialized in electronic music, the 5,230 users that follow the brand in this platform are very loyal as only the lovers of this kind of music have a profile on this platform. In addition the hotel offers audio streaming of its live parties on Facebook, so people who are not in the party can also enjoy it.

Mobile apps are a trend that has strengthened in recent years as a channel to achieve consumers. Ushuaïa Ibiza Beach Hotel, a pioneer in digital technology, has a web adapted to smartphones and tablet screens and it also has an own app (Ushuaïa Ibiza Mobile) for Apple and Android devices that does not copy the content of the corporate web.

The theme hotel also follows the gaming trend to involve its followers. It has created the game "Ushuaïa Dj Game," available on Facebook and in a mobile app.

Community managers also encourage the users to participate in social media where the brand is on and promote the engagement with the brand through competitions that are embraced with enthusiasm. In the same way, one of these initiatives in Twitter achieved a participation of 8,000 users and 10,000 tweets turning up Ushuaïa the first Spanish hotel trending topic.

Finally, another action promoted by Ushuaïa Ibiza Beach Hotel, promoting the link with the brand, is to select the hotel team through the fans community. Every season, the brand publishes job offers on Facebook and Twitter in order to make sure that the applicants are really fans.

CONCLUSION AND IMPLICATIONS

New technologies and social net are another important part when developing experiential marketing in Ushuaïa Ibiza Beach Hotel. In this sense, in the 2.0 environment the clue is that the brand does not sell a vacational accommodation, but an inspirational and emotional experience that connects at any time with its community, who are very loyal to the brand. Despite the summer season in Ushuaïa hotel lasting only 5 months and customers stay once or twice each summer, brand Community Managers offer relevant content all year round.

Ushuaïa Ibiza Hotel has perfectly understood that to be competitive and impact on their consumers, it has to develop a non-invasive publicity that generates an emotional link with the brand with the aim that users become scripters through the earned media.

Company community managers have brought the brand contents to the environment where the target is, offering an attractive content that has created passionate defenders of Ushuaïa Ibiza Beach Hotel, who not only spread their contents, but also generate brand content.

This fact confirms that in the 2.0 scenario, development of new products and services is not only a company matter, but the clients and their needs also take part in the brand structure.

Ushuaïa Ibiza Beach Hotel knows perfectly its target market and positions itself in the same level to mix with it. Not for nothing, the brand gets into conversations that take place on the internet and gives voice to users in their own media.

Also it should be noted that hotel community managers dominate storytelling perfectly, that is the art of telling stories. They do not persuade their target market by speaking of how nice their product is; the brand goes into the content context and is dependent on it, thanks to the fact that they offer relevant information to their followers to involve them and to connect with their lifestyle.

In conclusion, the value added by Ushuaïa Ibiza Beach Hotel is not the product or service itself offered, but is the ability to transfer the offline experiences to the online world and to create engagement with its fans' community through the branded content.

REFERENCES

Aguado, G. G. (2008). Branded content más allá del product placement en la televisión digital: Advertainment y licensing. *Revista del CES Felipe II, 8.*

Brakus, J. J., Schmitt, B. H., & Zarantonello, L. (2009). Brand experience: What is it? How is it measured? Does it affect loyalty? *Journal of Marketing, 73*, 52−68.

Hosteltur. (2013). *Las grandes cadenas refuezan su presencia en las redes sociales.* Retrieved from http://www.hosteltur.com/158030_grandes-cadenas-refuerzan-su-presencia-redes-sociales.html. Accessed on June 2013.

Infoadex. (2014). *Estudio Infoadex de la inversión publicitaria en España 2014*. Retrieved from http://www.infoadex.es/estudios.html. Accessed on February 2014.

Maciá, F., & Gosende, J. (2011). *Marketing con redes sociales: Guía práctica*. Madrid: Anaya Multimedia.

Pine, J., & Gilmore, J. (1999). *The experience economy*. Boston, MA: Harvard Business School Press.

Regueira Mourente, F. (2012). El contenido como herramienta eficaz de comunicación de marca. Análisis teórico y empírico (Tesis doctoral inédita, Universidad Rey Juan Carlos, Madrid).

Rhythm NewMedia. (2014). *Audience insights: Demographic trends in mobile video*. Retrieved from http://rhythmnewmedia.com/site/assets/files/1011/rhythm_mobile_video_demo graphics_q1_2014-1.pdf. Accessed on February 2014.

Sheehan, B. (2012). *Marketing online*. Barcelona: Ed. Blume.

Vallet Saavedra, G. (2006). E-Branding. La creación de una marca digital en la era de la conectividad (Tesis doctoral inédita, Universidad Autónoma de Barcelona).

CHAPTER 14

IDENTIFICATION OF ORGANIZATIONAL CULTURE IN THE HOSPITALITY INDUSTRY

Ali Bavik

ABSTRACT

A range of organizational culture scales have been developed and applied in various industries. However, the measurement of organizational culture is noticeably different according to industry. Measuring organizational culture, specifically as it relates to the hospitality industry, is also a research area that has remained relatively unexplored. The purpose of this chapter is to discuss some essential problems and gaps existing in the previous studies. This chapter also presents a new scale entitled the "hospitality industry organization culture scale" that applies specifically to the hospitality context, and contributes to our understanding of organizational culture within this context. A multidisciplinary and mixed-method research approaches were followed in order to develop a new organizational culture scale for the hospitality industry. The findings suggest that the hospitality industry has unique cultural characteristics that are distinguished from similar industries.

Keywords: Organizational culture; scale development; New Zealand

Tourism and Hospitality Management
Advances in Culture, Tourism and Hospitality Research, Volume 12, 197–210
Copyright © 2016 by Emerald Group Publishing Limited
All rights of reproduction in any form reserved
ISSN: 1871-3173/doi:10.1108/S1871-317320160000012015

INTRODUCTION

An understanding of organizational culture is considered to be one of the most important ways for shaping employee behavior and which could contribute positively to delivering organizational effectiveness (Lund, 2003). This implies that developing a concrete understanding of organizational culture and how this might best be measured is vital for a company's management so that the goals of their employees may be more accurately aligned with those of the organization.

The importance of organizational culture has received considerable attention in the field of organizational behavior. Over the past three decades, several researchers put their attention on conceptualization and measurement of organizational culture (Delobbe, Haccoun, & Vandenberghe, 2002; Schein, 1985; Wallach, 1983; Weinzimmer, Franczak, & Michel, 2008). The main areas of research on organizational culture to date focus on aspects of competitiveness, productivity, company sales, profitability, and growth of companies (e.g., Barney, 1986; Kotter & Heskett, 1992; Lund, 2003; Peter & Waterman, 1982). However the importance of industry, as a factor in defining organizational culture, has received considerably little attention (Tepeci & Bartlett, 2002). This holds especially true for the hospitality industry (which is one of the largest industries), where little attention has been paid to organizational culture. This is surprising because human involvement is considered an inherent and integral characteristic of the hospitality industry (Yavas & Konyar, 2003). In other words, the relationships between hosts and guests are more fragile than those in other industries (Hemmington, 2007; King, 1995; Walker & Miller, 2009). The distinct characteristics of the hospitality industry make organizational culture an important area of concern for this industry, particularly as organizational culture has the potential to affect employees' behaviors to a noticeable degree. There appears to be a discernible need for developing an understanding of organizational culture in this sector, as well as for developing a means for measuring this construct within the context of this industry (Dawson, Abbott, & Shoemaker, 2011; Tepeci & Bartlett, 2002).

THEORETICAL CONSIDERATIONS

Over the last three decades a range of organizational culture scales have been developed and applied in various industries. Despite the fact that there are several studies measuring organizational culture, two basic "typological" and "dimensional" approaches are presented in the literature.

The typological approach examines culture by means of classifying organizational culture according to various characteristics. Based on this approach, each organization is an amalgamation of different cultural dimensions and usually, one type of culture being noticeably more powerful or influential, compared with other culture types. For instance, Harrison's (1972) typology defines organizational culture as "organizational ideologies" that associate with employee behaviors and organizational change. Based on this cultural profile, the culture of organizations consists of four categories: power orientation, task orientation, person orientation, and role orientation. On the other hand, according to Wallach's (1983, p. 26) typology, organizational culture is "the shared understanding of an organization's employees — how we do things around here." This typology is also known as the "organizational culture index," which focuses on values, beliefs, and ethical behaviors and classifies culture as bureaucratic, innovative, and supportive forms.

Despite the fact that typological studies help define organizational culture and present a particular type of employee behavior (Lim, 1995), several studies argue that these studies are mainly descriptive, there is a potential to stereotype, categorize, and pass judgment on different types of culture. Therefore, the interpretation and implementation of the models in the more diverse industries are limited or problematic (Gregory, 1983; Henri, 2006; Smircich, 1983). According to Henri (2006), typological studies are not theory driven and focus on beliefs about how to manage rather than on beliefs about how to compete. Another difficulty about the typological studies is that classifications of cultural elements do not provide detail beyond the descriptive level of organizational culture (Xenikou, 1996). The potential problem is that organizational cultures may be misclassified, or necessary aspects may be ignored (Barney, 1991; Henri, 2006; Schein, 1990). Therefore, typologies of organizational culture make it complicated for researchers to choose the types of categories that researchers should use in an analysis (Jamieson, 1982).

The second type of approach is dimensional. In this approach, the main focus is finding organizational culture profiles (OCPs) by identifying cultural dimensions of organizations. Dimensional studies operationalize their studies based on validity and reliability. Therefore these studies preferred standardized questionnaires to gather survey data to identify cultural dimensions in organizations. Although there have been several studies on dimensional research in the literature, in terms of dimensional structure, a number of contradictions are evident from these studies (Chatman & Jehn, 1994).

One of the problems is that some studies focus on the one or more specific dimensions of organizational culture, while others present a more comprehensive range of dimensions. For example, Webster (1993) presents 34 items and 6 dimensions derived from factor analysis, with the 6 dimensions being service quality, interpersonal relationships, selling task, organization, internal communication, and innovation. On the other hand, Alexander (1978) presents 42 items and 10 dimensions: questions organizational and personal pride, performance excellence, teamwork and communication, leadership and supervision, cost-effectiveness and productivity, associate relations, citizen relations, innovation and creativity, training and development and candor, and openness.

Literature review indicates that the empirical formulation of organizational culture dimensions is also inconsistent with those dimensions that might be included in organizational culture models. The probable reason behind such inconsistency is that some organizational culture dimensions are unipolar while some are bipolar (Scott, Mannion, Davies, & Marshall, 2003). For example, some studies paired up a communication dimension with teamwork or openness (see Alexander, 1978; Tucker, McCoy, & Evans, 1990), whereas some researchers split communication into two dimensions, that is, "communication and openness" and "communication and teamwork" (see Christensen & Gordon, 1999; Glaser, Zamanou, & Hacker, 1987; Gordon, 1979). Therefore, studies explore different levels of organizational culture, resulting in different dimensions (Delobbe et al., 2002). In this sense, existing scales are inconsistent with dimensional structure and therefore generalization and content validity of these scales has been questioned (Weinzimmer et al., 2008).

Keeping this in mind, many of these studies adopt either a typological or a dimensional approach, yet a key question arises concerning the extent to which a scale developed for a selected industry can be generalized to another industry. A scale of organizational culture, initially developed, measured, operationalized in a specific industry and then applied to other industry settings, may be found to be not completely transferable in terms of the economic system, industry characteristics, context, and employee and/or customer relationships (Chatman & Jehn, 1994; Gordon, 1991). Therefore, developed scales that are appropriate for studying manufacturing businesses might be not applicable for service or hospitality industries due to these industries having different characteristics. Deal and Kennedy (1982) point out that industry characteristics and the nature of the business create different cultural types. In this regard, it would seem that a specific industry is being measured, the degree to which the related criteria are consistent with the nature of the industry, and internal as well as external factors, should be of paramount concern to the researcher.

Unlike other sectors, studies on organizational culture in the context of hospitality are limited. Among these studies there are two main approaches that have drawn researchers' attention. The first approach is the use of previously developed organizational culture scales for testing other organizational dimensions. For instance, Sparrowe (1994) focuses on the relationship between organizational culture and empowerment among employees in 33 hospitality organizations by using the Organizational Culture Inventory developed by Cooke and Lafferty (1989). Similarly, Iverson and Deery (1997) investigates on the existence of a turnover culture in the hotel industry using the scales developed by Agho, Mueller, and Price (1993) and Price and Mueller (1986), the researchers combine turnover variables (e.g., structural, pre-entry variables, environmental, union) with various organizational outcomes (e.g., job satisfaction, employee intention to leave).

The second approach is the development of industry-specific scales. For example, Kemp and Dwyer (2001) examine how organizational culture influences employee behaviors within the Regent Hotel in Sydney and how it affects organizational performance. Using Johnson's (1992) "Cultural Web" as a framework, they adopt qualitative methodology and interview 45 respondents including both bottom-line employees and managers. The study provides a clear picture of the organizational culture in the Regent Hotel in Sydney. In addition, they use multiple sources of data including document analysis of in-house publications, staff bulletin board notices, and advertising material as well as observed the interactions between both hotel staff and hotel staff and guests. A drawback of this research is that assumptions really cannot be made outside the scope of the selected hotel. Given the fact that their research is organization specific, generalizability of their conclusions is restricted (Janićijević, 2012).

Tepeci and Bartlett (2002) also develop industry-specific scale by combining various cultural dimensions in different scales and integrated them with those they developed for their study. The authors formed the Hospitality Industry Culture Profile based on O'Reilly, Chatman, and Caldwell (1991) OCP. To put more clearly, based on the OCP, they have added dimensions of valuing the customer, honesty, and ethics based on previous hospitality research (Woods, 1989) with a sample of 182 junior and senior hospitality management students. As the study only focuses on organizational values, it does not provide evidence particularly with regards the different layers of organizational culture, the artifacts, and the core assumptions.

It should be also noted that the OCP has been developed and tested in government agencies. There is a clear consensus in the literature that private and public sectors are different in terms of employee recruitment, employee motivation, intrinsic and extrinsic rewards, and management (Boyne & Walker, 2005; Budhwar & Boyne, 2004; Tansel, 2005). To illustrate, in terms of management, in the private sector the hierarchical order is a pyramid shape and the structure is based on top to bottom (Houston, 2000; Lewis & Frank, 2002). On the other hand, the public sector "is subject to the pressure of the press and to public scrutiny, it operates in a goldfish bowl" (Murray, 1975, p. 367). Therefore, the public sector has clear rules for employees while the private sector has more flexibility and employees are empowered to make decisions (Rainey, Backoff, & Levine, 1976). As highlighted earlier, industries have different values and assumptions; therefore using the OCP scale might be not applicable for service or hospitality industries due to these industries having very different characteristics.

There is also a specialized instrument for measuring organizational culture in the hospitality industry, which has been developed by Dawson et al. (2011). The aim of their study is to discover the attributes that are unique to hospitality organizations while identifying the characteristics and values of a person who would fit into hospitality industry culture. The researchers theoretically define relevant domains of the construct (organizational culture); invited hospitality professionals to review these, and to then rate and rank the identified items to confirm the final pool of items. Consequently, they identify six constructs that are unique to the hospitality industry.

While the studies of Tepeci and Bartlett (2002) and Dawson et al. (2011) make some progress in this area, they have some important methodological shortcomings. First, due to the terminological differences among instruments, drawing a clear boundary among them and differentiating them clearly from each other is nearly impossible. That is, alternative classifications and a variety of dimensions consisted in a scale is always possible, depending on the perspective taken by researchers. For example, Reynolds's (1986) scale emphasizes work values and work beliefs whereas Schall's (1983) communication. Such approaches lead to the problem of researchers shaping their analysis and mapping their methodology based on the scope of organizational culture adopted in previous studies. Second, both Tepeci and Bartlett (2002) and Dawson et al. (2011) administer their scales by inviting students as participants. As a sample, students possess only a very limited amount of industry work experience. Indeed, using students as subjects in empirical studies could lead to the problem of inadequate assessment of some on-job related variables such as job satisfaction and intent to quit (Dawson et al., 2011), as well as the issue of having a rather demographically homogenous sample (Tepeci & Bartlett, 2002). Here Gordon, Slade, and Schmitt (1986) critique this approach, claiming the use of students as subjects means the research suffers from a lack of external validity, thus the potential for generalizability to other populations, settings, and variables is compromised. Last but not least, although the two studies discussed above provide some conceptually and empirically sound results, the researchers only adopted a quantitative method for examining their scales. Therefore, the results of their studies are limited to the numerical descriptions provided without detailed description (Xenikou & Furnham, 1996).

METHOD

Considering the research gaps summarized above, this study develops a scale specifically for the hospitality industry. To overcome the shortcomings of adopting a single methodological approach, a hybrid methodological approach is adopted for guiding the current study. In fact, a multi-method (qualitative and quantitative) approach is extensively advocated among researchers in the (anthropology, sociology, and psychology) disciplines summarized below.

To identify organizational culture elements in the hospitality, the study primarily uses the scale development procedures of Churchill (1979), DeVellis (2003), Hinkin (1995), and Netemeyer, Bearden, and Sharma (2003). Initially, this entailed developing a preliminary definition of organizational culture, which was grounded in the existing literature on organizational culture. This helped specify the domain of the construct. The dimensional foundation of the constructs was an amalgamation of relevant literature and qualitative findings of the study. Guided by previous qualitative and quantitative research on organizational culture, this study combines interview approaches that have been developed in the fields of psychology, sociology, and anthropology. Consequently, 25 interview questions were generated in order to uncover different "layers" of organizational culture in the hospitality industry. These layers refer to the observable objects (artifacts), company philosophy (values), and beliefs, principles, patterns, and private conversations (assumptions).

Judgmental sampling was used to increase the participation rate. Particularly, the Qualmark New Zealand Hotel organization website was used for identifying where the majority of the hotels are located in New Zealand. Then, 18 interviews were conducted across different cities in New Zealand. The in-depth interviews sought to uncover culturally based values (Phillips, 1994), cultural beliefs, or knowledge structures (Sapienza, 1985). Data were collected from various departments of the hotels in order to grasp the characteristics of organizational culture as they pertain to the industry. Thematic analysis was used and items were coded based the method developed by Braun and Clarke (2006). This process results in 143 "items" with eight "dimensions." The items refer to a question or a statement used in a questionnaire; while dimensions relate to an abstract idea or an underlying theme that one wishes to measure using questionnaire items. Following the design of the first instrument, 14 "judges" were selected to check the content validity (Hair, Money, Samouel, & Page, 2007). These judges provide their comments based on content, readability, clarity, and representativeness criteria (Zaichkowsky, 1985). After rigorous analyses, 94 items are identified with eight dimensions. A Likert-type response format was used and five response categories are used in the questionnaire.

The next stage of the scale development procedure involves the first purification of the scale (DeVellis, 2003); this implies the computation of coefficient alpha for questionnaire items and each dimension. In addition to this it includes deletion of items whose item-to-total correlations are low and whose deletion increases coefficient alpha, and factor analysis to confirm the dimensionality of the overall scale (Churchill, 1979). By referring to previous studies, the researcher carried out a pilot study in order to produce more sound evidence to suit the purpose of the research. In the data collection process, 130 questionnaires are distributed, while 82 usable questionnaires are retrieved. Afterwards, exploratory factor analysis, item-to-total correlation, and Cronbach's alpha tests are used to analyze the data. These tests result in the generation of 58 items to form the questionnaire for main study.

The second stage purification of the scale is carried out with a new data set. The population for the main study consisted of employees who work in four, four plus, and five star accommodation establishments in New Zealand. Data are collected through convenience sampling technique. A total of 450 questionnaires are distributed to respondents. Consequently, 281 questionnaires were returned (62.4% response rate), and are used in the final analysis.

Similar to the pilot study for this research, rigorous data testing is employed in the main study, which includes the assessment of normality, Cronbach's alphas, and construct reliabilities. Subsequent to these being calculated convergent and discriminant validities are established. Consequently, confirmatory factor analysis is performed to verify the scale's dimensionality and to assess its psychometric properties.

FINDINGS

After the analysis, the nine dimensions were found, including: (1) level of cohesiveness, (2) ongoing-onboarding (3) work norms, (4) social motivation, (5) guest focus, (6) human resource management practices, (7) communication, (8) innovation, (9) job variety and each of these dimensions are briefly described below.

Dimension 1. Level of cohesiveness

The level of cohesiveness is defined as the degree, which organizational members tend to act jointly and cooperate with each other to accomplish the given tasks.

Dimension 2. Ongoing-onboarding

It is the ability of organizations to deliver its goals and objectives, through communication channel. In another words, organizations emphasize organizational standards about how things should be done through supervisors who possess a collective way of working.

Dimension 3. Work norms

Work norms are formal and informal rules, which are to protect the well-being of an organization.

Dimension 4. Social motivation

Social motivation refers to the managements' efforts in improving the well-being of subordinates as well as encouragement and motivation through social components, fostering individual and organizational effectiveness.

Dimension 5. Guest focus

Guest focus is defined as understanding and providing customized service based on their expectations. With other words, employees provide personalized service and aim to make guests feel at home and create them unique memories.

Dimension 6. Human resource management practices

Human resource management (HRM) practices refer to employee participation, empowerment, and job redesign, including team-based production systems, extensive employee training, and performance-contingent incentive compensation.

Dimension 7. Communication

Communication is defined as the way of sharing and exchanging of information with others.

Dimension 8. Innovation

Innovation dimension indicates the extent to which members are encouraged to produce new ideas to develop product/service and organization.

Dimension 9. Job variety

Job variety represents repeated patterns and the degree of work pace.

CONCLUSION AND IMPLICATIONS

Understanding the elements of organizational culture is important for executives as it helps these executives' direct activities and behaviors in a productive way and avoids the destructive influence of retaining employees who do not share the same set of values or who are not committed to the organization's goals. The hospitality industry organizational culture scale (HIOCS) can be considered a crucial instrument for the hospitality industry, which executives could consider in the management of employees in the hospitality industry. The HIOCS could be used as a diagnostic instrument to pinpoint areas where particular enhancements are necessary. The assessment of the scale can be used in the hospitality industry in several ways.

First, executives should be aware of the cultural elements on which their company relies on before they implement the HIOCS. This scale will enable executives to determine if there is a gap between organizational ideologies and the organization's actual culture. Second, assessing and profiling the dominant culture of an organization is essential for executives. The scale will help executives identify the core values that are held by most of the members in an organization. This will provide a better understanding about what happens behind the scenes within their organizations, and which might require improvement. Third, large organizations usually develop specific values or experiences that are unique to members of certain departments. The assessment of this scale could also potentially allow executives to identify if there are significant discrepancies among departments, and then identify which steps need to be taken, as an example, to improve communications, or more generally, to assist in streamlining communications between departments. In addition, it can be also used between different hierarchical levels, which may provide multilevel analysis of an organization's culture. Fourth, if an organization has numerous branches (hotels) in different geographic locations, OCPs for the individual branches can be used to identify the similarities and discrepancies with other branches. Finally, the assessment of the HIOCS can be used during the recruitment and selection efforts of an organization. The HRM department may compare perceptions of prospective applicants' personal characteristics with their company's culture.

To conclude, scholars have investigated organizational culture in different industries, but less attention has been paid to the hospitality industry. This study combines multidisciplinary approaches to uncover different layers of hospitality organizational culture while using multi-methodological research methods. The HIOCS, involving nine dimensions with 47 items, is shown to be clear, concise, and practical, and can be used as an assessment tool for the hospitality executives to diagnose their organizational culture compared with their company ideology.

REFERENCES

Agho, A. O., Mueller, C. W., & Price, J. L. (1993). Determinants of employee job satisfaction: An empirical test of a causal model. *Human Relations*, *46*(8), 1007–1027.

Alexander, M. (1978). Organizational norms opinionnaire. In J. W. Pfeiffer & J. E. Jones (Eds.), *The 1978 annual handbook for group facilitators* (pp. 81–88). La Jolla, CA: University Associates.

Barney, J. (1991). Firm resources and sustained competitive advantage. *Journal of Management*, *17*(1), 99–120.

Barney, J. B. (1986). Organizational culture: Can it be a source of sustained competitive advantage? *The Academy of Management Review*, *11*(3), 656–665.

Boyne, G. A., & Walker, R. M. (2005). Introducing the "determinants of performance in public organizations" symposium. *Journal of Public Administration Research and Theory*, *15*(4), 483–488.

Braun, V., & Clarke, V. (2006). Using thematic analysis in psychology. *Qualitative Research in Psychology*, *3*(2), 77–101.

Budhwar, P. S., & Boyne, G. (2004). Human resource management in the Indian public and private sectors: An empirical comparison. *The International Journal of Human Resource Management*, *15*(2), 346–370.

Chatman, J. A., & Jehn, K. A. (1994). Assessing the relationship between industry characteristics and organizational culture: How different can you be? *The Academy of Management Journal*, *37*(3), 522–553.

Christensen, E. W., & Gordon, G. G. (1999). An exploration of industry, culture and revenue growth. *Organization Studies*, *20*(3), 397.

Churchill, G. A. (1979). A paradigm for developing better measures of marketing constructs. *Journal of Marketing Research*, *16*, 64–73.

Cooke, R. A., & Lafferty, J. C. (1989). *Organisational culture inventory*. Plymouth, MA: Human Synergistic.

Dawson, M., Abbott, J., & Shoemaker, S. (2011). The hospitality culture scale: A measure organizational culture and personal attributes. *International Journal of Hospitality Management*, *30*(2), 290–300.

Deal, T., & Kennedy, A. (1982). *Corporate cultures: The rites and rituals of organizational life*. Reading, MA: Addison-Wesley.

Delobbe, N., Haccoun, R. R., & Vandenberghe, C. (2002). Measuring core dimensions of organizational culture: A review of research and development of a new instrument. Unpublished manuscript, Universite Catholique de Louvain, Belgium.

DeVellis, R. F. (2003). *Scale development – Theory and applications*. Thousand Oaks, CA: Sage.

Glaser, S. R., Zamanou, S., & Hacker, K. (1987). Measuring and interpreting organizational culture. *Management Communication Quarterly*, *1*(2), 173–198.

Gordon, G. G. (1979). *Managing management climate*. Lexington, MA: Lexington Books.

Gordon, G. G. (1991). Industry determinants of organizational culture. *The Academy of Management Review*, *16*(2), 396–415.

Gordon, M. E., Slade, L. A., & Schmitt, N. (1986). The "science of the sophomore" revisited: From conjecture to empiricism. *Academy of Management Review*, *11*(1), 191–207.

Gregory, K. L. (1983). Native-view paradigms: Multiple cultures and culture conflicts in organizations. *Administrative Science Quarterly*, *28*, 359–376.

Hair, J. F., Money, A. H., Samouel, P., & Page, M. (2007). *Research methods for business*. New York, NY: John Wiley.

Harrison, R. (1972). *Understanding your organisation's character*. Boston, MA: Harvard Business Review.

Hemmington, N. (2007). From service to experience: Understanding and defining the hospitality business. *The Service Industries Journal*, *27*(6), 747–755.

Henri, J.-F. (2006). Organizational culture and performance measurement systems. *Accounting, Organizations and Society*, *31*(1), 77–103.

Hinkin, T. R. (1995). A review of scale development practices in the study of organizations. *Journal of Management*, *21*(5), 967.

Houston, D. J. (2000). Public-service motivation: A multivariate test. *Journal of Public Administration Research and Theory*, *10*(4), 713–728.

Iverson, R. D., & Deery, M. (1997). Turnover culture in the hospitality industry. *Human Resource Management Journal*, *7*(4), 71–82.

Jamieson, I. (1982). The concept of culture and its relevance for an analysis of business enterprise in different societies. *International Studies of Management & Organization, 12*(4), 71−105.

Janićijević, N. (2012). The influence of organizational culture on organizational preferences towards the choice of organizational change strategy. *Economic Annals, 57*(193), 25−51.

Johnson, G. (1992). Managing strategic change − Strategy, culture and action. *Long Range Planning, 25*(1), 28−36.

Kemp, S., & Dwyer, L. (2001). An examination of organisational culture − the Regent Hotel, Sydney. *International Journal of Hospitality Management, 20*(1), 77−93.

King, C. A. (1995). What is hospitality? *International Journal of Hospitality Management, 14*(3−4), 219−234.

Kotter, J. P., & Heskett, J. L. (1992). *Corporate culture and performance.* New York, NY: Free Press.

Lewis, G. B., & Frank, S. A. (2002). Who wants to work for the government? *Public Administration Review, 62*(4), 395−404.

Lim, B. (1995). Examining the organizational culture and organizational performance link. *Leadership & Organization Development Journal, 16*(5), 16−21.

Lund, D. B. (2003). Organizational culture and job satisfaction. *Journal of Business & Industrial Marketing, 18*(3), 219−236.

Murray, M. A. (1975). Comparing public and private management: An exploratory essay. *Public Administration Review, 35*(1), 364−371.

Netemeyer, R. G., Bearden, W. O., & Sharma, S. (2003). *Scaling procedures: Issues and applications.* London: Sage.

O'Reilly III, C. A., Chatman, J., & Caldwell, D. F. (1991). People and organizational culture: A profile comparison approach to assessing person-organization fit. *Academy of Management Journal, 34*, 487−516.

Peter, T. J., & Waterman, R. H. (1982). *In search of excellence: Lessons from America's best-run companies.* New York, NY: Warner Book.

Phillips, M. E. (1994). Industry mindsets: Exploring the cultures of two macro-organizational settings. *Organization Science, 5*, 384−402.

Price, J. L., & Mueller, C. W. (1986). *Absenteeism and turnover of hospital employees.* Greenwich, CT: JAI Press.

Rainey, H. G., Backoff, R. W., & Levine, C. H. (1976). Comparing public and private organizations. *Public Administration Review*, 233−244.

Reynolds, P. D. (1986). Organizational culture as related to industry, position and performance: A preliminary report. *Journal of Management Studies, 23*(3), 333−345.

Sapienza, A. M. (1985). Believing is seeing: How culture influences the decisions top managers make. In R. Kilmann, R. Saxton, & M. J. Serpa (Eds.), *Gaining control of the corporate culture* (pp. 66−83). San Francisco, CA: Jossey-Bass.

Schall, M. S. (1983). A communication-rules approach to organizational culture. *Administrative Science Quarterly, 28*(4), 557−581.

Schein, E. H. (1985). How culture forms, develops, and changes. In R. Kilmann, R. Saxton, & M. J. Serpa (Eds.), *Gaining control of the corporate culture* (pp. 17−43). San Francisco, CA: Jossey-Bass.

Schein, E. H. (1990). Organizational culture. *American Psychologist, 45*(2), 109.

Scott, T., Mannion, R., Davies, H., & Marshall, M. (2003). The quantitative measurement of organizational culture in health care: A review of the available instruments. *Health Services Research, 38*(3), 923−945.

Smircich, L. (1983). Concepts of culture and organizational analysis. *Administrative Science Quarterly, 28*(3), 339—358.

Sparrowe, R. T. (1994). Empowerment in the hospitality industry: An exploration of antecedents and outcomes. *Journal of Hospitality & Tourism Research, 17*(3), 51—73.

Tansel, A. (2005). Public-private employment choice, wage differentials, and gender in Turkey. *Economic Development and Cultural Change, 53*(2), 453—477.

Tepeci, M., & Bartlett, A. (2002). The hospitality industry culture profile: A measure of individual values, organizational culture, and person-organization fit as predictors of job satisfaction and behavioral intentions. *International Journal of Hospitality Management, 21*(2), 151—170.

Tucker, R. W., McCoy, W. J., & Evans, L. C. (1990). Can questionnaires objectively assess organisational culture? *Journal of Managerial Psychology, 5*(4), 4—11.

Walker, J. R., & Miller, J. E. (2009). *Supervision in the hospitality industry: Leading human resources.* New York, NY: John Wiley.

Wallach, E. J. (1983). Individuals and organizations: The cultural match. *Training & Development Journal, 37*, 29—36.

Webster, C. (1993). Refinement of the marketing culture scale and the relationship between marketing culture and profitability of a service firm. *Journal of Business Research, 26*(2), 111—131.

Weinzimmer, L. G., Franczak, J. L., & Michel, E. J. (2008). Culture-performance research: Challenges and future directions. *Journal of the Academy of Business & Economics, 8*(4), 152—162.

Woods, R. H. (1989). More alike than different: The culture of the restaurant industry. *Cornell Hotel and Restaurant Administration Quarterly, 30*(2), 82—97.

Xenikou, A. (1996). A Correlational and factor analytic study of four questionnaire measures of organizational culture. *Human Relations, 49*(3), 349—371.

Xenikou, A., & Furnham, A. (1996). A correlational and factor analytic study of four questionnaire measures of organizational culture. *Human Relations, 49*(3), 349—371.

Yavas, B. F., & Konyar, K. (2003). Cultural and economic determinants of managerial perceptions of quality. *Journal of Asia-Pacific Business, 4*(4), 3—23.

Zaichkowsky, J. L. (1985). Measuring the involvement construct. *Journal of Consumer Research, 12*(3), 341—352.

PART III
TOURISM EDUCATION AND TRAINING

CHAPTER 15

DEVELOPING TRAINING PROGRAMS FOR DISABLED GUESTS: AN INDUSTRY PERSPECTIVE

Funda Cengiz

ABSTRACT

As an alternative way of tourism, disabled tourism has its own character-istics due to the fact that disabled tourists are likely to have different needs and expectations throughout their vacations at a destination. Therefore, this chapter aims to provide a generic overview of disabled tourism and identify if there would be any requirements for developing training programs and examine their contexts. The discussion of results is based on undertaking an interview survey among the executive man-agers of travel agencies and hotel businesses operating in a resort town of Turkey. Although the respondents emphasize the importance of train-ing programs, unfortunately there is much less improvement in terms of facilities for disabled visitors.

Keywords: Disabled tourism; tourism education; disabled tourists; destination management

Tourism and Hospitality Management
Advances in Culture, Tourism and Hospitality Research, Volume 12, 213–222
ISSN: 1871-3173/doi:10.1108/S1871-317320160000012021

INTRODUCTION

Both as a result of the size of the market with 133 million people (ITB Berlin, 2012) and of the support the countries provided for this market on the legal basis (Burnett & Baker, 2001), disabled tourism has significantly become one of the alternative types of tourism that has rapidly developed all over the world. Ranked as the 6th in 2013 out of international tourism figures, Turkey is one of the countries that is eager to play an active role in this market, as a branch of health tourism. Disabled Tourism is a type of tourism that has its own characteristics. Varying disabilities of the disabled individuals cause them to have different needs and requests from the beginning of their vacations to the end (Buhalis & Michopouloub, 2011).

The academic research on disabled tourism mainly focuses on those obstacles that the disabled individuals encounter on their travels, and the body of related research underlines the necessity of eliminating such obstacles in order to increase the disabled individuals' participation in tourism activities (Israeli, 2002; Mckercher, Packer, Yau, & Lam, 2003). One of these obstacles is the service staff who constitutes the subject of tourism. Just as in other types of health tourism, a difference in competition through disabled tourism depends on human resources as well. The ability of Turkey to accomplish the objective in respect to disabled tourism will only be possible by means of training, supplied for the service staff working in the tourism business, in order to understand the needs and problems of disabled visitors, and to help them in accordance with different types of obstacles they have (Artar & Karabacakoğlu, 2003). As a consequence, this study aims to underline those challenges the disabled customers are mainly likely to face and to consult them and tourism authorities so as to determine what types of training programs need to be developed for employees providing services for this cluster.

THEORETICAL CONSIDERATIONS

A significant proportion of disabled people within the world's population has directed countries and organizations to become more sensitive about the travel rights of these people (Burnett & Baker, 2001). The Manila Declaration released by the World Tourism Organization in 1980 indicates "the ultimate aim of tourism is to improve the quality of life, and to create better living conditions for all people" (World Tourism Organization, 1980). The European Commission has similarly adopted a sensitive sector approach in 1996 with its slogan "tourism for all" and attracted the attention to meeting the needs of disabled tourists and their families and noted the economic potential of the market in the manual it published (Var, Yeşiltaş, Yaylı, & Öztürk, 2011). Some other countries have tended to release their own legislations on this issue. While the United States of America put "the Law for Americans with Disabilities Act" into effect in 1990, England put "the Law of the Disability Discrimination Act" into practice in 1995. Both codes also play an important role for the tourism industry (Miller & Kirk, 2002). Chen (2005) states that it is the responsibility of the government to ensure barrier-free tourism for disabled people (Poria, Reichel, & Brandt, 2011).

Despite a quantitative increase in the movements of disabled people, a qualitative increase that will facilitate the movements of disabled people also constitutes a great significance for the development and continuity of this type of tourism because for a disabled individual, accommodation is not an action as simple as buying a ticket, booking or paying for a package tour (Yau, McKercher, & Packer, 2004). There are many practical and social barriers preventing the full participation of disabled individuals and accompanying people (Yau et al., 2004). In earlier research conducted on disabled people, the researchers have focused on identifying the most significant obstacles that the disabled individuals encountered while traveling. It is frequently described that there is a direct negative relationship between travel barriers and disabled individuals' intention to participate in a travel. The body of earlier research suggests the need to eliminate such obstacles so as to increase the participation of disabled people in tourism movements (Israeli, 2002; Mckercher et al., 2003). Tourism barriers consist of factors that reduce the participation in such activities, and that impede the enjoyment of participants.

Having been increasingly important in the world, disabled tourism is considered to be a part of health tourism (Gonzales, Brenzel, & Sancho, 2001). While understanding the needs and expectations of tourists is important in all types of tourism, it becomes more important in health tourism (Zattan & Gül, 2012). The distinct importance of disabled tourism from other parts of health tourism (e.g., medical tourism, thermal tourism, and elderly tourism) is that disabled individuals have a more heterogeneous structure. The disabled can be categorized in four distinct groups: individuals with hearing-impaired, visually impaired, physically impaired, and mentally impaired (Daniels, Rodgers, & Wiggins, 2005). Although each group has its own distinct needs, in a more general manner, the disabled should not be considered as a homogenous group with similar needs (Buhalis & Michopouloub, 2011). Just as in other parts of health tourism, it only depends on human resources that destinations offering similar products in such a rapidly evolving competitive environment can make a difference in a competition in disabled tourism, as well.

In a survey conducted in Antalya in 2012 with the purpose of investigating the demand and supply for the development of disabled tourism, items such as "guidance, and knowledge and education level of the supporting staff" are indicated among products and services that disabled tourists are less pleased with (http://apgem.akdeniz.edu.tr). In the same survey, among the expectations of disabled tourists with hearing-impaired, visually-impaired, physically-impaired, and mentally-impaired, the average value of the proposition of "the staff need to be informed sufficiently," concerning the adjustments in accommodation facilities, was "4.81" out of 5.00, and this indicates an important issue. As far as seen, in Turkey aiming to become a regionally attractive destination in health tourism, the staff working in tourism businesses and in tourism-related services should be trained according to the distinct types of disabilities that disabled tourists have, in a way that they understand their needs and problems, and that they can help them with their disabilities. The staff should receive adequate training concerning the implementation and the control of these services provided for their clients. The staff should be trained in a way to inform their disabled visitors about services and facilities, and in a way to provide necessary assistance for their disabled visitors about the challenges they may face (Artar & Karabacakoğlu, 2003).

In a survey, conducted in 2012 by the European Network for Accessible Tourism, which is one of the major organizations for the development and the increased accessibility of disabled tourism all over the world, disabled tourists are likely to demand, at the highest rate, the helpfulness and hospitality of service providers (European Network for Accessible Tourism, 2012). This important organization, on behalf of the development of the disabled tourism all over Europe, has started the project on improving accessibility through training in tourism. The main objective of the project emphasizing the importance of staff training is to carry out the training and practices for tourism employees so as to improve the accessibility to services in tourism for disabled tourists (http://www.accessibletourism.org).

METHOD

This study aims to carry out the overall evaluation of disabled tourism, and to determine and identify the content of the education-based requirement in disabled tourism. For this purpose, the study employed a semi-structured interview method. Through a literature review and opinions of expert academics, we aimed to search for answers as response to a list of 10 specific questions that were formulated on thoughts and views of senior executives of tourism businesses and organizations. The executive managers of travel agencies and hotel businesses were directed questions related to their general opinions about disabled tourism, evaluation of Kuşadası as a destination in terms of disabled tourism, marketing and promotional activities for this type of tourism, and questions related to the challenges that disabled tourists have faced. Moreover, additional questions were directed – questions related to the knowledge and education level of the tourism staff about disabled tourism, the content of training to be provided on disabled tourism, the types of challenges that training should cover, and whom this training should be given.

Interviews were carried out between 13 and 20 of April 2014 with eight senior executives working in those businesses and organizations operating in Kuşadası (four general managers at five-star hotels, one president of a tourism association, one president of a tourism union, one senior local government administrator, one senior executive responsible of room division). Each interview took 45–60 minutes on average. The interviews started with brief information about the purpose of research. The responses were recorded in the form of short notes, and later were detailed in order to prevent wasting time and avoiding distraction. Considering the possibility of having the necessary equipment and feasibility of disabled tourism, the hotel businesses selected for interviews were limited only to five stars. The organizations selected for interviews were limited to the unions and associations that dominate the current states of hotel businesses and travel opportunities in tourism, and those who dominate the local government and the economy, and those who can give direction to disabled tourism in Kuşadası.

FINDINGS

From the results of interviews, primarily an overall evaluation was carried out considering disabled tourism and its conditions in Kuşadası. When the responses are considered in the context that disabled tourism is an important type of tourism, is both a profitable market and a type of tourism which creates social benefits and a positive image, and moreover is an important market when considered in the context of health tourism. It seems that there is unlikely to have a special marketing effort for disabled tourism in Kuşadası, and that the general profile of tourists visiting Kuşadası is mostly composed of those whose disabilities stem from their old ages (physical, visual, hearing, allergic, and diabetic disabilities), physical disabilities, visual and hearing impaired, and very rarely with mental disabilities. The general condition of disabled tourism is considered mediocre, and awareness is considered to be low by both tourism businesses and organizations. Physical conditions of the city are emphasized to be unsuitable for the disabled, and the substructure and upper structure facilities are especially inadequate. It is indicated that professional service is provided for the disabled at the airport, but right after leaving the airport and starting their vacations, disabled tourists start to face problems with transportation, unconscious attitudes and behaviors of the local people and other tourists, the resort itself, the lack of facilities they need in the city and in hotels, the lack of experts, and security.

A participant, the president of a union and serving as an active person in the industry for 30 years, expresses his opinion about disabled tourism in Kuşadası as follows:

> ... Kuşadası has inadequate physical facilities, and has problems that can cause troubles for even healthy tourists. There are some negative conditions that may be listed as such sidewalks, never ending road works, narrow and congested roads and traffic problems as a result of unplanned housing and unconsciousness of the local people, in particular. I think an awareness should initially be achieved covering the nongovernmental civic organizations and the administrative institutions in the city. (Tourism Union, 53, Male, 30 years)

In this regard, a participant who is the general manager of a five-star hotel and has served for 11 years in the industry, articulates his views on the problems of disabled tourists as follows:

> ... There are times that disabled tourists do not even get out of hotels during their vacations due to the problems they face ... They want to join the culture tours, but what they hear is that the conditions are not suitable for them. If they join these tours despite warnings, the result is an unhappy ending. It is not right to blame anyone. It is a must to constitute a collective consciousness in order to work for this market. Our efforts alone will be insufficient or if an agency wants to move into this market, it will not find available hotels, and will divest itself of the market. I think we need to act collectively for the sake of disabled tourism in particular, which is a type of tourism requiring the creation of surplus values. (General Manager, 35, Male, 9 years)

In the survey, the first question for the determination of any training needs and for identifying its content concerning disabled tourism was about: "knowledge and training level of staffs about disabled tourism." In general, it was noticed that the service staff have a low level of knowledge and training. There are serious problems not only about disabled tourism as a specific type of tourism, but also about tourism in general; the employees focus on quantity rather than quality due to the fact that Kuşadası mainly operates in mass tourism. The response to this question of the participant, vice-president of the local administration in Kuşadası, was as follows:

> ... We think that the education level is low in general. The staff first should be provided with the general tourism training, and then training on disabled tourism should be given. The level of awareness and education of both the local community and the staff should be improved. We do never think that success can be achieved without training and awareness. (Vice-president of the local administration, 61, Male, 24 years)

Considering the responses to the questions in order to determine the content of training about disabled tourism, training should be the one that will constitute awareness about disabled visitors; that will enable us to clarify the needs according to the different types of disabilities; that will inform us about the psychology of disabled visitors; that will instruct us how to act about security and emergency cases; that will include information about promotion, marketing, and current conditions of this type of tourism, and relevant laws. The response to this question by the general manager of a five-star hotel is as follows:

> Training needs to provide us with the recognition of different types of disabilities and learning their needs. Disabled visitors are much more sensitive than our other guests, and their expectations about their vacations are too high. Therefore, it is very important to learn and understand their psychology. Security is a very significant issue. There emerge some problems we face especially with physically disabled visitors from time to time. the staff need to be trained to know how to cope with such emergency cases. (Hotel general manager, 61, Male, 35 years)

Similar responses, but in different expressions, were received to the question "on the basis of destination and hotel, which departments, and who the training program should cover," "all the service staff from top to bottom should receive training." The response provided by the head of a tourism association to this question was as follows:

> ... a holistic integrated training should be given to all staff in hotels, but relevant units in the institutions as well may be subject to such a training in this regard. In cities, on the other hand, the awareness of local community about the disabled may be increased

through associations and NGOs, and those who wish may be provided with training. (Hotel general manager, 61, Male, 35 years)

The response to the question by a vice-president of the local government administration in Kuşadası is as follows:

Each agency and organization must approach to this issue sensitively. Even if training is free, businesses often provide tepid welcome to such training activities as they are consuming the labor force. Thus, firstly senior executives should be trained about the importance of this training and then every employer should make their own staff to participate in this training. (Vice-president of the local administration, 61, Male, 24 years)

The last question posed about training was "which organization or institution they want to provide them with training on disabled tourism." The responses received indicate that the Ministry of Culture and Tourism is the most highly preferred institution for training issues about the tourism industry. Beside the Ministry of Culture and Tourism which is the mostly preferred one, the Ministry of Health, Universities, and NGOs are also thought to take part in training. The response to this question by the general manager of a five-star hotel was as follows:

… I think that the Ministry of Culture and Tourism will be the most authoritative and most influential institution in this regard, and a commission of experts may be constituted on this subject. Organizations of paramedics, academics and the disabled can provide training collectively. (Hotel general manager, 61, Male, 35 years)

CONCLUSION AND IMPLICATIONS

In this chapter, as the example of Kuşadası that is one of the key destinations in Turkey, we aimed to determine priorities and contents of a training program that will be provided for the development of disabled tourism. As a result of the interviews carried out with the executives of businesses and institutions in Kuşadası, disabled tourism appears to be as an important type of tourism, but further and detailed research on this segment is lacking due to various reasons, for example, the lack of infrastructure and superstructure, lack of awareness and education, etc. Only a limited number of projects have been conducted on disabled tourism, yet they are not sufficient to have a voice in the market. One of the significant results obtained is that all organizations and businesses need to be in cooperation for the development of disabled tourism, and that especially the projects led by the Ministry of Culture and Tourism and the Ministry of Health will be supported.

Findings claim that related to disabled tourism, both the local community and the service staff should be provided with training. Training should be covering the whole destination in order to increase the awareness and knowledge on distinct types of disabilities. In light of the results obtained, it is possible to suggest that a significant progress will be achieved by the administration of training programs and projects related to disabled tourism. The research is envisaged to cover different destinations and participants in the future and allows to make comparisons between them. It also seems to become important to examine certain destinations abroad that are considered as best practices in the application of disabled tourism practices and conduct comparative studies in Turkey.

REFERENCES

Artar, Y., & Karabacakoğlu, Ç. (2003). Türkiye'de engelliler turizminin geliştirilmesine yönelik konaklama tesislerindeki altyapı imkanlarının araştırılması, *Engelsiz Turizm Raporu, Engellilerin Toplumsal Gelişimin Yönelik Proje*, Dünya Engelliler Vakfı, Ankara.

Buhalis, D., & Michopoulou, E. (2011). Information-enabled tourism destination marketing: Addressing the accessibility market. *Current Issues in Tourism, 14*(2), 145–168.

Burnett, J., & Baker, B. H. (2001). Assessing the travel related behaviors of the mobility disabled consumer. *Journal of Travel Research, 40*, 4–11.

Chen, R. J. (2005). Uses of hospitality and leisure services: Voices of visitors with disabilities. *Advances in Hospitality and Leisure, 1*, 89–102.

Daniels, M. J., Rodgers, E. B. D., & Wiggins, B. P. (2005). Travel tales: An interpretive analysis of constraints and negotiations to pleasure travel as experienced by persons with physical disabilities. *Tourism Management, 26*(6), 919–930.

European Network for Accessible Tourism. (2012). The social tourist's profile, market expectations & needs, growth opportunities for tourism in the low season, Malta.

Gonzales, A., Brenzel, L., & Sancho, J. (2001). Health tourism and related services, Caribbean development and international trade, Final Report, 20.

Israeli, A. A. (2002). A preliminary investigation of the importance of site accessibility factors for disabled tourists. *Journal of Travel Research, 41*(1), 101–104.

ITB Berlin. (2012). *World travel trends report 2012/2013*. Retrieved from http://www.itb-berlin. de/media/itbk/itbk_media/itbk_pdf/WTTR_Report_2013_web.pdf

Mckercher, B., Packer, T., Yau, M. K., & Lam, P. (2003). Travel agents as facilitators or inhibitors of travel: Perceptions of people with disabilities. *Tourism Management, 24*, 465–474.

Miller, G. A., & Kirk, E. (2002). The disability discrimination act: Time for the stick? *Journal of Sustainable Tourism, 10*(1), 82–88.

Poria, Y., Reichel, A., & Brandt, Y. (2011). Dimensions of hotel experience of people with disabilities: An exploratory study. *International Journal of Contemporary Hospitality Management, 23*(5), 571–579.

Var, T., Yeşiltaş, M., Yaylı, A., & Öztürk, Y. (2011). A study on the travel patterns of physically disabled people. *Asia Pacific Journal of Tourism Research*, *16*(6), 599−618.

World Tourism Organization. (1980). *Manila declaration on world tourism (Manila, Philippines)*. Retrieved from http://www.e-unwto.org/content/k4222x788q51/

Yau, K. M., McKercher, B., & Packer, T. L. (2004). Travelling with disability − More than an access issue. *Annals of Tourism Research*, *31*(4), 946−960.

Zattan, U., & Gül, Y. (2012). Sağlık turizminde entelektüel sermaye. *II. Disiplinlerarası Turizm Araştırmaları Kongresi*. 10−12 Nisan, Kemer.

INTERNET SOURCES

Antalya'da Engelli Turizminin Gelişimi İçin Arz ve Talep Üzerine bir. http://apgem.akdeniz.edu.tr/v2/template/content/projeler/eaet/ciktilar/kitap_engelli_son_kapali.pdf

Araştırma [A study on supply and demand for the development of disabled tourism in Antalya]. http://docplayer.biz.tr/4200382-Antalya-da-engelli-turizminin-gelisimi-icin-arz-ve-talep-uzerine-bir-arastirma.html. Retrieved January 12, 2015.

CHAPTER 16

MOTIVATIONS OF SOUTH ASIAN STUDENTS TO STUDY TOURISM AND HOSPITALITY IN THE UNITED KINGDOM

Roya Rahimi, Vipin Nadda, Blerton Hyseni and Dirisa Mulindwa

ABSTRACT

The economic ramifications of tourism and hospitality have led to the considerable growth of global education in this industry. The ever-changing needs of this industry for appropriate skills and expertise have made it more competitive in nature, which has led to the increase in studies exploring the motivations for students to choose a specific destination. This chapter explores the motivations of South Asian students to undertake tourism and hospitality qualifications in the United Kingdom. The research was based on mixed method approach through two sequential phases of focus group and questionnaire among the students of a higher education provider in London. The results revealed a set of motivational factors influencing South Asian student's choices to study tourism and hospitality in the United Kingdom.

Keywords: Motivation; international students; higher education

Tourism and Hospitality Management
Advances in Culture, Tourism and Hospitality Research, Volume 12, 223–234
Copyright © 2016 by Emerald Group Publishing Limited
All rights of reproduction in any form reserved
ISSN: 1871-3173/doi:10.1108/S1871-317320160000012017

INTRODUCTION

The twenty-first century has seen a sustained growth of globalisation and internationalisation which have considerably influenced the higher education sector across the world (Knight, 2006), although with variable degrees ranging from attaining economic advantage, enhancing global brand image, better quality of life and global competitiveness. Globalisation has further led to the development of 'transnational education programmes' pioneered by nations like the United Kingdom and offered to international students (Altbach, 2004). In the last two decades, the number of international students has almost doubled to 2.7 million globally and intends reaching 7.2 million by 2025 (Organization for Economic Co-operation and Development [OECD], 2006) with the priorities ranging from Law, Engineering, and Chemistry to tourism and hospitality.

Tourism and hospitality today has become a global phenomenon. The economic importance of these industries has created ever-increasing demand for skilled and qualified human resources in the labour market thus convincing the education providers to offer them as part of wider programs at various levels. Tourism was introduced as a subject by European universities in 1930s (Faulkner, 2003) although there has been — considerable increase in the demand reflected in the supply offerings (Barron, Baum, & Conway, 2007). A wide range of literature about changing demographics especially the international students have greatly influenced the demand for tourism and hospitality education in the United Kingdom, which has made many academic institutions to operate on corporate models rather than traditional societal concept of education (Hobson, 2008; O'Mahony, Whitelaw, & McWilliams, 2008) thereby necessitating the need to analyse the motivations of international students to come to United Kingdom for tourism and hospitality education.

The focus of this chapter is the students from South Asia including Bangladesh, Pakistan, India and Nepal; put together these countries represent almost 25% of the world's total population. However, their strength is not only in the big number of people, but also in the youthfulness of their populations. The governments of these countries put a lot of investment in their efforts to increase primary and secondary education enrolment, today their youth are seeking for higher education. Many countries today recognise that higher education is the key to the development of knowledge societies as well as their knowledge intensive industries (OECD, 2006). The ever-increasing need for skilled people both in terms of quality and quantity has led to demand in higher education which in return has resulted in a rapid growth of transnational student mobility (Altbach, Reisberg, & Rumbley, 2009).

At the same time the tourism and hospitality industries of these countries are also thriving, south Asia is one of the fastest emerging destinations recording 8.2% growth in international tourists arrival between 2005 and 2012 (UNWTO, 2013). This growth means that the region has a big demand for skilled people to work in its ever-expanding tourism industry. Many of the aspiring students who would like to work in this industry seek higher education abroad. The purpose of this chapter is to be able to understand what motivates the students from South Asia to choose the United Kingdom as their education destination, and why they choose to study tourism and hospitality in particular. The study was carried out on students of a UK higher education provider in London, which is 100% international, and with a big percentage of the students coming from the South Asia region.

THEORETICAL CONSIDERATIONS

Alongside other western nations, the United Kingdom has also experienced a significant increase in the number of international students for higher education qualifications in the last decade (UK Council for international Affairs, 2013). The percentage of international (non EU) students in the United Kingdom has risen from 8.6% in 2003–2004 to 12.1% with 2.5 million students across 163 higher educational institutions in 2011–2012 (HESA, 2013).

Wide ranges of logics have been cited by the experts for these trends in the form of nature of the course curriculum, research focus and competitive market conditions (Smith & Frankland, 2000). They have been the research focus for some time (Altbach & Knight, 2006) due to the substantial commercial implication of international student's income to supplement the declining government funding and hence increasing importance of monitoring the student's motivations to come to the United Kingdom (Cooper & O'Keefe, 2005).

While Anderson, Johnson, Milligan, and Stephanou (1998) explored the motivations from career enhancement, professional advancement and skills development perspective, Suvantola (2004) found them then to be self-development and knowledge enhancement. Further, Coulthard (2000) and Moogan and Baron (2003) happen to find students motivated due to subject interest and enhancement of professional practice. Some other research indicated towards increase in the employment and travel opportunities, career advancement and wage improvements (Hannam, Mitsche, & Stone, 2004). Mazzarol and Soutar (2002) carried out a wide research and pointed out that other factors influencing the selection of a country have been a commonality of language, the availability of science or technology-based programmes and the geographic proximity of the home and host countries. According to Mazzarol and Soutar (2002), the decision to study abroad is carried out by many members within the family and this even varies for postgraduate and graduate levels. They further highlighted in their research that the parental influence is higher among undergraduate students when they are choosing a country or a destination to study. To some extent the decision of the students choosing the destination can be influenced so much by others that the students end up studying in the countries or disciplines that would not necessary would have been their choice if they were to make their own decision.

In many cases parents sacrifice everything within their means to provide the best education to the children and hence the children may choose to study abroad to please them (Li, 2001). Also foreign qualification from some countries could be considered a guarantee for better future (Ashley & Jiang, 2000) through better skills and employment prospects upon returning home (Gareth, 2005).

The economic ramifications of tourism and hospitality have led to the considerable growth of global education in this sector. The ever-changing needs of this industry for appropriate skills and expertise have made it more competitive in nature, which has led to the increase in studies exploring the motivations for students to choose specific destinations. Further, from the providers' perspective also, various academic institutions in the United Kingdom need to understand the changing trends in the recruitment market in order to maintain a competitive advantage with the need to identify and explore various push and pull factors influencing potential students from South Asian market (Hung, Shive, Wang, & Diu, 2005).

METHOD

The research was conducted with mix method approach through two sequential phases. It started with a qualitative phase via a focus group to find in-depth information about student's motivations. In the second phase with quantitative approach the results of the focus group proceeded to design a questionnaire. During the first phase for gaining a variety of perspectives, 15 undergraduate and postgraduate Indian, Bangladeshi, Pakistani, and Nepali students were selected. With the moderation of two lecturers the focus group discussion was conducted for an hour and students were encouraged to talk about their motivations to study abroad, reasons to select the United Kingdom and study tourism and hospitality here. The focus group was recorded, transcribed and the data were analysed via inductive approach and content analysis (Ritchie & Lewis, 2003). A list of students' motivations emerged and was used for the second phase and designing questionnaire to investigate the most important motivational factors influencing student's decision. The questionnaire was based on a 5-point Likert-Scale. The questionnaire comprised four parts. The first part included questions related to study abroad; the second part included the motivational factors for selecting the United Kingdom; and the third part the motivational factor to study tourism and hospitality. The final part included demographic questions of the respondents. Online survey tools were used (Survey Monkey) and the link of the questionnaire was distributed among 375 undergraduates and postgraduate South Asian students in a higher education provider in London in May 2014. One week after, a reminder e-mail was sent. After two weeks a second reminder was sent and eventually after four weeks the final reminder was sent stating the importance of the participant's input for the study. In total 133 responses were collected. Incomplete questionnaires were disregarded and 128 responses considered for analysis. SPSS Software (Version 21) was used and the data were subjected to descriptive and factor analysis.

FINDINGS

Qualitative Study

The results of focus group showed different factors play role for students to study abroad. The first factor mentioned by students was the values and reputations of certificates from abroad. One of them mentioned that: 'In Asian countries foreign degrees and certificates from abroad specially England is valuable and you can easily find jobs'. Whereas a female student from Pakistan said 'in my home country you cannot work unless you have a degree but here you can study and work and also support your family'; she also added that having a degree from abroad gives more opportunities in future to work as a woman in Pakistan. One of the students mentioned that going abroad is a culture. He added that 'when you finish high school everyone starts to ask which country you want to go to study'. They also mentioned experiencing different cultures, making friends and meeting different people as important factors. One of the students said, 'The travel was my big motivation, I wanted to go to other countries to understand their culture and understanding yourself better'. They also mentioned that family encouragement and hoping for a better future are the main reasons to study abroad.

Selecting the United Kingdom

The students mentioned that they selected the United Kingdom as they have friends and relatives in the United Kingdom and it is close to Asia in comparison to other countries like Australia or Canada. One of the students mentioned 'it is just few hours on flight'. Having friends and relatives were specially persisted by Indian and Pakistani students which matches the 2011 UK Census showing that there are approximately 3,039,470 South Asias in England and Wales, representing around 4.9% of the population, and those of Indian origin comprised 2.3% of the population, with those people of Pakistani origin comprising 1.9%, and around 0.75% were of Bangladeshi origin. One of the Indian students said 'by coming to the UK I can study, I cans see my relatives and I also can save money as I do not need to pay for accommodation and I can earn money as well'.

As well as the above reasons, visa process was one of the important factors mentioned by students. While courtiers like Australia, Canada, and the United States asked for a lot of supporting documents and bank statements, the United Kingdom has an easier visa process in comparison. One of the students mentioned, 'for applying UK visa we need £9000 deposit in our bank accounts while for Australia we need US$50000' another student added 'UK accept IELTS score 6 while other countries ask for 6.5 or 7'. Students mentioned visa-processing time was important as it currently takes up to two months for the British Embassy to issue students visa and it can take up to six months in other countries like Canada. Language of the country being English was mentioned by students as important factor. Having a multi-cultural environment and equal opportunities was mentioned by one of the students as important factor for selecting the United Kingdom. Currently full-time students can work up to 20 hours per week and it is one of the important factors among international students for selecting the United Kingdom. One of the students said 'I have friends in other countries and they do not have right to work and I decided to come her as I can work and study'. Good reputations of UK universities were also mentioned as the main reasons for selecting the United Kingdom. One of the student mentioned, 'UK classify among one of the high quality education providers and having a degree from UK means a better future'.

Studying Tourism and Hospitality

Tourism and hospitality is one of the first preferences among Indian, Bangladeshi, Pakistani and Nepali students. Different factors were mentioned by students as their main reasons to study tourism and hospitality. Students mentioned that there is more job opportunity during study and after graduation in tourism and hospitality compared to other disciplines. One of them said, 'With a tourism and hospitality degree I can secure a job in the Europe or Dubai as there are a lot of multinational tourism and hospitality businesses and opportunities'. Most of the students mentioned that they decided to study tourism and hospitality as they have previous work experience in tourism and hospitality. Having previous qualifications in tourism and hospitality was also mentioned by students as currently international students can complete the first two years in their home countries and join UK universities for the final year (top-up) and get the qualification from UK universities. The nature of the tourism field that might be easier in comparison to other fields like business (unless math is involved) was mentioned by students. One of the students said 'I cannot study engineering or physic as it is too difficult for me and I wanted something easier so I selected Tourism and Hospitality'. They also mentioned that tourism is more practical than theoretical. However it needs to be mentioned that they found tourism more difficult than what they were thinking about it before joining the university. One of the students said 'I thought it is tourism you can write anything you want in your assignment and I found it hard to cope with the modules'. One of the other students added that 'when I tell my friends I study tourism and hospitality and I need to study hard they make fun out of me'. Most of the students in tourism and hospitality enjoy travelling and this was one encouragement to study it, as they are interested in investing in it as a career. Students also mentioned that encouragement and influence from friends and families and the agency and consultants in their home countries influence their decision.

Quantitative Study

The descriptive analysis of the data (Table 1) demonstrated that 48% of the students were from India, 24% from Bangladesh, 14% from Nepal and 14% from Pakistan. 62% of respondents were undergraduate and 38% postgraduate students and 63% of respondents were between 25 and 30 ages and 28% between 18 and 24 and 8% between 35 and 44.

Towards reliability analysis of the questionnaire Cronbach's alpha test was conducted and the results of .88 were among the accepted range >.70 suggested by Nunally (1978). Table 2 shows the mean, standard deviation and factor loading of motivational factors among Indian, Bangladeshi, Pakistani and Nepali students. According to the mean scores the majority of the students decide to study abroad because of encouragement from their families. Students mentioned that in their home country study abroad is a trend and cultural issue and most of the young generation are encouraged to it.

As Table 2 demonstrates the visa process of the United Kingdom is the most important motivational factor for student to select it. The second important factor is the job opportunities in the United Kingdom that let students work and study at the same time. Having relatives in the United Kingdom and the distance of the United Kingdom to Asia were the third and fourth important factors for studying in the United Kingdom. Based on the mean scores of the motivational factors, the most important factors to study tourism and hospitality is the encouragement from the agents, consultants and families. It shows that very low percentages of students select tourism and hospitality independently. Currently most of the universities and colleges in the United Kingdom have agents in Asia that encourage students to study abroad and select that specific higher education provider. They also help students with application process and selecting the courses. Considering that the role of student recruitment agency has been mentioned several times by the students during the focus group, in the questionnaire we asked whether students would have preferred to study Tourism

Table 1. Demographic Distribution of Respondents.

Undergraduate (degree or top-up)	62%
Postgraduate (Master)	37%
18−24	28%
25−34	63%
35−44	8%

Table 2. Mean, Standard Deviation and Factor Loading of Motivational Factors.

Motivation Items	Factor Loading	Mean	S.D.	Cumulative %	Alpha
Study abroad				15.76	0.78
I would like to experience different cultures.	0.642	1.38	0.85		
I would like to make more friends.	0.632	1.98	0.71		
I would like to meet different people.	0.627	1.62	0.62		
Certificates from abroad have a better value.	0.618	1.35	1.09		
It was a culture and trend back home.	0.579	2.40	1.05		
My family encouraged me to come.	0.559	2.37	0.617		
It will open doors for global job opportunities in the future.	0.559	1.33	0.884		
It can lead my family and me to a quality life.	0.538	1.72	1.43		
Selected UK for study				32.17	0.71
I have friends in the UK.	0.487	2.96	1.08		
I have relatives in the UK.	0.478	3.06	0.933		
The visa process is easier.	0.470	3.43	0.789		
It is easy to find a job in the UK.	0.439	3.34	1.35		
UK education has a global brand reputation.	0.409	1.44	0.845		
It is close to home in comparison to other countries such as Australia, USA.	0.469	3.05	0.921		
It can be like a platform to move to a better country	0.455	1.85	1.11		
I like to improve my English	0.704	1.95	0.777		
I can settle in the UK after study.	0.591	2.77	1.13		
UK is a multi-culture country.	0.576	1.56	0.805		
Decided to study tourism and hospitality				40.29	0.80
There are a lot of job opportunities in this field.	0.448	1.56	1.38		
It is easier in comparison to other fields.	0.492	2.47	1.40		
Travelling is my hobby and I wanted it as a career.	0.487	1.65	1.15		
I have previous experience in tourism and hospitality field.	0.492	2.41	1.11		
I have previous related qualifications in the field.	0.487	2.66	0.919		
My family encouraged me to study this field.	0.404	3.36	1.12		

Table 2. *(Continued)*

Motivation Items	Factor Loading	Mean	S.D.	Cumulative %	Alpha
My friends influenced my decision.	0.458	3.48	1.10		
I believed this field is practical rather than theoretical in nature.	0.436	2.03	0.852		
My agency (consultants) encouraged me.	0.392	3.74	0.714		
The influence from agents was very high.	0.487	3.87	0.629		

Notes: Extraction Component Method with Principal Component analysis.
Kaiser-Meyer-Olkin: .617 with Sig. 0.00.

and Hospitality courses without the influence of an agent. The results showed that 95% of the students were still interested in studying tourism and 4% said they preferred to study business, human resource and fashion. Having previous qualifications in tourism and hospitality and the nature of the discipline being easier compared to other major were the next important factors.

CONCLUSION AND IMPLICATIONS

This chapter has found a considerable range of motivating factors influencing South Asian students' decision to undertake tourism and hospitality education in the United Kingdom and thus provided valuable insight into their relative importance with regards to the destination location. Some very interesting factors evolved in the findings, which reflect back to the origin of student's motivation from their culture, society, family background, awareness level followed by the competitive advantages offered by United Kingdom as a multi-cultural global destination for quality education and their perceptions about a career in tourism and hospitality sector. This has obvious implications for marketing and recruiting international students thus opening further opportunities for the UK higher educational institutions. Also, it indicates towards collaborating the destination promoter's efforts with the tourism and hospitality education marketers.

The research is conducted in the frame of a case study with focus on South Asian students, therefore the findings cannot be generalised to a larger population. This research is conducted in the context of higher education provider and the result might be different for further educations. According to the UK Council for International Student Affairs (UKCISA),

Romania and Bulgaria are among the top 10 EU countries when it comes to sending people for higher education in the United Kingdom. Currently one in six college applicants is Romanian or Bulgarian and more than 5,000 apply for vocational courses, that makes 5,000 students from the two countries on vocational courses in England accounting for a staggering one in six of all applicants. Further research with different samples such as East European students can be conducted and the results can be compared.

REFERENCES

Altbach, P. G., & Knight, J. (2006). Visión panorámica de la internacionalización en la educación superior: motivaciones y realidades. *Perfiles educativos*, *28*(112), 13–39.

Altbach, G. P., Reisberg, L., & Rumbley, L. E. (2009). *Trends in global higher education: Tracking an academic revolution*. A report prepared for the UNESCO 2009 world conference on higher education.

Altbach, P. (2004). Higher education crosses borders. *Change*, *36*(2), 18–24.

Anderson, D., Johnson, R., Milligan, B., & Stephanou, A. (1998). *Access to postgraduate courses: Opportunities and obstacles*. Canberra: Higher Education Council, Australian Government Publishing Service.

Ashley, D., & Jiang, Y. (2000). *Mao's children in the New China*. Beijing: Routledge.

Barron, P., Baum, T., & Conway, F. (2007). Learning, living and working: Experiences of international postgraduate students at a Scottish university. *Journal of Hospitality and Tourism Management*, *14*(2), 85–101.

Cooper, B., & O'Keefe, S. (2005). The importance of credit transfer in the decision to undertake post-compulsory education: An exercise in experimental choice analysis. Paper presented to the Australian Vocational Education and Training Research Association Conference, Brisbane, Australia.

Coulthard, D. (2000). *Identifying the changing needs of Australian coursework postgraduate students*. Melbourne: Evaluations and Investigations Programme Higher Education Division, School of Management Information Systems, Deakin University. Retrieved from http://www.dest.gov.au/archive/highered/eippubs/eip99-9/default.htm. Accessed on February 20, 2014.

Faulkner, B. (2003). *Progressing tourism research*. Clevedon: Channel View Publication.

Gareth, D. (2005). Chinese students' motivations for studying abroad. *International Journal of Private Higher Education*, *2*, 16–21.

Hannam, K., Mitsche, N., & Stone, C. (2004). Critical issues in tourism education: Conference of the association for tourism in higher education. In J. Tribe & E. Wickens (Eds.), *Tourism employability and the European social fund*. (pp. 39–52). Buckinghamshire: Missenden Abbet.

HESA. (2013). *Patterns and trends 2013 in UK higher education*. Retrieved from http://www. universitiesuk.ac.uk/highereducation/Documents/2013/PatternsAndTrendsinUKHigher Education2013.pdf. Accessed on February 19, 2014.

Hobson, J. S. P. (2008). Internationalisation of tourism and hospitality education. *Journal of Hospitality & Tourism Education*, *20*(1), 4–5.

Hung, F. S., Shive, G., Wang, X., & Diu, J. (2005). *A report on the export potential of Hong Kong's education services*. Hong Kong: A Consultancy Study for the Hong Kong Trade and Development Council.

Knight, J. (2006). Cross-border education: Conceptual confusion and data deficits. *Perspectives in Education, 24*(4), 15–27.

Li, J. (2001). Expectations of Chinese immigrant parents for their children's education: The interplay of Chinese tradition and the Canadian context. *Canadian Journal of Education, 26*(4), 477–494.

Mazzarol, T., & Soutar, N. G. (2002). "Push-Pull" factors influencing international students' destination choice. *The international Journal of Educational Management, 16*(2), 82–90.

Moogan, Y. J., & Baron, S. (2003). An analysis of student characteristics within the student decision making process. *Journal of Further and Higher Education, 27*(3), 271–287.

Nunnally, J. C. (1978). *Psychometric theory*. New York, NY: McGraw-Hill Book Company.

OECD. (2006). *Improve skills to build fairer, more inclusive societies - OECD*. [Online]. Available at: http://www.oecd.org/skills/improve-skills-to-build-fairer-more-inclusive-societies.htm. Accessed on July 22, 2016.

O'Mahony, B., Whitelaw, P. A., & McWilliams, A. (2008). The drivers of program selection in hospitality management at Victoria University. *Journal of Hospitality & Tourism Education, 20*(3), 5–10.

Ritchie, J., & Lewis, J. (2003). *Qualitative research practice: A guide for social science students and researchers*. London: Sage.

Smith, B., & Frankland, M. (2000). *Marketisation and the new quality agenda: Postgraduate coursework at the crossroads*. Australian Universities' Review. Retrieved from http://0-files.eric.ed.gov.opac.msmc.edu/fulltext/EJ623399.pdf. Accessed on April 8, 2014.

Suvantola, J. (2004). Self-determination theory in charting students' motivation. In J. Tribe & E. Wickens (Eds.), *Critical issues in tourism education: Proceedings of the 2004 conference of the Association for Tourism in Higher Education* (pp. 139–144). Buckinghamshire: Missenden Abbet.

UK Council for International Affairs. (2013). *International student statistics: UK higher education*. Retrieved from http://www.ukcisa.org.uk/Info-for-universities-colleges–schools/Policy-research–statistics/Research-statistics/International-students-in-UK-HE/#. Accessed on February 25, 2013.

UNWTO. (2013). *UNWTO tourism highlights*, 2013 edition. Retrieved from unwto.org

CHAPTER 17

EFFECT OF WORK EXPERIENCE ON STUDENTS' ATTITUDES TOWARD HOSPITALITY CAREERS

Marlena A. Bednarska and Marcin Olszewski

ABSTRACT

There is an essential link between the success of hospitality organizations and the availability of appropriate labor resources, making employee attraction a critical concern for the industry. The purpose of this chapter is to investigate the role of work experience, both inside and outside the hospitality industry, in shaping students' attitudes toward hospitality careers. The study was conducted on the group of 338 undergraduates and graduates enrolled in tourism and hospitality studies in Poznan, Poland. The findings suggest that work experience displays a stronger relationship with preferred than with perceived job and organization attributes. It is also related to perceptions of hospitality career attractiveness both in the long and in the short run as well as to intentions to apply for a job after graduation. The results underline the importance of providing students with quality work experience by the hospitality industry stakeholders as it can influence future career decisions.

Keywords: Work experience; hospitality career; tourism and hospitality students; Poland

Tourism and Hospitality Management
Advances in Culture, Tourism and Hospitality Research, Volume 12, 235–249
ISSN: 1871-3173/doi:10.1108/S1871-317320160000012018

INTRODUCTION

There is a broad consensus that the success of hospitality firms, being high-contact service organizations, lies to a great extent in the quality of their human resources. In line with service-dominant logic the real sustainable competitive advantage in today's market is realized through an increased focus on operant resources, which are capable of acting and producing effects in other resources, and constitute the essential component of differentiation (Lusch, Vargo, & O'Brien, 2007). Therefore, the issue of attracting and retaining employees with proper competences who can become the primal source of innovation, organizational knowledge, and value is of critical importance to hospitality business. As the hospitality industry traditionally relies on young workforce (Baum, 2007; Solnet, Kralj, & Kandampully, 2012), it appears meaningful to investigate career-related expectations and perceptions of tourism and hospitality students as prospective employees.

While much academic work has been devoted to the topic of understanding tourism and hospitality students' attitudes toward the industry, this has been undertaken in Western countries (e.g., Barron, Maxwell, Broadbridge, & Ogden, 2007; Hjalager & Andersen, 2001; Jenkins, 2001), and more recently in Asian context (e.g., Jiang & Tribe, 2009; Richardson & Butler, 2012), with scarce studies conducted in the context of Central and Eastern Europe. The novelty of present research therefore lies in looking at students' perceptions of hospitality employment in one of the transition economies — in Poland. In addition, empirical studies provide evidence that prior work experience influences students' attitudes toward tourism and hospitality careers (e.g., Kim, McCleary, & Kaufman, 2010; Kusluvan & Kusluvan, 2000; Maxwell, Ogden, & Broadbridge, 2010). However, they are limited to industry-related experience. This study seeks to contribute to the body of literature by investigating the role of work experience both inside and outside the hospitality industry in shaping hospitality career attractiveness perceptions and job pursuit intentions.

THEORETICAL CONSIDERATIONS

In recent years the career choice behavior of tourism and hospitality students has received an increasing attention in academic literature, which is stimulated by the fact that tourism and hospitality organizations across the world face the growing problem of attracting and retaining employees with desired skills and commitment (cf. Bednarska, 2013; Enz, 2009; Walsh & Taylor, 2007). Current research undertaken to understand students' industry perceptions has revealed a number of factors that influence prospective employees' decisions and determine the industry's image, work experience being one of them (Chuang & Dellmann-Jenkins, 2010; Koyuncu, Burke, Fiksenbaum, & Demirer, 2008; Kwan, 2005; Richardson, 2010; Wan, Wong, & Kong, 2014).

Students search for employment while completing their degrees for a variety of reasons. Apart from those financially related, enhancing employability through gaining real-world experience appears to be the leading one (Barron, 2007; Martin & McCabe, 2007; Schoffstall & Arendt, 2014). Engaging in employment while studying is an element of industry-based experiential learning, which has been documented to offer numerous benefits to students. It gives the opportunity to apply what they learn in the classroom in an actual work environment. It helps understand how organizations function on a daily basis and enables enhancing on-the-job skills demanded by employers, such as communication, problem-solving, and teamwork skills. Finally, experiential learning provides students with the requirements they will need to comply with to function effectively in a later career, so it allows them to view career expectations realistically and assess how they fit into specific organization or industry (Lee, 2007; Leslie & Richardson, 2000; Zopiatis & Constanti, 2007).

Considering the above-mentioned experiential learning outcomes, it is unsurprising that many researchers link industry-based experience to students' attitudes toward tourism and hospitality employment. However, the evidence of relationships between work experience and commitment to careers in the industry is inconclusive. While some studies suggest that as the degree progresses and students gain relevant work experience, their perception of the industry deteriorates; others advocate that early work experience positively affects students' intentions to apply for a job in tourism and hospitality organizations following graduation.

Many previous studies indicated that having direct work experience can lower student intentions to remain in the tourism and hospitality industry and can have a major negative impact on intentions to pursue career after graduation (Barron et al., 2007; Richardson, 2008; Wang, Chiang, & Lee, 2014; Zopiatis, 2007). Jenkins (2001) reported that hospitality students became considerably less interested in selecting hospitality as their first choice career field after exposure to work experience. According to Kusluvan and Kusluvan (2000) students' negative attitudes toward different aspects of working in the tourism industry are formed after the practical work experience. Barron et al. (2007) addressed the differences between students' expectations and their internship experience. After attending an unsatisfying internship, many students leave with a negative perception of the career opportunities, treatment by management staff, monetary rewards and job satisfaction in the hospitality industry. These findings concur with those of Richardson (2008) who found that working in the industry is turning potential employees away. Many of those with work experience claimed that this experience had left them with a negative attitude toward a career in the industry and more than one-third of respondents declared that they would not work in the tourism and hospitality industry after graduation. Kim and Park's (2013) research also implies that students, having faced the reality of the hospitality and tourism industry during their internships, may be left with unfavorable perceptions of working in the industry. However, the results suggest that desirable social experiences during students' internship periods can even lead to a change in students' perceptions, thereby decreasing negative perceptions regarding various factors relating to a career in the hospitality and tourism industry.

Negative impact of first work experiences on hospitality and tourism image as an employer stems from the nature of these experiences. Students are often treated as a solution to a labor-shortage problem and considered as a source of low-cost labor while they are on their placements. Low-quality internships can alienate them from a career in hospitality when their expectations do not match reality (Wang et al., 2014).

On the other hand, it has been also argued that a positive internship experience encourages hospitality and tourism students to join the industry after graduation and promotes job satisfaction and willingness to stay in the industry (Chuang & Dellmann-Jenkins, 2010; Fong, Lee, Luk, & Law, 2014). Wang et al. (2014) found significant relationships between internship outcomes and career commitment in hospitality college students. Chuang and Dellmann-Jenkins (2010) studied undergraduate hospitality and tourism students and their career intentions within the industry. The authors reported 83% of the respondents planned to pursue hospitality careers following their college graduations, and in addition, students who currently worked in the industry showed stronger intentions than their peers who were not employed. Koyuncu et al.'s (2008) research also implies that students having more tourism experience held more favorable views on careers in tourism.

Undoubtedly, gaining experience during the study allows students enhance their understanding of the workplace (Wang et al., 2014) and improve insights into reality so they become "industry-wise" (Busby, Brunt, & Baber, 1997, p. 108). According to Kim et al. (2010) "work experience" has the highest mean scores as information sources for career decisions, which highlights the importance positive work experiences have on newer generations in the workplace. This issue deserves detailed attention, especially as pointed out by Kusluvan and Kusluvan (2000), students' attitudes may spell negative consequences for the students, the tourism industry, the government, and tourism and hospitality education providers. Hence, understanding potential employees' perceptions, and specifically, whether students differ in their opinion if they experienced working in non-tourism and hospitality industries deserve further investigation.

This study examines tourism and hospitality students' perceptions of the industry and it was conducted in one of the leading centers for higher education in Poland — Poznan. The range of employment opportunities in the industry has increased significantly, along with various degrees related to tourism and hospitality offered by the Polish universities, making this topic a timely one to examine. While much academic work has been devoted to exploring the industry's attractiveness as a place to work and intentions to enter it upon graduation, many questions about differences in students' attraction to the hospitality industry remain largely unaddressed (Bednarska & Olszewski, 2013). Research questions established for the purpose of this study are as follows:

- Is type of work experience related to preferred and perceived job and organization attributes in the hospitality industry?
- Is type of work experience related to perceptions of hospitality career attractiveness?
- Is type of work experience related to intentions to apply for a job in the hospitality industry?

Examining those issues will further contribute to understanding the role of work experience both inside and outside the hospitality industry in shaping perceptions of hospitality organizations as workplaces and job application intentions.

METHOD

The research reported in the chapter represents a part of a larger study examining complementary person-environment fit as a predictor of tourism and hospitality students' job pursuit intentions. The target population comprised undergraduates and graduates enrolled in tourism and hospitality studies in Poznan, one of the leading centers for higher education in Poland. In the academic year 2012/2013 eight public and private universities in Poznan offered bachelor and master degrees in tourism (a total of 4,150 students). To obtain a representative subset of the target population a single-stage cluster sampling was employed. Tourism and hospitality courses' providers were contacted and they all agreed to facilitate accessing their students.

A survey was designed for the purpose of this study. A measurement instrument was developed based on a review of previous research on employer image (Berthon, Ewing, & Hah, 2005; Schlager, Bodderas, Maas, & Cachelin, 2011). Participants evaluated 19 items representing five core dimensions of employer attractiveness (see Appendix for the dimensions and the items), that is, job content (3 items), economic benefits (4 items), development opportunities (5 items), social relations (5 items), and reputation (2 items). As applicants are attracted to a firm based on the extent to which they believe that the firm possesses the desired attributes and the relative importance they place on those attributes (Backhaus & Tikoo, 2004), respondents were requested to assess both perceived and preferred job/organization characteristics. Next, students rated general career attractiveness and their willingness to search for a job in the hospitality industry. A seven-point Likert scale, ranging from "strongly disagree" (1) to "strongly agree" (7), was employed for gradations of opinions. At the end of the survey, questions about students' work experience and demographic characteristics were included.

Prior to administration, the survey was pre-tested on a group of 30 tourism and hospitality students. The pilot testers were asked to complete the questionnaire as well as provide feedback regarding understandability. On the basis of the comments a few minor modifications were made to clarify questions and reduce completion time. Data for full-scale study were collected through paper-based questionnaires administered in the controlled environment of formal class time and under the supervision of researchers. A total of 348 respondents were recruited, yielding a response rate of 66.3%. Due to incomplete or incoherent information 10 questionnaires were excluded, which resulted in 338 usable questionnaires for further analysis. As can be seen from Table 1, the sample was diverse. Females represented the majority of participants (70%) and the median age equaled 21 years. Full-time students outnumbered part time students by five to one and 78% of respondents were pursuing bachelor degree. Most of surveyed students had some type of work experience (82%), 49% of them worked in the hospitality industry.

Table 1. Characteristics of Survey Sample.

Variable	Category	N	%
Gender	Female	234	69.6
	Male	102	30.4
Age	20 and less	126	37.5
	21–22	124	36.9
	23–24	65	19.4
	25 and more	21	6.3
Study mode	Full-time	280	83.3
	Part-time	56	16.7
Study degree	Bachelor	262	78.0
	Master	74	22.0
Year of study	First	89	26.5
	Second	82	24.4
	Third	91	27.1
	Fourth	9	2.7
	Fifth	65	19.3
Work experience	Hospitality-related only	38	11.3
	Hospitality-unrelated only	111	33.1
	Hospitality-related/unrelated	125	37.3
	No experience	61	18.2

The survey data analysis involved descriptive statistics and correlations to portray the main features of variables under study and relations between them. In order to examine the differences between groups, one-way ANOVA followed by Tukey's post hoc tests was conducted. In this study, four sub-groups of students were compared – with hospitality-related experience only, with hospitality-unrelated experience only, with experience both in hospitality and in other sectors, and with no working experience.

FINDINGS

The results of the preliminary analysis are reported in Table 2, which presents the descriptive statistics and the correlations between the variables of interest. As far as career expectations are concerned, respondents rate social relations the highest, reputation – the lowest. Regarding perceptions

Table 2. Variable Means, Standard Deviations, and Correlations.

Variable	Mean	Standard Deviation	Correlations											
			1	2	3	4	5	6	7	8	9	10	11	12
Expectations														
1. Job content	5.60	0.82												
2. Economic benefits	6.09	0.90	0.30**											
3. Development opportunities	5.95	0.87	0.36**	0.67**										
4. Social relations	6.15	0.88	0.23**	0.60**	0.66**									
5. Reputation	5.55	1.19	0.25**	0.48**	0.56**	0.51**								
Perceptions														
6. Job content	5.03	1.19	0.25**	0.16**	0.18**	0.14**	0.24**							
7. Economic benefits	5.19	1.15	0.08	0.23**	0.22**	0.18**	0.26**	0.49**						
8. Development opportunities	5.21	1.02	0.11*	0.19**	0.28**	0.23**	0.30**	0.55**	0.80**					
9. Social relations	5.13	1.07	0.11*	0.20**	0.24**	0.27**	0.30**	0.50**	0.74**	0.78**				
10. Reputation	5.23	1.10	0.23**	0.30**	0.39**	0.26**	0.50**	0.54**	0.64**	0.70**	0.67**			
11. Long-term career attractiveness	4.31	1.58	0.08	0.06	0.10	0.02	0.13**	0.56**	0.36**	0.42**	0.38**	0.35**		
12. Short-term career attractiveness	5.01	1.53	0.11*	0.07	0.06	0.08	0.16**	0.57**	0.29**	0.35**	0.33**	0.33**	0.75**	
13. Job pursuit intentions	4.28	1.81	0.11*	0.07	0.05	0.02	0.14**	0.45**	0.26**	0.32**	0.29**	0.28**	0.61**	0.61**

Significant ** at the 0.01 level; * at the 0.05 level (two-tailed).

of hospitality employment, students report the highest mean score for reputation, the lowest − for job content. In general, investigation showed that participants do not believe the hospitality industry would respond to their career needs − in all dimensions under study expectations exceed perceptions. Students are particularly pessimistic about social relations in the workplace, while holding relative optimism about reputation. Respondents find hospitality employment moderately attractive and they are less positive toward the industry as a long-term career option comparing to short-term one. Only half of those surveyed claim they plan to seek employment in hospitality upon graduation. Correlation coefficients indicate that both perceptions of hospitality career attractiveness and intentions to apply for a job in the industry display the strongest relationship with perceived job content and development opportunities.

Analysis of variance results are provided in Table 3. Post hoc multiple comparison procedure determined more significant mean score differences concerning preferred than perceived job and organization attributes. Students who experienced working life, regardless of the industry, have notably higher expectations toward four out of five facets of employer image, that is, job content, economic benefits, development opportunities, and social relations. The analysis further revealed the largest mean differences between those with and without work experience with regard to salary and stable employment conditions (constituents of economic benefits), prospects for promotion within the organization and possibility of long-term professional development (constituents of development opportunities). Students with working experience in the hospitality industry rate job content higher both as expected and as perceived attribute, particularly job that matches individual interests and tasks that are challenging. One striking result is that in the eyes of the students the main strength of hospitality job, in each sub-group of participants, is that it offers useful experience for future employment in other sectors.

Post hoc tests also revealed that type of work experience is related to perceptions of hospitality career attractiveness both in the long and in the short run. Those who gained direct experience in hospitality hold much more favorable attitudes to the industry as a career field than their colleagues who did not. Finally, type of work experience is related to intentions to apply for a job after graduation. Students with hospitality-related experience only declare the highest commitment to the industry as a workplace, students with hospitality-unrelated experience only − the lowest one. It is noteworthy that with regard to job pursuit intentions the mean difference between these two sub-groups is larger than with regard to any other variable under study.

Table 3. Variable Means – Comparison of Students with Different Types of Work Experience.

Variable	Hospitality-Related Experience	Hospitality-Unrelated Experience	Hospitality-related/ Unrelated Experience	No Experience	ANOVA F-Value
Expectations					
1. Job content	5.80^a	5.59^1	5.70^b	5.28^{ab1}	4.53**
2. Economic benefits	6.25^a	6.19^b	6.13^c	5.69^{abc}	5.16**
3. Development opportunities	5.98^1	6.02^a	6.04^b	5.57^{ab1}	4.71**
4. Social relations	6.27^1	6.20^2	6.20^3	5.86^{123}	2.90*
5. Reputation	5.70	5.54	5.64	5.28	1.49
Perceptions					
6. Job content	5.37^1	4.91	5.18	4.80^1	2.91*
7. Economic benefits	5.25	5.06	5.24	5.25	0.65
8. Development opportunities	5.28	5.19	5.24	5.12	0.24
9. Social relations	5.16	5.11	5.14	5.18	0.08
10. Reputation	5.43	5.23	5.20	5.11	0.68
11. Long-term career attractiveness	4.88^a	3.92^{ab}	4.54^b	4.21	5.02**
12. Short-term career attractiveness	5.37^1	4.78^a	5.34^{ab}	4.61^{b1}	5.08**
13. Job pursuit intentions	5.16^{a1}	3.85^{a2}	4.41^2	4.24^1	5.48**

Notes: Significant ** at the 0.01 level; * at the 0.05 level (two-tailed).
Means with the same superscript letter (a, b, c) differ significantly at the 0.05 level (two-tailed).
Means with the same superscript number (1, 2, 3) differ significantly at the 0.1 level (two-tailed).

CONCLUSION AND IMPLICATIONS

The hospitality industry is a highly labor-intensive sector that relies on the abilities of employees to identify and satisfy customers' needs. Hence, attracting and maintaining high caliber staff is of critical importance for hospitality organizations. As the image of employment is regarded as a significant determinant of the effective recruitment of quality labor, this study examines attitudes toward hospitality careers of students as prospective employees and the effect of early work experiences on their career plans.

The present investigation revealed that students are more positive toward the hospitality industry as a short-term career option compared to long-term one. This finding corresponds with those reported by Jiang and Tribe (2009) and Hjalager and Andersen (2001). Such attitude is typical for generation Y, who moves jobs to experience new challenges and finds job switching an appealing alternative (Barron et al., 2007; Solnet et al., 2012). As noted by Lyons (2010) career mobility within and beyond the tourism and hospitality industry is a fast growing global phenomenon. Consequently, implementing human resource practices that are in alignment with work-related needs and preferences of generation Y employees and make them committed to organizations which employ them appears to be a major challenge for the hospitality industry.

Students' perceptions of career paths in the hospitality and tourism industry can be seriously influenced by first impressions formed during their experiential learning, which can either enhance or damage the industry's reputation (Kim & Park, 2013). Considering that the study confirmed relationships between work experience and career attractiveness perceptions, hospitality employers should bear in mind the importance of making a good first impression on new employees, particularly when they are in their first job. The success or failure of the various internship programs determines the quantity and quality of the hospitality graduates and the future leaders of this sector (Zopiatis, 2007). The positive first work experiences result in the industry's future success in recruiting and retaining the qualified graduates and this will have a favorable effect on gaining competitive advantages through the increase in service quality and consumer loyalty.

Companies should make the undergraduates' placements offer more attractive to ensure they are receiving positive experiences while working during their degree. For the industry, positive attitudes toward tourism jobs after students' internships result in the short- and the long-term benefits. The short-term benefits include: the possibility of acquiring experienced staff which are familiar with the company; availability of high caliber and committed staff; opportunity to bring into the organization someone who is not steeped in a different organizational culture nor one who probably needs re-training. This results in cost and time savings due to newcomers who are ready to take on all their responsibilities at once. Moreover, enterprises know the candidates as they checked them in a real work environment so the probability of choosing the wrong candidate is lower. The long-term benefits for companies resulting from providing positive experience to students include: increase in their pool of qualified candidates, reduction in their cost-per-hire and building a positive image of a company that is friendly to young people.

The results of this study should be considered in the light of certain limitations that could be addressed in future research. First, the investigation identified significant differences in students' opinions on hospitality careers based on type of work experience gained. However, it did not examine underlying reasons for these different views. Further research could address more closely the quality of industry-based experience and critical aspects that affect the desire to continue employment upon graduation. Second, the cross-sectional nature of the present study means that direction of causality cannot be unambiguously determined. It would be of value to conduct a longitudinal research following students as they progress through their degrees and gain more work experience to explore the causality of the identified relationships. Third, all variables were measured with self-reports and based on the same source, thus there exists the possibility of common method variance occurring, including social desirability and consistency motif. Another aspect to keep in mind when interpreting the findings is that the study was carried out only in one city in Poland. Therefore, due to unique characteristics of the population, results may not generalize to tourism and hospitality students in other regions of the country. Finally, the findings identified a group of respondents who were interested neither in gaining experience, nor in searching for employment in the hospitality industry after graduation. This may suggest that students are committed to careers in other sectors of the tourism industry or they enroll in tourism and hospitality program for other reasons than career interest. Future research should seek for insights into these areas.

ACKNOWLEDGMENT

The research reported in this chapter is a part of the project "Quality of work life in competitive potential development in the tourism industry" financed by the National Science Centre, Poland (decision no. DEC-2012/07/B/HS4/03089).

REFERENCES

Backhaus, K. B., & Tikoo, S. (2004). Conceptualizing and researching employer branding. *Career Development International*, 9(5), 501–517.
Barron, P. (2007). Hospitality and tourism students' part-time employment: Patterns, benefits and recognition. *Journal of Hospitality, Leisure, Sport and Tourism Education*, 6(2), 40–55.

Barron, P., Maxwell, G., Broadbridge, A., & Ogden, S. (2007). Careers in hospitality management: Generation Y's experiences and perceptions. *Journal of Hospitality and Tourism Management*, *14*(2), 119–128.

Baum, T. (2007). Human resources in tourism: Still waiting for change. *Tourism Management*, *28*(6), 1383–1399.

Bednarska, M. A. (2013). Quality of work life in tourism — Implications for competitive advantage of the tourism industry. *Journal of Travel and Tourism Research*, 13(1/2) (Spring & Fall), 1–17.

Bednarska, M. A., & Olszewski, M. (2013). Organisational determinants of employer image: A case of the tourism industry in Poland. *Anuario Turismo y Sociedad*, *14*, 17–31.

Berthon, P., Ewing, M. T., & Hah, L. L. (2005). Captivating company: Dimensions of attractiveness in employer branding. *International Journal of Advertising*, *24*(2), 151–172.

Busby, G., Brunt, P., & Baber, S. (1997). Tourism sandwich placements: An appraisal. *Tourism Management*, *18*(2), 105–110.

Chuang, N.-K., & Dellmann-Jenkins, M. (2010). Career decision making and intention: A study of hospitality undergraduate students. *Journal of Hospitality & Tourism Research*, *34*(4), 512–530.

Enz, C. A. (2009). Human resource management: A troubling issue for the global hotel industry. *Cornell Hospitality Quarterly*, *50*(4), 578–583.

Fong, L. H. N., Lee, H. A., Luk, C., & Law, R. (2014). How do hotel and tourism students select internship employers? A segmentation approach. *Journal of Hospitality, Leisure, Sport and Tourism Education*, *15*, 68–79.

Hjalager, A.-M., & Andersen, S. (2001). Tourism employment: Contingent work or professional career? *Employee Relations*, *23*(2), 115–129.

Jenkins, A. K. (2001). Making a career of it? Hospitality students' future perspectives: An Anglo-Dutch study. *International Journal of Contemporary Hospitality Management*, *13*(1), 13–20.

Jiang, B., & Tribe, J. (2009). Tourism jobs — Short-lived professions: Student attitudes towards tourism careers in China. *Journal of Hospitality, Leisure, Sport and Tourism Education*, *8*(1), 4–19.

Kim, B., McCleary, K. W., & Kaufman, T. (2010). The new generation in the industry: Hospitality/tourism students' career preferences, sources of influence and career choice factors. *Journal of Hospitality & Tourism Education*, *22*(3), 5–11.

Kim, H., & Park, E. J. (2013). The role of social experience in undergraduates' career perceptions through internships. *Journal of Hospitality, Leisure, Sport and Tourism Education*, *12*(1), 70–78.

Koyuncu, M., Burke, R. J., Fiksenbaum, L., & Demirer, H. (2008). Predictors of commitment to careers in the tourism industry. *Anatolia: An International Journal of Tourism and Hospitality Research*, *19*(2), 225–236.

Kusluvan, S., & Kusluvan, Z. (2000). Perceptions and attitudes of undergraduate tourism students towards working in the tourism industry in Turkey. *Tourism Management*, *21*(3), 251–269.

Kwan, F. V. C. (2005). Effect of supervised work experience on perception of work in the tourism and hospitality industry. *Journal of Human Resources in Hospitality & Tourism*, *4*(2), 65–82.

Lee, S. A. (2007). Increasing student learning: A comparison of students' perceptions of learning in the classroom environment and their industry-based experiential learning assignments. *Journal of Teaching in Travel & Tourism*, *7*(4), 37–54.

Leslie, D., & Richardson, A. (2000). Tourism and cooperative education in UK undergraduate courses: Are the benefits being realised? *Tourism Management*, *21*(5), 489–498.

Lusch, R. F., Vargo, S. L., & O'Brien, M. (2007). Competing through service: Insights from service-dominant logic. *Journal of Retailing, 83*(1), 5−18.

Lyons, K. (2010). Room to move? The challenges of career mobility for tourism education. *Journal of Hospitality & Tourism Education, 22*(2), 51−55.

Martin, E., & McCabe, S. (2007). Part-time work and postgraduate students: Developing the skills for employment? *Journal of Hospitality, Leisure, Sport and Tourism Education, 6*(2), 29−40.

Maxwell, G. A., Ogden, S. M., & Broadbridge, A. (2010). Generation Y's career expectations and aspirations: Engagement in the hospitality industry. *Journal of Hospitality and Tourism Management, 17*(1), 53−61.

Richardson, S. (2008). Undergraduate tourism and hospitality students' attitudes toward a career in the industry: A preliminary investigation. *Journal of Teaching in Travel & Tourism, 8*(1), 23−46.

Richardson, S. (2010). Generation Y's perceptions and attitudes towards a career in tourism and hospitality. *Journal of Human Resources in Hospitality & Tourism, 9*(2), 179−199.

Richardson, S., & Butler, G. (2012). Attitudes of Malaysian tourism and hospitality students' towards a career in the industry. *Asia Pacific Journal of Tourism Research, 17*(3), 262−276.

Schlager, T., Bodderas, M., Maas, P., & Cachelin, J. L. (2011). The influence of the employer brand on employee attitudes relevant for service branding: An empirical investigation. *Journal of Services Marketing, 25*(7), 497−508.

Schoffstall, D. G., & Arendt, S. W. (2014). Benefits and challenges encountered by working students. *Journal of Hospitality & Tourism Education, 26*(1), 10−20.

Solnet, D., Kralj, A., & Kandampully, J. (2012). Generation Y employees: An examination of work attitude differences. *Journal of Applied Management and Entrepreneurship, 17*(3), 36−54.

Walsh, K., & Taylor, M. S. (2007). Developing in-house careers and retaining management talent: What hospitality professionals want from their jobs. *Cornell Hotel and Restaurant Administration Quarterly, 48*(2), 163−182.

Wan, Y. K. P., Wong, I. A., & Kong, W. H. (2014). Student career prospect and industry commitment: The roles of industry attitude, perceived social status, and salary expectations. *Tourism Management, 40*, 1−14.

Wang, Y.-F., Chiang, M.-H., & Lee, Y.-J. (2014). The relationships amongst the intern anxiety, internship outcomes, and career commitment of hospitality college students. *Journal of Hospitality, Leisure, Sport and Tourism Education, 15*, 86−93.

Zopiatis, A. (2007). Hospitality internships in Cyprus: A genuine academic experience or a continuing frustration? *International Journal of Contemporary Hospitality Management, 19*(1), 65−77.

Zopiatis, A., & Constanti, P. (2007). "And never the twain shall meet": Investigating the hospitality industry — Education relationship in Cyprus. *Education + Training, 49*(5), 391−407.

APPENDIX

Dimensions and Items	Alpha Coefficient	
	Expectations	Perceptions
1. Job content	0.51	0.81
Your job matches your individual interests. Your job involves tasks that are challenging. You are provided with a variety of work activities.		
2. Economic benefits	0.79	0.89
Your job guarantees high salary. You are provided with attractive fringe benefits. You are equipped with modern devices for performing tasks. Your job offers stable employment conditions.		
3. Development opportunities	0.80	0.88
You are given possibilities of enhancing qualifications. Your job offers prospects for promotion within the organization. You can influence decisions that are important for your work. Your job guarantees long-term professional development. Your job provides you with experience for future employment.		
4. Social relations	0.83	0.89
Your job offers friendly atmosphere. You have the feeling of trust and cooperation at the workplace. Your work fits in with your family or social commitments. You have the feeling of integration and belonging. You work with competent supervisors.		
5. Reputation	0.72	0.77
Your employer offers high-quality products. Your job enjoys high social prestige.		

CHAPTER 18

THE ROLE OF EDU-TOURISM IN BRIDGING RACIAL DIVIDES IN SOUTH AFRICA

Julia C. Wells

ABSTRACT

The tourism industry in South Africa today faces the dual challenges of finding ways to extend tourism spending into previously marginalised communities and to redress the imbalances in cultural representations of those communities. The legacy of formal racial segregation is extremely difficult to reverse. The study investigated the potential of Edu-tourism to fundamentally change tourism dynamics. This approach targets young, intelligent, 'new tourists' who choose different types of visitor experiences and contribute to changing the way South Africans value and use their own cultures. The method used included requiring students to design tourist packages, in consultation with tour guides, visitors and local community members. The outcomes provide stimulation for new research, widely distributed income generation and building bridges between divided communities.

Keywords: Edu-tourism; cultural tourism; pro-poor tourism; public history; South Africa

Tourism and Hospitality Management
Advances in Culture, Tourism and Hospitality Research, Volume 12, 251–263
Copyright © 2016 by Emerald Group Publishing Limited
All rights of reproduction in any form reserved
ISSN: 1871-3173/doi:10.1108/S1871-317320160000012019

INTRODUCTION

This chapter explores efforts currently being made to develop a robust Edu-tourism industry in the small, historic town of Grahamstown in South Africa's Eastern Cape Province. The concept arises from the town's unique combination of hosting a university, numerous libraries and museums, the annual South African National Arts Festival and lying in close proximity to relatively unspoilt natural features. The surrounding area is also the site of numerous frontier wars from the late 1700s through the mid-19th century.

While people from diverse cultural backgrounds have occupied the area in different historical periods, the English prevailed, through military conquest, in 1812. In 1820, nearly 5,000 British settlers arrived, resulting in a long-standing tourism brand of 'settler country'. The Grahamstown city centre consists of mostly Victorian buildings and an imposing Anglican cathedral. Until the end of apartheid, all historical information in the public domain was geared towards the glorification of European domination and achievements, while people, events, place names and places of cultural significance for the majority African population scarcely received any mention.

Since the advent of democracy in South Africa in 1994, the inclusion of all population groups into the domain of public memory has been a high priority of the government. Yet in the vicinity of Grahamstown, this has been difficult to achieve because of the domination of British culture in the entire built environment. This cultural monopoly is echoed throughout the tourism industry. Very few facilities for visitors have any character other than Victorian English and most are in the hands of English descendants. In recent years, private game farming has become quite popular, but has developed around a generic African look and feel with virtually no reference to the earlier local human inhabitants or their history.

On achieving the 20th anniversary of democracy in 2014, there was a widespread sense that progressive change has been far too superficial. The ideals of commitment to shared humanitarian values have not brought the anticipated changes, leaving untouched some of the legacies of the deeply divided past. Issues such as both blatant and subtle forms of racist behaviour, widespread corruption, vandalism of public property, a culture of dependency and entitlement and eruptions of violent conflicts centred around social services all indicate that something is still not right. The national government is now placing a good deal of emphasis on building social cohesion through new forms of 'active citizenship'. The potential of using knowledge of the past in a sensitive and transformative way is the core mission of the heritage sector in South Africa. Thoughtfully done, it serves to highlight the achievements of the marginalised black majority, put colonialism into a different perspective and offer a cathartic release from past injustices.

Working constructively with the past, however, competes with numerous other urgent priorities and is often under-funded. Using tourist spending to help finance and maintain cultural and heritage resources is a cornerstone of government policy, as outlined in its National Heritage and Culture Tourism Strategy (*Strategy*, 2012). South Africa has high expectations that tourism revenue will grow as a key economic driver (Binns & Nel, 2002; Kirsten & Rogerson, 2002). It is already reported to be a larger industry than the gold-mining economy (*Annual Report*, 2013–2014). The Department of Tourism has set a target of creating a quarter of a million new jobs in tourism by 2020, mostly in the hospitality industry (*Annual Report*, 2013–2014). The creation of sustainable jobs is the target of such policies.

The Edu-tourism model seeks to include local people from diverse backgrounds in packaged tours targeting visitors who seek an intelligent and well-informed introduction to South Africa as it is today. Innovative packaging creates space for a variety of voices and viewpoints, allowing previously marginalised people to become involved on a small, but eminently do-able scale, as experts with valuable knowledge to share. The designing of such packages offers a chance for South Africans to reflect on the past in ways that can help them heal and move forward. Edu-tourism offers such a space because it self-consciously seeks a break from old views and promotes debates, while providing an economic incentive to do so.

THEORETICAL CONSIDERATIONS

The well-developed concept of the 'new tourism' fits contemporary conditions in South Africa quite well. The universal appeal of coming to witness the national context of Nelson Mandela's 'triumph of the human spirit' (the branding slogan of the Robben Island Museum) results in attracting visitors who want to see how the changes are evolving. Erve Chambers describes the new tourists as well-educated elites who 'will increasingly value principles of environmental sustainability, human equality and cultural diversity, and will, as a result, be more sensitive than any other generation of recreational tourists to the consequences of their travels'

(Chambers, 2008). He sees these tourists as consumers of products that are intellectually challenging as well as offering some sense of self-improvement (Chambers, 2008). Such tourism is viewed as inviting new types of inputs from the host countries. Poon further describes the new tourism as characterised by a demand for flexibility, authenticity and respect for the environment, rejecting rigid packaging and superficial exposures (Poon, 1994).

This is a far cry from the cold, objectifying 'tourist gaze' so aptly described by John Urry (Urry, 1990). Since Dean MacCannel opened the debates on the damaging potential of tourists' quest for authenticity in 1976, the concept has been effectively teased out. Wang, writing in 1999, for example, cites important differences in objective authenticity, constructive authenticity and existential authenticity (MacCannel, 1976; Wang, 1999 as described by Cole, 2007, p. 944). Writers like Chhabra et al. and Yu Wang show how fluid and flexible the consumers' need for authenticity can be, as they readily accept that contemporary events are indeed an evolved form of long-lost traditions (Chhabra, Healey, & Sills, 2003; Wang, 2007).

Tourism in South Africa today remains stubbornly in the hands of the already-privileged. Most efforts to extend the economic benefits to black people take the form of either simply creating more entry-level jobs for unskilled workers or to give whole communities some form of shared ownership, usually via a community trust, while responsibility for the management of accommodation facilities remains with people with professional expertise (Mahoney & Van Zyl, 2002). The tourism industry in South Africa has included previously disadvantaged people in a number of other ways: cultural villages which claim to recreate traditional ways of living, the emergence of arts and crafts projects near game parks and training tour guides for sites of significance in the struggle against apartheid (Tomaselli, 2014). All of these, however, perpetuate existing cultural stereotypes (Rassool, 2000).

Martin Mowforth and Ian Munt's *Tourism and Sustainability*, now in its 3rd edition, asks how the gap between rich and poor of the world can be closed by tourism (Mowforth & Munt, 2009). They see the emergence of new forms of tourism as offering an important alternative to inherited patterns of exploitation as visitors self-consciously choose to avoid all the pitfalls of old-fashioned tourism. While pro-poor tourism has been around since 1999, it cannot be said to have achieved as much as was originally hoped for (Ashley & Goodwin, 2007). It recognises the need for strong, financially supported interventions to make a dent in industry norms. One of the advantages of the Edu-tourism concept is that it does not require major investments in capital, such as the construction of lodges, because it is a knowledge-based approach.

In South Africa, new tourists face the extra challenge of transcending the lingering stereotypes of the apartheid past. 'A World in One Country' was the official tourism slogan of the newly democratic South Africa in 1994. It capitalised on its first world qualities of wealth and comfort, as the leader in bringing modernity to Africa, where the world of the poor was portrayed as fascinating 'real Africa', all surrounded by fantastic wildlife and breath-taking scenery (Rassool & Witz, 1996). This allowed for black poverty to appear as normal, simply to be gazed upon. Bheki Peterson warns of the temptation to bypass everyday realities in South Africa by using slogans which refer to the 'South African Miracle' and the 'Rainbow' nation (Peterson, 2012). When communities participate in constructing their own stories, they generally reject the simplistic notion of a suddenly happy South Africa, instead articulating more honest and inclusive versions of the past which include 'complexity, controversy and contestation' (Rassool, 2000, 1; Rassool, 2009). Edu-tourism aims to offer a corrective by both raising tough questions and allowing the previously marginalised to speak for themselves.

A substantial body of writing exists about the overwhelming need in South Africa today to allow people to tell their stories as a form of healing from the pains of the past (see, e.g., Colvin, 2004; Field, 2006; Marschall, 2010; Meskell, 2008). But places and spaces to do so are scarce and often fall into the realm of NGOs who run intensive 'reconciliation' workshops. The use of a wide range of experts from previously disadvantaged communities within Edu-tourism packages partially serves this function. Telling one's own stories about cultural practices and personal experiences is in itself empowering, while also bringing the possibility of economic benefit.

Critics of how South Africa uses its past today bemoan the fact that the late 20th century struggle against apartheid dominates the public terrain, to the exclusion of numerous other issues (Meskell, 2008). An important component of the Edu-tourism approach in Grahamstown is to tap into the much longer legacy of the interaction of different cultures over a 200-year period. During this time, engagements between black and white ranged from aggressive to assimilative, defying a simplistic story line.

METHOD

The idea of creating tourist attractions which would combine fairly serious educational content with traditional recreational activities such as action sports, hiking, game viewing and visiting sites of historical significance emerged in Grahamstown in 2005. The Edu-tourism concept aimed to use the expertise available among university staff as an attraction, especially for young people who might be students themselves. The initial idea was to offer formal lectures within the university setting, possibly for degree credits, to visitors who would then spend parts of their days and weeks doing more traditional tourist outings, but within easy reach of Grahamstown. Funding from the European Union supported the creation of an Edu-tourism website, through which attractions could be advertised. Over time, however, it became evident that this approach tended to reproduce the status quo and failed to touch much of the potential of the Grahamstown area.

As both a university lecturer in Public History and a local government Councillor, I was familiar with the concepts of Edu-tourism and interacted with its key role players from the start. Over the years, many conversations took place with the designers of the Edu-tourism project, tour guides, the local tourism office, municipal tourism staff, academics with relevant interests, the university international office, the local museum and several groups of visiting international students with whom I worked as a historical consultant.

In 2013 and 2014, students of Public History in the History Department of Rhodes University undertook to develop special packages for potential Edu-tourism customers under my guidance. The approach arose from the recognition that the Edu-tourism website mostly captured existing tourist facilities, without developing new offerings tailored specifically to visitors with educational interests. In 2013, students produced seven-day packages for hypothetical groups of 15 students from overseas universities. These covered the themes of the frontier character of Grahamstown, the legacy of the Khoekhoe and San people, as well as eco-history. Each package included a balance of both educational and recreational offerings, using local museums, travelling to near-by places, meeting people with expertise and engaging in hands-on participatory activities. Central to the planning was a requirement that the packages should provide a good mix of black and white experts, regardless of formal educational qualifications, each to be paid a standard fee. This allowed people from previously disadvantaged backgrounds to speak about cultural and personal experiences as equal participants.

In the second year of the project, students used the original packages as a foundation, but redesigned them as stand-alone one-day packages with some key improvements. The first change required the development of digital inputs. When an international student group leader indicated that visiting young people would prefer to spend as much time as possible travelling to places, with limited time in classrooms, a decision was made to switch to more digital formatting. As most visiting students would have either tablets or smart phones, the new plan was to package information that they could carry with them and view onsite instead of spending time inside classrooms. Since international student group leaders often spend as much as a full semester preparing their students, another addition was to develop pre-travel reading lists, so that visitors could arrive well-prepared. Their time would then be spent primarily viewing and experiencing first-hand the places and issues they had read about.

The biggest innovation in the second round was the requirement that each one-day package should include a 'Ghost Story'. Ideally, this would be a relatively short performance done by 1–3 actors around an evening campfire. The goal was to create an opportunity to explore the experiences of obscure historical characters, mostly from the silenced black majority of the population. The idea was to allow artistic interpretation to fill in the silences, based on what is knowable about the person's historic context. As the home of South Africa's National Arts Festival, Grahamstown is well-endowed with actors coming from low-income backgrounds, as well as the Rhodes University Drama Department. The student designers of packages had to develop a Ghost Story concept and provide documentation about the historic figure for use by actors, who would, in turn, develop the actual scripts. Working closely with the Edu-tourism project and the Makana Tourism office, students developed comprehensive package plans, giving as much detail as possible. They had to provide daily activity plans, maps, marketing flyers, pre-reading lists, digital inputs, background readings for Ghost Stories and costing.

FINDINGS

The experience of developing Edu-tourism packages reveals a great deal about where South Africa is today in relation to altering the tourism status quo. Deep social and economic differences remain difficult to transcend. Today's South African students have little first-hand experience of the world outside university walls, and have not been exposed to viewing people of low-income status as having valuable knowledge to share. While some saw the inclusion of black people mostly in terms of voluntourism acts of charity, others learned the value of meeting people with expertise which they respected. Another limitation came from black students who felt that digging too deeply into the apartheid past is still too painful because economic and racial divides remain harsh realities.

It proved to be quite difficult for the students to think in terms of potential job creation and extending the benefits of tourism more widely to people from disadvantaged backgrounds. Instead, they readily grasped the services of existing tourism professionals. In many of the packages, the only 'black' component was the Ghost Story, which at times felt like an uncomfortable add-on to tourism-as-usual. Using black people in digital interviews was seldom done, mostly due to student unfamiliarity with relevant informants.

Initially, the South African students were wary of their international student counterparts, assuming that they would bring only superficial understanding into the local context. However, after meeting a few 'volunteer' international students, an alternate view emerged, that they were less tainted, open to trying new things and meeting new people, offering more of a 'clean slate' on South African dynamics.

The project also exposed several barriers to quick implementation. In some instances, low-income people could not easily develop useful products due to their poverty and social distance from the world of tourism. In order to create a cultural balance, it was found that a much greater effort is needed to find and help develop activities for tourists from within the black community. The wide gap in the skills and experience base between lower and higher-income tourism service providers became evident in several ways. In one instance, where a rural community under a traditional chief had already developed hiking trails to historic caves, the Edu-tourism planners were not allowed to visit the site without paying the full commercial fees. Therefore, it was left out of the relevant package. This reveals a lack of understanding of the potential value of marketing and its relationship to attracting more visitors.

In another instance, women who were eager to organise traditional African cooking lessons and who could readily explain the meaning and value of all the foods and techniques admitted that they had none of the necessary equipment themselves and could only meet any demand by borrowing or hiring from others. A small investment in start-up capital to make such service providers self-sufficient would go a long way.

People from low-income groups are also unfamiliar with what their more affluent visitors might enjoy. The idea of teaching guests how to do things, instead of simply demonstrating them, is hard to convey to those who have been servicing traditional tourists. The potential of developing activities such as African dancing, drumming, trying out contemporary

African fashions, trying to do rock art, testing indigenous medicinal plants or doing bead-work instead of simply buying it is unlikely to be realized without focused training.

Similarly, local tour guides, both black and white, were not very responsive to the possibilities inherent in Edu-tourism. They were not amenable to sharing tourist spending with a range of other 'experts', preferring instead to be the sole voice of authority. Although fees for guides were factored into the financial planning, the reluctance to move out of familiar patterns remained. No matter how well trained, the guides would not have the same level of first-hand experience and expertise as other participants, thus leaving space for a watered-down experience. The shift to design smaller packages made it easier to have one-day tours which could be largely self-guided, moving between experts. The smaller packages also had the advantage of not needing to include as much effort in planning accommodation and meals.

Many academics with expertise also were not willing to take the time to share it with the Edu-tourism planners, lacking sufficient incentive. While many lecturers already enjoy giving specialist lectures to visitors for a small fee, they did not wish to take time to participate in planning and developing packages. The break from set ways of teaching and tour guiding might be difficult to make at first.

In the design of the packages, it was often hard to find digital inputs that genuinely complimented what visitors would actually be seeing. The potential for recording numerous interviews to use while travelling and viewing places is enormous and offers an opportunity for the inclusion of multiple points of view and a range of expertise from all population groups. In a few cases, telephonic audio interviews with people who are not local were used, but too often students chose to record the same person who would be meeting visitors face-to-face. Using museum and academic experts tends to reproduce the racial divide, where white people speak extensively about black people. While all public institutions today have goals to transform the composition of their staff, these have not yet been met in many instances. Further ways and means need to be sought to break down this dichotomy. It also became clear that several local historic sites, including rock art and the ruins of an old mission station, are located on private land where access is severely limited.

A number of successes can also be noted. Firstly, students generally designed well-balanced packages which included good variety, from travel to interesting places, to do-it-yourself participatory activities, to hiking and wildlife viewing and creative eating experiences. Secondly, creating

Edu-tourism packages also revealed areas where interpretations of the past are still contested and undeveloped, but worthy of extensive further research and exploration. With its goal of creating culturally inclusive packages, the Edu-tourism initiative has stimulated new interest in local history. From working on projects, students experienced first-hand how heavily weighted the current historical record is towards the colonial European culture. Virtually nothing existed about the lower-income communities, other than a mention of prominent buildings, such as schools and churches.

Through long processes of digging through old records, talking to people and developing an exhibition for the local Albany Museum on the first 50 years of Grahamstown's history, a few new story-lines have emerged. For example, much of the local African community are descendants of ancestors who were refugees, who in turn became the first participants in Christian missions. Over time, they became the earliest elites in Southern Africa, producing prominent teachers, preachers and journalists. Another newly uncovered story is about people of mixed-cultural backgrounds (during apartheid classified as 'coloureds') who, after 50 years of trying, gave up on efforts to assimilate into English-dominated society and went into a very bitter open rebellion in 1851. The history of the white lower-classes also offers another untold story. Only fragments of tales of bars, brothels and bootlegging are known. The integration of the human history, both black and white, into today's world of game farming still remains to be done. All of these topics, as well as several others, can only be fully developed and incorporated into Edu-tourism when a good deal more research has been done. But at least the direction for such a research agenda has been clearly set, stimulating a good deal of local discussion and debate.

While these larger narratives are still being explored, some of the micro-details of buried stories can be used through the Ghost Story concept, even before extensive research takes place. The Ghost Stories are by far the most creative part of the Edu-tourism packages. They require a sophisticated audience who can appreciate the blending of fact and fiction, in the guise of creative entertainment — ideal for new tourists. The Ghost Stories allow for exploration of little-appreciated dynamics and obscure characters. Examples used by the students include a conversation between a Xhosa woman and the British settler who kidnapped her in 1820 when she sought traditional decorative clays within the colonial boundary; a love story between a French explorer and a Khoekhoe woman in the 1780s and an argument between two brother Xhosa chiefs over whether or not to convert to Christianity. In other cases, students invented stories using talking animals and dreams to transcend human barriers.

CONCLUSION AND IMPLICATIONS

The development of Edu-tourism packages reveals the potential within the concept. By targeting young international students, the dynamics of the global new tourists come into play, inviting a level of complexity and diversity in presentation. Chambers sees new tourists as enjoying activities which offer 'a playful disregard for the presumed reality of any tourism object or event, allowing for both ambiguity and entertainment in the interpretive process' (Chambers, 2008). These new tourists understand that it is important to engage with previously disadvantaged communities and to see that a portion of their spending is used to make an economic difference. This type of tourist serves the needs of South African society today, as it creates a rare space for speaking about contested issues, touching on unofficial silences of the troubled past and showing respect for the indigenous knowledge and lived experiences of the black majority population. In meeting the intellectual interests of the Edu-tourists, South Africans can engage with their own past in new, innovative and healing ways.

The Ghost Story approach provides an invitation to think creatively about what is left out of the written records and to deeply imagine how the events of the past might have felt from both sides of the story. The use of multiple digital interviews makes it possible to provide both diversity and an element of controversy in safe and managed ways. The variety of people and views do not have to be all gathered in one place for face-to-face confrontations, but can still be heard.

The development of the packages also shows exactly how funding support could best be used. To date, the packages remain on paper only. As with other attempts at pro-poor tourism, implementation needs focused interventions to bring about meaningful change. But unlike many other pro-poor tourism projects, this one does not need massive investment in infrastructure. Investments in harnessing existing knowledge and expertise are most appropriate, including:

- Ghost Story development
- Start-up capital for modest cultural activities
- The wider inclusion of black instructors in museum offerings
- Training black tour guides in how to talk about complex ideas, diversity of views and unresolved debates

- Modest payments for interviewees for digital inputs
- Securing the services of IT experts
- Marketing at all levels

Tourists offer an opening for fresh looks and new stories when it is still hard for South Africans to imagine a change. Through working on packages, within the general targets of social empowerment, inclusivity and job creation, South Africans can move towards a different way of being.

Edu-tourism should not be expected to alleviate the deepest pains of injury and insult from the apartheid past, but it can gently create space for previously marginalised people to find forms of self-affirmation and economic empowerment. The prospect of financial return offers an important incentive to develop the necessary skills.

ACKNOWLEDGEMENTS

Appreciation must be expressed to all the students of Public History who, have diligently explored ways to share local historical content and experience with international visitors. Most of the thinking around the possibilities inherent in Edu-tourism has arisen from extensive conversations with a range of tourism and museum staff, too numerous to mention.

REFERENCES

Ashley, C., & Goodwin, H. (2007). 'Pro-poor tourism': What's gone right and what's gone wrong? Overseas Development Institute Opinion Paper, June.

Binns, T., & Nel, E. (2002). Tourism as a local development strategy in South Africa. *The Geographical Journal, 168*(3), 235–247.

Chambers, E. (2008). From authenticity to significance: Tourism on the frontier of culture and place. *Futures, 41*, 353–359.

Chhabra, D., Healey, R., & Sills, E. (2003). Staged authenticity and heritage tourism. *Annals of Tourism Research, 30*(3), 702–719.

Cole, S. (2007). Beyond authenticity and commodification. *Annals of Tourism Research, 34*(4), 943–960.

Colvin, C. (2004). Ambivalent narrations: Pursuing the political through traumatic storytelling. *Political and Legal Anthropology Review, 27*(1), 72–89.

Department of Tourism, Republic of South Africa. (2012). National heritage and cultural tourism strategy, p. 51.

Department of Tourism, Republic of South Africa. (2014). Annual Report 2013–2014, p. 170.

Field, S. (2006). Beyond "healing": Trauma, oral history and regeneration. *Oral History*, *34*(1), 31–42.

Kirsten, M., & Rogerson, C. M. (2002). Tourism, business linkages and small enterprise development in South Africa. *Development Southern Africa*, *19*(1), 29–59.

MacCannell, D. (1976). *The tourist, a new theory of the leisure class*. New York, NY: Schochen Books.

Mahoney, K., & Van Zyl, J. (2002). The impacts of tourism investment on rural communities: Three case studies in South Africa. *Development Southern Africa*, *19*(1), 83–103.

Marschall, S. (2010, September 23). The memory of trauma and resistance: Public memorialization and democracy in post-apartheid South Africa and beyond. *Safundi: The Journal of South African and American Studies*, *11*(4), 361–381.

Meskell, L. (2008). Heritage as therapy, set pieces from the new South Africa. *Journal of Material Culture*, *13*(2), 153–173.

Mowforth, M., & Munt, I. (2009). *Tourism and sustainability: Development, globalization and new tourism in the third world* (3rd ed.). London: Routledge.

Peterson, B. (2012). Dignity, memory and the future under siege: Reconciliation and nation building in post-apartheid South Africa. Paper presented to seminar, Witwatersrand Institute for Social and Economic Research, University of the Witwatersrand, Johannesburg, September 10, 2012. Also published in Opondo, S. O., & Shapiro, M. J. (Eds.). (2012). *The new violent cartography: Geo-analysis after the aesthetic turn*. London: Routledge.

Poon, A. (1994). The 'new tourism' revolution. *Tourism Management*, *15*(2), 91–92.

Rassool, C. (2000). The rise of heritage and the reconstitution of history in South Africa. *Journal of Cape History*, *26*, 1–21.

Rassool, C. (2009). Power, knowledge and the politics of public pasts. Paper presented to seminar at Nelson Mandela Centre of Memory, April 7, 2009, 17 pp.

Rassool, C., & Witz, L. (1996). South Africa: A world in one country. *Cahiers d'Etudes Africaines*, *143*(XXXVI-3), 335–371.

Tomaselli, K. (2014). Who owns what? Indigenous knowledge and struggles over representation. *Critical Arts*, *28*(4), 631–647.

Urry, J. (1990). *The tourist gaze, leisure and travel in contemporary societies*. London: Sage.

Wang, N. (1999). Rethinking authenticity in tourism experience. *Annals of Tourism Research*, *26*, 349–370.

Wang, Y. (2007). Customized authenticity begins at home. *Annals of Tourism Research*, *34*(3), 789–804.

CHAPTER 19

HIGHER EDUCATION TOURISM COURSES IN BRAZIL

Teresa Catramby and Priscilla Dutra

ABSTRACT

In Brazil, higher education Tourism courses emerged in the 1970s as a teaching and research field aiming to raise the students' critical awareness toward a contextualized learning within the political, economic, and sociocultural scenario of the country. This chapter discusses the structure of higher education Tourism courses based on a new academic structure. The data are drawn from the monthly informative bulletins of the Center of Tourism Research (CEPETUR) of the Catholic University of Petrópolis, Rio de Janeiro, wherein a group of teachers report their activities in both professional and academic sector of Tourism. The findings show that undergraduate students are encouraged to produce conceptual texts enabling their insertion in scientific research projects under a new conception of academic field.

Keywords: Higher education; knowledge production; teaching and research; professional qualification

Tourism and Hospitality Management
Advances in Culture, Tourism and Hospitality Research, Volume 12, 265–273
ISSN: 1871-3173/doi:10.1108/S1871-317320160000012020

INTRODUCTION

In order to understand the path and the main conceptions of higher education Tourism courses in Brazil, an analysis of the structure of the Brazilian university as a whole is necessary. Different from the American model which associates teaching and research (ideas) with services (functional), the Brazilian model adopts an entrepreneurial view of Tourism in order to graduate specialists to meet the interests of the State's productive sector and its ideology. While the German model focuses on the indissolubility of teaching, research and qualification (the Humboldtian model), the French one proposes less State power and ideology. The latter models inspire institutions all over the world and are later influenced by the American model wherein the instrumental rationality and the fragmentation of the intellectual work replace the German ideal.

Ever since the creation of higher education Tourism courses in Brazil, research has never been a priority and the available courses are merely ways to create technical and political personnel. From 1968 onward, different views regarding the importance of academic research starts to change the didactic structure of the universities which adopts the American model as reference for producing knowledge and student's critical awareness.

This chapter aims at providing an overview of the structure of higher education Tourism course in Brazil from its origins to its actual status. Based on the new academic structure, we conduct an analysis of the monthly bulletins of the Center of Research in Tourism (CEPETUR, acronym in Portuguese) of the Catholic University of Petrópolis (UCP), Rio de Janeiro, in the 1970s. In these bulletins, a group of faculty members reports both the professional and academic activities of the Tourism sector and also encourages undergraduates to produce conceptual texts so as to engage them in scientific research projects within a new academic conception.

The chapter presents the contextual background that results in the creation of the higher education Tourism courses in Brazil, provides the development of such courses within an institutional and academic context, analyses the contents of the CEPETUR bulletins and its relevance for the professional and academic Tourism sector, and concludes with critical insight into the actual status of the sector in Brazil.

THEORETICAL AND INSTITUTIONAL CONSIDERATIONS

The 1960s is marked by important political and educational changes in Brazil. In the political context, there are urban guerillas based on the student movements, governmental repression and control of the university's activities. Given this scenario, the military dictatorship enacts Law 5.540/1968 under pressure proposing a deep reorganization in the Brazilian higher education system. The government orders specialists some studies on the matter, such as the Meira Mattos Report elaborated by the American professor Rudolph Atcon, and the report of the Higher Education Council, integrating Brazilian and American professors. The so-called MEC-USAID Agreements are then signed between the Ministry of Education and Culture (MEC) and the United States Agency for International Development (USAID).

On the organizational level, the reform includes several elements from the American universities: the departments extinguish the professorship system; the credit system eliminates the serial and annual program courses; the academic career is institutionalized and the legislation links faculty admission and career progression to academic title. All institutions should follow this model. The educational authorities then create the budget and legal conditions for full-time faculty hiring though some part-time faculty migrates to a full-time position without improving their academic qualifications.

Before the 1968 reform, private higher education is organized the same way as public education. It has a semi-state character by which the institutions of Catholic higher education, for example, keeps depending on public financing to support their activities (Martins, 2008). The structure arisen out of this demand tends to be qualitatively different from the previous one. "As it is another system in terms of nature and objectives, structured in terms of educational enterprises" (Martins, 2008, p. 3), it subverts the articulation of teaching, research and student academic autonomy. It is also worth pointing out that teaching at the institutions of Catholic higher education does not aim at expansion to meet a general demand but rather remain as institutions to meet the local elite's demands.

Based on a utilitarian characteristic, the reform establishes a direct relation between education and productive system providing workforce and consumers. De Paula (2002, p. 12) adds that:

> The idea of rationalization was the basic principle of the 1968 Reform, which resulted in other policies, all of them based on own categories of technical and entrepreneur language: efficiency, efficacy, productivity, etc. This is why the educational process was associated with the production of goods which, as in all economic process, implied in cost and benefit.

Due to the national socio-economic development and driven by an expanding sector seen as a field of professionalization, the first higher education Tourism course opens in a private institution in Brazil in 1971 under the military regime. Barreto (2004) argues that, at that moment, there is a persecution of the "thinking courses" which may oppose the government's proposal and thus the incentive is toward the creation of courses to somehow promote technology and a superficial understanding of society.

In the process of the institutionalization of higher education Tourism courses in Brazil, four favorable variables include: (a) the creation of the Brazilian Tourism Enterprise (EMBRATUR, acronym in Portuguese) in 1966; (b) the investment for improving the touristic infrastructure with the creation of the Investment Fund to graduate qualified workforce; (c) the expansion of private higher education institutions; and (d) leisure valorization.

The institutionalization of Tourism in Brazil occurs with the creation of the EMBRATUR through Deliberation no. 35/1971 of the Ministry of Education and Culture (MEC), which regulates the first higher education Tourism course in the country. Matias (2002, p. 5) points out that,

> After the creation of the regulatory laws, there were some discussions to insert the Tourism course in the Business Administration Colleges but, due to the reality of Tourism in Brazil, this idea was abandoned.

In 1971, the Morumbi College, now University of Anhembi Morumbi, in São Paulo, opens the first Tourism course in Brazil with full autonomy as "the first Tourism courses were either implemented in autonomous university units or linked to the equally new Communication and Arts courses" (Matias, 2002, p. 4). It is "a new course for a promising country, [...], the country of the future has met the profession of the future," argues Trigo (2000, p. 245). In the following years, other courses are created in the University of São Paulo (1973) and the Catholic institutions by request of the National Commerce Confederation and supported by then Minister of Education, Jarbas Passarinho. Table 1splays the timeline of the opening of the higher education Tourism courses in Brazil.

As far as curricula are concerned, Matias (2002, pp. 13–19) explains the bureaucratic path of the implementation of minimum curricula of the Tourism courses through the unnumbered Resolution of January 28, 1971, which sets forth the minimum contents and the duration of the courses. In 1981, the Commission of Curricula and Programs proposes the elaboration of a new curriculum with qualifications to the III Congress of Brazilian Tourism (Embetur). The proposal is sent to the Federal Council of Education (CFE) and forwarded to get then EMBRATUR's opinion which in turn seeks advice of businessmen, undergraduates and graduate students, and institutions. The terms of the Resolution 35/1971 remain with the suggestion of a minimum curriculum based on basic and professional subjects

Table 1. Timeline of the Opening of Higher Education Tourism Courses in Brazil.

Year	Higher Education Institutions	City – State
1971	Faculdade de Turismo no Morumbi	São Paulo – SP
1972	Universidade Católica de Petrópolis	Petrópolis – RJ
1973	Faculdade de Turismo da Guanabara	Rio de Janeiro – RJ
	Faculdade Ibero-Americana	São Paulo – SP
	Faculdade de Ciências Exatas, Administrativas e Sociais, União Pioneira de Educação social.	Brasília – DF
	Escola de Comunicação e artes da Universidade de São Paulo	São Paulo – SP
1974	Pontifícia Universidade de Campinas	Campinas – SP
1975	Universidade Católica de Pernambuco	Recife – PE
1976	Faculdade Associação do Litoral Santista	Santos – SP
	Faculdade Capital de Administração e Estatística	São Paulo – SP
1977	Faculdade Hélio Alonso	Rio de Janeiro – RJ
1980	Associação Educacional Veiga de Almeida	Rio de Janeiro – RJ
	Faculdade de Turismo Embaixador Paschoal Carlos Magno	Campinas – SP
	Pontifícia Universidade Católica de Campinas	Campinas – SP
1981	Instituto Cultural Newton Paiva Ferreira	Belo Horizonte – MG
1984	Faculdade de Turismo da Bahia	Salvador – BA
1985	Faculdade de Ciência de Foz do Iguaçu	Foz do Iguaçu – PR
	Universidade de Fortaleza	Fortaleza – CE

Source: Adapted from Turismo (2014).

(optative subjects). In 1995, the Brazilian Association of Bachelor's Degree in Tourism (ABBTUR/National) presents a new proposal with a minimum curriculum comprised of a common core and diversified subjects based on emphasis, and also elective subjects. In the second semester of 1996, the ABBTU, jointly with the Association of Tourism Managers and Hospitality Schools (CNE), puts forward a new proposal to the CNE with mandatory implementation from 1998 onward. It proposes a minimum 3,000 hours/class course load with the duration of four years to be concluded in up to seven years.

Critics of higher education in Tourism and the lack of focus on different levels makes it difficult to interpret the differences in technical, technological and Bachelor's degree education. As research is not a priority, higher education in Tourism courses do not duly consider scientific research and student critical awareness. As pointed out in Trigo (2002, p. 2),

> ... some people criticize the courses claiming that they are too "theoretical" and very little linked to the "market." I have an opposite analysis as a scholar. The most operational courses, that is, the most practical ones linked to the "market" should be technical, sequential and technological courses. The Bachelor's degree courses should be really theoretical and I think our students need to read much more. The Bachelor's degree aims at giving initial conditions so as the profession can have a strategic view of the touristic phenomenon, have conditions to do management work and a bear a critical and reflexive stance on the area. In short, a solid theoretical basis is fundamental. The contents of the Tourism courses are based on the tripod human sciences, management subjects and specific subjects. There is no (or there should not be) a dichotomy between theory and practice in the university, but rather a work that assures maturity and knowledge to the future professional. ... The Bachelor's degree Tourism courses should require more theory from their students so as to justify the four-year education and the title of "Bachelor's degree in Tourism" or "tourismologist."

Recent proposals have changed the national contexts of higher education in Tourism including the reduction of course load and the diversification of the own qualification. In the 2000s, the Tourism courses change their course load enabling the creation of technological courses, most of them based on the presented proposal. The Bachelor's degree courses offered by private institutions opt for reducing course load but nowadays the most common is full-time undergraduate education (both Bachelor's degree and Licentiate's degree) in public institutions.

With the government's incentive, Brazilian universities assign a priority to the insertion of Tourism undergraduates in the market and their qualification in the area, different from the current proposal which has a more scientific view of Tourism with focus on its intellectual character and concern about knowledge production. It is worth pointing out that the current academic degree in Tourism, even with the several changes throughout the years, still does not prioritize the professionals' intellectual knowledge. As only a few Brazilian public universities offer post-graduation courses, they try to engage the undergraduates in scientific research projects, as in the case of the Center of Tourism Research (CEPETUR) in the Catholic University of Petrópolis.

METHOD AND FINDINGS

The need to qualify workforce in Tourism results in the opening of the first higher education Tourism course in Brazil at the Catholic University of

Petrópolis (UCP), in the State of Rio de Janeiro, in partnership with the Universidad Autonoma de Guadalajara, Mexico in 1972. The UCP welcomes the professor Rosa Maria de La Fuente, responsible for the teaching Hospitality Management and Food and Beverages, and which also helps to structure the course. In 1973, the first Center of Tourism Research (CEPETUR) is created in the same institution aiming at collecting data, articles, interviews published by scholars and undergraduates, and any type of relevant information related to the sector to support the undergraduates and the academic community in general. The main goal of the CEPETUR is to provide undergraduates and professors with relevant touristic information of the cities directly related to Tourism, such as new laws, decrees, and regulations which influence areas of touristic interest.

In 1978, the CEPETUR launches monthly bulletins, reaching a total of 3,000 printed issues, and distributes them to several educational institutions, enterprises, and public bodies. The analysis of the bulletins evidences the attempt to spread information about the sector's activities while, at the same time, enabling the student's participation in the publication of conceptual texts since the military dictatorship in Brazil in the 1970s. The bulletins also establish a greater relationship among the Tourism undergraduates of other institutions so as they can share a general view of all the elements involved in the area.

The contents of the CEPETUR bulletins cover the sectors of leisure, urbanism, ecology, historical heritage, museum, Brazilian art and cultures, folklore, transport, hospitality, and economy. In leisure, the bulletins give several suggestions of touristic attractions integrated to the cultural context of the country. As far as urbanism is concerned, the Center claims that urban planning is needed to integrate the cities further away from the city centers since they play an important role in local history and culture. Ecology has been a much-discussed theme since the 1970s with concerns about the human action in the environment, essential to the implementation of tourism, and care of using ecosystem resources within ecological possibilities. Historical heritage, museum, Brazilian art and cultures, and folklore gain more room in the bulletins because the CEPETUR is located in the historical city of Petrópolis. Their concern includes the conservation and restoration of historical heritage buildings, the incentive for visiting cultural events, projects in museums sponsored by FUNARTE and EMBRATUR, and folklore valorization which directly portraits the local culture mainly to tourists, as it is also the case of Salvador.

The transport sections provide information about the new technologies in the aviation sector, port maintenance, and bike paths as a new tourist option to reduce fuel costs. Regarding hospitality, the bulletins discuss the expansion of the SENAC hotel-schools engaging the Tourism under-graduates into joining their professional training centers to work in hotels. In regard to economy, which directly influences Tourism, they present the debates between the government and entrepreneurs, and the promises and news to turn Tourism into one of the country's source of wealth.

On the whole, the CEPETUR bulletins deliver knowledge to Tourism undergraduates concerning the course they have chosen, show them the several sectors related in touristic activities and provide them with a critical look on several human, environmental, administrative, historical and social actions, which result in positive and negative aspects in both professional and academic areas.

CONCLUSION AND IMPLICATIONS

To fully understand knowledge production nowadays in any area, it is necessary to understand how the universities come to life and how they produce knowledge within its structure. Since its origins until today, the new Brazilian university structure and the new intellectual social actors have gone through deep reforms and changes.

This chapter provides an overview of higher education Tourism courses in Brazil within an institutional and academic framework. Some educational policies are also described so as to contextualize the creation of higher education Tourism courses. In particular, we analyze the monthly bulletins published by the Center of Tourism Research (CEPETUR) at the Catholic University of Petrópolis, Rio de Janeiro, which is considered a reference in the Brazilian tourism and academic sector.

In the current globalized world, the American standard of university model, based on curricularization, departmentalization and *campi*, is widely spread in order to optimize the continuous production of qualified under-graduates for specific professions. Likewise, higher education Tourism courses in Brazil have gone through changes both in their curricular struc-tures to meet legal demands and course loads. For example, most of the institutions have changed their Bachelor's degree courses to technologi-cal ones.

The claim is to consider the university as a site of cultural transforma-tion. Therefore, the Humboldtian model resurfaces in the need of associat-ing teaching and research to reformulate knowledge to be taught.

REFERENCES

Barreto, M. (2004). *Discutindo o ensino universitário de Turismo*. São Paulo: Papirus.

De Paula, M. de F. C. (2002). A influência das concepções alemã e francesa em suas fundações. *Tempo Social, 14*(2), 147–161.

Matias, M. (2002). *Turismo: formação e profissionalização (30 anos de história)*. Barueri: Manole.

Martins, C. B. (2008). A Reforma Universitária de 1968 e a abertura para o ensino superior privado no Brasil. *Educação e Sociedade, Campinas, 30*(106), 15–35.

Trigo, L. G. G. (2000). A importância da educação para o Turismo. In B. H. G. Lage & P. C. Milone (Eds.), *Turismo: Teoria e Prática*. São Paulo: Atlas.

Trigo, L. G. G. (2002). *Turismo Básico*. São Paulo: Senac.

Turismo, R. (2014). Retrieved from http://www.revistaturismo.com.br/. Accessed on October 17, 2014.

CHAPTER 20

DEVELOPING INTERCULTURAL SKILLS FOR HOSPITALITY STUDENTS IN CHINA

Alan Wong and Cathy H. C. Hsu

ABSTRACT

Intercultural awareness and skills are important competencies for hospitality and tourism management program graduates due to the internationalization of the tourism industry. Graduates will work with coworkers and serve customers from diverse cultural backgrounds. With the exponential growth of China's tourism industry, an examination of intercultural awareness and skills education in China's hospitality and tourism higher education is needed. This study employed a qualitative approach by interviewing 11 educators in Chinese mainland universities on their views of the current status of intercultural awareness education, their role in this learning process, and how their program offerings enhance students' learning of cultural diversity. Implications for administrators and faculty members are discussed.

Keywords: Cultural sensitivity; intercultural awareness; diversity; student competency; China

Tourism and Hospitality Management
Advances in Culture, Tourism and Hospitality Research, Volume 12, 275–291
Copyright © 2016 by Emerald Group Publishing Limited
All rights of reproduction in any form reserved
ISSN: 1871-3173/doi:10.1108/S1871-317320160000012016

INTRODUCTION

Intercultural awareness and skills are becoming essential work competencies for hospitality and tourism management graduates at different levels. With the growth of globalization and cultural diversity in the workplace, there is the need for employees to have a better understanding of fellow employees from different ethnic and cultural backgrounds. In addition, those working in the hospitality and tourism industry will encounter tourists from different parts of the world (Gannon, 2008; Taylor & McArthur, 2009; Wong, 1992; Wong & Chan, 2010; Ye, Zhang, & Yuen, 2012).

China's tourism industry has opened up since 1978, and was ranked fourth as one of the World's Top Tourism Destination in 2013 (UNWTO, 2014). In light of this trend, China's tourism and hotel industry will definitely face diversity in terms of international customers, multinational business operations, and the workforce. There will be more cross-cultural interactions between Chinese staff and tourists and colleagues from different cultures. In 2013, the number of foreign inbound tourists to China was 26.29 million. Although Asians make up 61.19% of the foreign inbound market, international tourists come from a diverse range of countries. The top eight countries generating between 1 and 4 million visitors to China are Korea, Japan, Russia, the United States, Vietnam, Malaysia, Mongolia, and Philippines (Table 1).

Tourists from diverse cultural backgrounds may have different needs which Chinese staff may not be well prepared to handle. At the end of 2013, there were 3,100 five- and four-star hotels in China (CNTA, 2014). Despite the growth in the number of local customers and talent, most multinational hotels serve international tourists and employ expatriate managers in key positions, such as general manager, resident manager, food and beverage manager/director, director of sales and marketing, executive chef, and human resources manager. "Developing cultural awareness is a professional obligation for managers in order to help them become more aware of other values, habits, customs, and lifestyles that must be understood for an effective working environment" (Welch, Tanke, & Glover, 1988 quoted in Gamio & Sneed, 1992, p. 13). Wong and Chan (2010) indicated that "cultural sensitivity" is one of the key elements which constitute employees' perception of a professional hotel manager. However, these managers receive little cross-cultural training (Dewald & Self, 2008). Also, Horng and Lu (2006) indicated that "international service" skills will be one of the most important professional competencies in the future. The literature indicates that there is limited research in this area, particularly in the China context.

Table 1. 16 Major Tourist Source Countries for Mainland China in 2013.

	Country	Inbound Tourist No. (Millions)
1	Korea	3.97
2	Japan	2.88
3	Russia	2.19
4	USA	2.09
5	Vietnam	1.37
6	Malaysia	1.21
7	Mongolia	1.05
8	Philippines	1.00
9	Singapore	0.97
10	Australia	0.72
11	Canada	0.68
12	India	0.68
13	Thailand	0.65
14	Germany	0.65
15	UK	0.63
16	Indonesia	0.61

Source: CNTA (2014).

THEORETICAL CONSIDERATION

Previous research has mainly focused on the cultural training needs of and the benefits of training to expatriates or managers, not local or front-line employees (Dewald & Self, 2008; Gamio & Sneed, 1992; Lee & Chon, 2000). Dewald and Self (2008) suggested that "Cross cultural training should not be limited to expatriate managers, but should also include local management and staff to enable local managers to better understand the expatriate" (p. 361). Researchers are now concerned whether our curriculum in hospitality and tourism schools meets this need of the industry (Gannon, 2008; Heares, Devine, & Baum, 2007).

Drawing from two previous studies, one conducted among hospitality and tourism educators and the other across international hotel companies, Gannon (2008) concluded that both sets of respondents lacked a rigorous understanding of the importance of intercultural awareness and communication skills. Heares et al. (2007) argued that hospitality and tourism educators face the challenge of redesigning their curricula to meet the industry's need for interculturally competent employees. Strategies in curriculum development have included preparing students to become competent intercultural communicators and encouraging the development of cultural awareness and cultural sensitivity. Heares et al. (2007) proposed a conceptual model of cultural diversity in the curriculum as a pathway to investigate the integration of cultural diversity within tourism programs. The model includes four themes:

1. *Training requirements of tomorrow's hospitality graduates*: For example, are they sensitive about cultural diversity, including values and beliefs; do they have the skills to deal with diverse cultures, including communication skills; do they understand discriminatory/legislative requirements?
2. *Educators' training needs*: There is a need to understand educators' development needs. Educators must be trained how to teach cross-cultural interactions and handle learning experiences among diverse students. Resources are required to deliver such training.
3. *Program content/learning outcomes*: Program content could include cultural sensitivity and awareness, communication and language training, negotiation skills, diversity values, and legislation.
4. *Program assessment and methods of delivery*: Possible approaches include on-the-job versus off-the-job training, field trips, partnerships among educators/employers/other stakeholders, workshops/seminars in small groups, interactive TV/video/film, mentoring, and problem-solving scenarios.

Similarly, Black (2004) suggested that there are four areas that contribute to the internationalization of hospitality management education:

1. *Faculty* (faculty exchange, undertaking joint international research, consultancy and publications with overseas partners).
2. *Students* (exchanging students, operating double degree and integrated joint programs).
3. *Curriculum content* (internationalization of disciplines, adding international courses to the curriculum, adding language courses, providing work or study opportunities).
4. *International alliances* (exchanging faculty, exchanging students, setting up programs).

In the Asian context, Sangpikul (2009) also indicated that faculty, students, curriculum development, and international alliances are the key elements in internationalizing Thai higher education. Internationalization could be a tool for developing global human resources and enhancing the intercultural understanding of human society.

Twenty years ago, some of the problems faced by hospitality and tourism education in mainland China's colleges and universities were related to the curriculum and courses. To a certain extent, these problems were related to the limited experience of most of the faculty members (Zhao, 1991). Most faculty members had been transferred to tourism programs from other disciplines such as economics, management, and foreign trade. There were also some professionals who worked in the industry and fresh college graduates who assumed the role of tourism and hospitality educators. In 2000, researchers still found that "A key dilemma of tourism education in China is poor curriculum design. Graduates from tourism education institutes and vocational training schools cannot fulfill industry needs and demands" (Lam & Xiao, 2000, p. 291). In reviewing the problems and challenges that tourism higher education in China was facing, Zhang and Fan (2005) concluded that "China's higher education in tourism needs to be integrated with the international tourism program practice, especially in curriculum design, internship, and opportunity for relevant working experiences" (p. 131).

To meet the needs of the industry, hospitality and tourism programs need to produce graduates with intercultural awareness and skills. To develop strategies of intercultural awareness and skills development for hospitality and tourism higher education in China, this study aims to provide some baseline information on the status of intercultural education in selected tourism programs in mainland China. Specifically, this study was designed to answer the following research questions:

1. What is the current situation regarding intercultural awareness or cultural diversity education in China's hospitality and tourism management programs?
2. What are educators' perceptions of their role in this learning process?
3. How do the program offerings in hospitality and tourism management departments in mainland China enhance students' learning of intercultural awareness knowledge and skills?

METHOD

A qualitative approach was adopted for this exploratory study. Nine individual in-depth interviews and one group interview with two informants were carried out with heads and faculty members of hospitality and tourism management programs from seven universities in mainland China to seek their perceptions of the current status of intercultural awareness or cultural diversity education, their role(s) in such education, and the design and effectiveness of their offerings in providing such education. The interviews were conducted in the interviewees' offices in six cities in China from February to July 2012. An interview guide, which included the study's objectives and semi-structured questions, was emailed to each participant 2–3 days before the interview. Data collection was completed when a theoretical saturation was reached and no significantly different insights were obtained (Strauss & Corbin, 1998). The conversations were voice recorded, and the transcription content was analyzed manually by two researchers independently. The researchers compared and discussed their coding to reach an agreement on the final categorizations. Each of the emerging themes from the data was listed and categorized. Items from the data were classified under an existing category if they were related to any of the themes; otherwise, items were classified as new themes. The frequency of each theme was also counted. The interviews and data analysis were conducted in Chinese. The results were translated into English for reporting purposes.

FINDINGS

The selected universities included those located in more developed coastal provinces as well as ones located in less developed inland provinces in order to provide a diverse range of institutions. Five of the interviewees were professors, four were associate professors, and two were lecturers. All of the participants were teaching one or two subjects for undergraduate students in their schools and so they interacted with students frequently. Nine of the respondents were deans or directors providing vision and direction to tourism education in their universities and guiding their schools' faculty members.

The qualitative data were analyzed in terms of the three research questions, and each question is discussed below.

Q1. What is the current situation regarding intercultural awareness or cultural diversity education in mainland China's hospitality and tourism management programs?

As shown in Table 2, three key themes were identified from the conversations: (a) perceived importance of intercultural awareness education; (b) intercultural awareness education activities, mainly focusing on three

Table 2. Current Situation regarding Intercultural Awareness
Education in Mainland China.

Theme	Frequency of Interviewee Comments	Subthemes
Importance of intercultural awareness education	11	More and more important given economic development in China; especially important for hotel and tourism students.
Intercultural awareness education activities	11	Faculty exchange, student activities, curriculum design.
Uneven development in China	6	International cities have more resources and information, remote areas have less; other disciplines have more resources.

areas, namely faculty, students, and curriculum; and (c) the uneven development of intercultural awareness education in different regions of China.

1. *Perceived Importance of Intercultural Awareness Education*

All respondents indicated that intercultural awareness or cultural diversity education is important in hotel and tourism management programs. With the development of the hotel and tourism industry, intercultural awareness education has become more and more important, especially for hotel and tourism education. Respondent #4 reviewed the development of intercultural education:

> During the 1980s, intercultural education focused on introducing foreign cultures to students or comparing the differences between Chinese and foreign cultures. However, in the 1990s, more and more universities, especially Beijing International Studies University and Sun Yat-Sen University, emphasized cultural education. Many intercultural educational activities were held, such as faculty outbound visits and studies, inbound and outbound student exchanges, and so on.

Respondent #1 also stated that intercultural awareness education is strategically important for hotel and tourism subjects:

> The tourism and hotel management school has already included intercultural study into the program as we are providing qualified human resources with intercultural awareness and communication skills to tourism and hotel businesses.

2. *Intercultural Awareness Education Activities*

There are three main aspects of intercultural activities: (1) faculty exchange activities, such as attending international conferences, outbound visiting scholar schemes, and joint research with scholars abroad; (2) student exchange activities, such as outbound study programs, inbound exchange student programs, and student-organized foreign cultural events; and (3) the integration of intercultural knowledge and skills into the program curriculum.

(1) Faculty activities: All of the respondents indicated that their institutions have faculty members with international education or work experience. For instance, respondent #2 stated:

> All of our staff have international education or work experience. Our school provides funding for faculty overseas exchange activities.

Respondent #3 added

> We have faculty members with work experience in international organizations such as PATA and UNWTO. In their classes, they can share their international experience with our students.

Meanwhile, several respondents mentioned that their schools have related policies on inviting overseas scholars for visits, research, and teaching. For example, respondent #2 described the situation in her school:

> The Dean of our school is a foreigner, a top researcher in his field. He has good connections to invite top scholars to be guest lecturers in our school.

However, it is interesting to note that one of the barriers to faculty members going overseas for cultural exchange activities is government policy restrictions. The Chinese Government allows only a small quota of faculty members in each university to go abroad, even when a faculty has financial support for a project. The policy is not consistent year by year; it can be changed temporarily and suddenly, and therefore faculties cannot apply to attend international conferences in advance as required. Respondent 3# stated:

> The government only allows a small quota of faculty members to go overseas each year. The whole university is under this restriction and we cannot control it.

(2) Student activities: All of the respondents pointed out that students' outbound visits are a great help in intercultural education and that students benefit from overseas educational and working experiences. For example, respondent #3 stated:

> We have partnerships with foreign universities or sister universities such as The Hong Kong Polytechnic University, Queensland University, and Purdue University. Our students can participate in exchange studies for one or two semesters.

All of the seven universities studied had inbound exchange students. Respondent #5 stated:

> We have foreign undergraduate and postgraduate students studying in our tourism school: 60–70 Korean students and several students from Thailand, Mongolia, and Japan. They have little Chinese language ability, but we provide bilingual (Chinese and English) courses for them. The Chinese Government provides funding for foreign students' studies in our university.

In addition to inbound and outbound exchange activities, various cultural events are held on campus to benefit students' intercultural awareness and improve their intercultural skills. For instance, respondent #2 commented:

> We initiate cultural-related seminars and activities for students, such as an "international tourism week," and students organized the events themselves. They usually invite guest lecturers and foreign students to participate or share their interests at these events.

(3) Curriculum integration: Intercultural awareness no longer only focuses on language studies, as was previously the case; it is now integrated into many subjects in tourism education. For example, respondent #1 reported:

> In our school, cultural diversity is included as a topic in many subjects, such as management science, even though it is not set as a separate subject.

Respondent #5 shared the practices in his school:

> We import textbooks from overseas universities for some subjects, such as International Hotel Industry and Cross-Cultural Studies. The content is first taught in Chinese and then bilingually to make students aware of up-to-date knowledge from abroad.

3. *Uneven Development of Intercultural Education*

Concerns were expressed by the interviewees that intercultural education resources are unevenly distributed among different geographic regions and disciplines. First, universities in remote areas have fewer resources, such as less qualified teaching staff to deliver intercultural knowledge to students, fewer opportunities to set up international alliances with overseas universities, and less financial support for student exchange activities. For instance, Respondent #9 stated:

> Our teaching staff faces language barriers when supervising students' exchange
> activities as most of our faculty members in the tourism school can only speak
> Chinese and very little English. Such language barriers limit our attendance at inter-
> national conferences and our overseas visiting activities.

Colleagues from the same university (Respondents #10 and #11) added:

> We have an accessibility issue as well. As we are located in a small city in the south-
> west of China, some invited visiting scholars cannot travel to our city directly, and
> this seriously holds back our intercultural activities.

Respondent #3 observed the uneven development and stated:

> In general, I think the importance of intercultural education among universities in
> China is improving gradually; however, there are still differences among different
> universities in different locations. For example, a university in an international city,
> such as Beijing or Shanghai, enjoys more resources than a university in a
> remote area.

Second, hotel and tourism management programs are not as competitive
as other disciplines in terms of receiving universities' attention. Respondents
#6 and #7 made the following comments:

> The tourism school in our university is a young school; the university assigns less
> financial resources to tourism subjects. For example, the university sets a quota of
> 25–30 faculty members per year for visiting activities, but we have 21 schools in the
> university, which makes this very competitive. So, there is less chance for the tour-
> ism faculty. (Respondent #6)

> Our university has cooperation activities with about 60 institutions abroad; how-
> ever, the tourism school does not have a successful project for student exchange
> activities at this moment. (Respondent #7)

Q2. What are educators' perceptions of their role in this learning
process?

As summarized in Table 3, when discussing the role of educators in
intercultural awareness education, five major roles emerged from the data,
namely (1) information provider, (2) curriculum planner, (3) coordinator,
(4) influencer, and (5) participant.

1. *Information Provider*
When the interviewees were asked to describe their roles in intercultural
awareness education, most of them responded that they were lecturers
or information deliverers first. For example, respondent #4 stated:

Table 3. Role of Educators in Intercultural Awareness Education.

Theme	Frequency of Interviewee Comments	Subthemes
Information provider	11	Lecturer, information deliverer
Curriculum planner	6	Planner
Coordinator	6	Initiator, coordinator
Influencer	4	Influencer
Participant	4	Participant in intercultural activities

We teach students intercultural knowledge and educate them about proper attitudes toward intercultural education. After studying, students can identify real and fake foreign cultures and use the knowledge in their future work.

Respondent #1 added:

We are not only lecturers of knowledge in the classroom but also information deliverers, delivering what we have personally experienced and observed from our own intercultural educational and work experience.

2. *Curriculum Planner*

As teaching faculty members and administrators of tourism schools, six respondents emphasized their role as curriculum planners. For instance, respondents #1 and #2 made the following comments:

Based on the students' needs, we offer courses related to intercultural education, such as an international hotel industry course, and we also have a policy of letting students freely select subjects run by other departments, such as Japanese language study. (Respondent #1)

We make decisions on the teaching methods and modes. For example, some courses about theories are taught 100% in Chinese, and some courses related to cultural comparisons are taught in bilingual mode. (Respondent #2)

3. *Coordinator*

Six of the respondents pointed out that they meet international educators at conferences or on other occasions. After discussions with these educators, they initiate faculty or student exchange programs and then act as coordinators for intercultural activities. Two of the respondents explained their roles:

> I am an organizer, and I contact overseas universities to arrange cooperation activities. (Respondent #7)

> We contact other universities and provide exchange opportunities for faculty members and students. (Respondent #2)

4. *Influencer*

In addition to teaching students intercultural knowledge, educators influence students' attitudes toward intercultural study, as illustrated in the following comments:

> We educate students to have proper attitudes toward intercultural study. For example, students may not realize the importance of foreign culture study or have no interest in it. We spark their interest in studying it. (Respondent #5)

> We encourage students to participate in overseas exchange activities. (Respondent #2)

5. *Participant*

Some respondents perceived themselves as participants in intercultural education, as respondent #6 explained:

> Educators are participants in intercultural awareness education. We have outbound visits to overseas universities and attend their classes to learn. We also participate in international conferences, research seminars, and cultural events.

Q3. How do the program offerings in the hospitality and tourism departments in mainland China enhance students' learning of intercultural awareness knowledge and skills?

In terms of how the program offerings in hospitality and tourism institutions enhance students' learning of intercultural knowledge and skills, three key themes were identified from the interviewees' responses: (1) exchange program, (2) language ability, and (3) overseas internship (as indicated in Table 4).

1. *Exchange Program*

All respondents agreed that an exchange program can enhance students' intercultural knowledge and skills. For example, respondent #1 stated:

> Our returning exchange students have said that they are more comfortable when talking with foreigners, and they can integrate themselves into a foreign culture through an exchange program faster than they could through studying a foreign culture in their home country. Some students even obtain part-time job offers in the host country. Students can learn to think in foreign ways and communicate with foreigners effectively.

Table 4. How Program Offerings Enhance Students' Knowledge
and Skills.

Theme	Frequency of Interviewee Comments	Subthemes
Exchange program	11	Experiential study
Language ability	7	Language skills
Overseas internship	4	Knowledge application and enhancement

2. *Language Ability*

According to some of the interviewees, language study is a basic but important means of communication. As elaborated in the following comments, a curriculum that emphasizes foreign language ability benefits students' understanding of intercultural knowledge and their ability to apply skills in the multicultural hospitality and tourism field:

> Our university stems from language education. Our students majoring in hospitality and tourism are also required to master English and pass a national English exam. With the help of English language skills, students can read English literature broadly and understand foreign culture directly without the interpretation of others. (Respondent #3)

> Most of our students master a foreign language of Southeast Asia, such as Vietnamese or Thai. They can participate in overseas study in Southeast Asian countries and can easily find a job after graduation as they can speak Chinese and can serve Chinese guests in these countries. (Respondent #9)

3. *Overseas Internship*

All of the tourism institutions represented by the interviewees have internship programs which require students to have at least a 3−6-month internship in the tourism and hospitality industry. Many of the institutions offer opportunities for overseas internships; for example, respondent #6 stated:

> Our students who have one year of study overseas can gain internship opportunities in the host country. For example, internships jobs lasting about one to three months are arranged by the host university in Vietnam.

Students' foreign cultural knowledge and communication skills are enhanced during internships. As respondent #8 stated:

> Through internships in a business environment, such as a hotel or travel agency, students can experience the real world. Students are the real staff. They apply

the knowledge learned in the classroom and broaden their knowledge through interaction with the guests; they benefit a lot from this.

CONCLUSION AND IMPLICATIONS

Overall, the results from this study indicate that the current situation
regarding intercultural awareness or cultural diversity education in mainland China's hospitality and tourism management programs is on the right
track. Senior hospitality and tourism educators in China are aware of the
importance of intercultural awareness education. They have taken actions
to implement policies to realize this idea, mainly by providing support to
faculty members and students through exchange activities and better curriculum design. To a certain extent, the four areas that Black (2004) suggested contribute to the internationalization of education have all been
utilized. Based on the examples provided in the model by Heares et al.
(2007), more can be done to integrate cultural awareness and diversity
issues into the curriculum.

Mirroring the uneven economic development of the country, intercultural awareness education is developing unevenly in different geographic
areas of China. Universities in less developed regions mainly lack the
required resources and face a bigger language barrier to engage in exchange
activities with universities overseas. The implication for Chinese hospitality
and tourism educators in these regions is that they need to fight for more
resources or support from the government. At the university level, administrators should communicate with government officials at the national level
to request a review of its funding polices so as to help disadvantaged remo-
tely located institutions.

At the program and departmental levels, hospitality and tourism administrators need to convince universities to channel more resources to this field
of education. Otherwise, China will lag behind in nurturing sufficient hospitality and tourism management students with the competencies to work in a
culturally diverse workplace and provide culturally sensitive service to tourists from different parts of the world. International experience indicates that
internationalization and cultural diversity education needs long-term commitment from faculties and educational institutions (Gannon, 2008).

For educators, one of the strategies might be to lobby support from various departments of local government to bid for international conferences
to be held in their city. Cooperation among universities in the same region
could help them pool resources together to organize events that they would

not be able to host individually. To bid for events that are a good fit with their geographic region will give them a competitive advantage in winning the bid; for example, ecotourism-related conference holders are likely to look for less developed areas in order for participants to experience unexploited destinations.

In terms of curriculum design, the current practices of hospitality and tourism institutions in China that help students develop intercultural awareness mainly focus on exchange programs, overseas internships, and raising the foreign language ability of students. The barriers to further development are still a lack of information and resources. Educators are encouraged to make full use of the Internet to source information as well as to explore more exchange and collaboration opportunities. For example, online networking groups, such as Trinet, could be useful platforms for contacting potential collaborators. Faculty members can also search for virtual Internet conferences where they can meet foreign scholars and discuss pertinent issues. Of course, they will still have to remove the language barrier by improving their English language skills.

It is interesting to note that the senior hospitality and tourism educators in this study perceived that they played different roles – information provider, curriculum planner, coordinator, influencer, and participant – in the process of developing intercultural awareness and skills for hospitality and tourism students. Such awareness of multiple roles definitely helps the current and future development of student cultural sensitivity in a positive way. What educators from outside of China can take away from this study is that hospitality and tourism educators in China have positive attitudes toward international collaboration. Thus, for those who are interested in collaborating with Chinese institutions, opportunities abound.

This is an exploratory study using a qualitative approach with a small number of selected tourism and hospitality programs in mainland China. The small sample size is a limitation of the study. Future research could use a quantitative survey involving a larger number of hospitality and tourism programs in China. Other future studies could examine further details of the curricula of different programs, including an analysis of the syllabi, to gain a fuller understanding of how intercultural awareness and skills are integrated into students' overall learning. As this study has identified that one of the barriers is the restrictions faced by institutions when seeking permission (or be allocated a quota) for faculty members to go overseas for exchange activities, it would be beneficial to examine how the government perceives this issue and how government officials understand their roles in developing the intercultural awareness of future professionals.

ACKNOWLEDGMENT

Funding for this project was provided by a grant from the School of Hotel and Tourism Management, Hong Kong Polytechnic University. Project Code: 2011 G.24.37.UA08.

REFERENCES

Black, K. (2004). A review of factors which contribute to the internationalisation of a programme of study. *Journal of Hospitality, Leisure, Sport & Tourism Education, 3*(1), 5–18.

CNTA. (2014). *China tourism statistical bulletin 2013.* Beijing: China National Tourism Administration. Retrieved from http://www.cnta.gov.cn/html/2014-9/2014-9-24-%7B@hur%7D-47-90095.html

Dewald, B., & Self, J. (2008). Cross cultural training for expatriate hotel managers: An exploratory study. *Journal of Hospitality & Tourism Administration, 9*(4), 352–364.

Gamio, M., & Sneed, J. (1992). Cross-cultural training practices and needs in the hotel industry. *Journal of Hospitality and Tourism Research, 15*(3), 13–26.

Gannon, J. (2008). *Developing intercultural skills for international industries: The role of industry and educators.* Oxford: Hospitality, Leisure, Sport and Tourism Network. Retrieved from http://www.heacademy.ac.uk/assets/bmaf/documents/publications/Case_studies/gannon.pdf

Heares, N., Devine, F., & Baum, T. (2007). The implications of contemporary cultural diversity for the hospitality curriculum. *Training and Education, 49*(5), 350–363.

Horng, J. S., & Lu, H. Y. (2006). Needs assessment of professional competencies of F&B/hospitality management students at college and university level. *Journal of Teaching in Travel and Tourism, 6*(3), 1–26.

Lam, T., & Xiao, H. (2000). Challenges and constraints of hospitality and tourism education in China. *International Journal of Contemporary Hospitality Management, 12*(5), 291–295.

Lee, C., & Chon, K. (2000). An investigation of multicultural training practices in the restaurant industry: The training cycle approach. *International Journal of Contemporary Management, 12*(2), 126–134.

Sangpikul, A. (2009). Internationalization of hospitality and tourism higher education: A perspective from Thailand. *Journal of Teaching in Travel & Tourism, 9*(1–2), 2–20.

Strauss, A., & Corbin, J. (1998). *Basics of qualitative research: Grounded theory procedures and techniques* (2nd ed.). Newbury Park, CA: Sage.

Taylor, M., & McArthur, L. (2009). Cross-cultural knowledge, attitudes and experiences of hospitality management students. *Journal of Hospitality & Tourism Education, 21*(4), 6–14.

UNWTO. (2014). *UNWTO tourism highlights 2014 edition.* Retrieved from http://www.unwto.org

Welch, T., Tanke, M., & Glover, G. (1988). Multicultural human resources management. *Hospitality Education and Research Journal, 12*(2), 337–345.

Wong, A. (1992). *A study on intercultural attitudes and communication between travel consultants and their Asian clients.* Unpublished Graduate Diploma thesis, James Cook University, Townsville.

Wong, A., & Chan, A. (2010). Understanding the leadership perceptions of staff in China's hotel industry: Integrating the macro and the micro-aspects of leadership contexts. *International Journal of Hospitality Management, 29*(3), 437–447.

Ye, B. H., Zhang, H. Q., & Yuen, P. (2012). An empirical study of anticipated and perceived discrimination of Mainland Chinese tourists in Hong Kong: The role of intercultural competence. *Journal of China Tourism Research, 8*(4), 417–430.

Zhang, W., & Fan, X. (2005). Tourism higher education in China. *Journal of Teaching in Travel and Tourism, 5*(1–2), 117–135.

Zhao, J. L. (1991). A current look at hospitality and tourism education in China's colleges and universities. *International Journal of Hospitality Management, 10*(4), 367.